How Well Does Your Child READ, WRITE, AND DO MATH?

*Step-by-Step Methods for Parents to Assess
and Develop their Child's Skills*

Ann Cook

**GALAHAD BOOKS
NEW YORK**

CONTENTS

How Well Does Your Child Read?

A Step-by-Step Assessment of Your Child's Reading Skills and Techniques to Improve Them

an,

C

For referral to a qualified testing or
tutoring center, call 800-457-4255 or e-mail
anncook@americanaccent.com

For Nate

Special thanks to Kim Ebner, Pat Weideman, Christie Savage, and Joan Di Giacomo.

Contents

Introduction

You've probably noticed that times have changed since you were in school. The work your child brings home seems quite different from what you were learning at that age. Children today are expected to know more and possess more advanced skills at an earlier age. You're left to wonder: "What is normal for a child in my child's grade?" or "What are the national standards in reading?"

You also begin to worry that report cards and scores on standardized tests aren't telling you enough about how your child is *really* performing academically. After all, news reports are assaulting you with discouraging statistics about American education. In 1998, the National Assessment of Educational Progress (NAEP), an arm of the U.S. Department of Education that monitors academic achievement through periodic testing of 4th, 8th, and 12th graders, reported that barely 36 percent of 12th graders, only 31 percent of 8th graders, and fewer than half of all 4th graders could read at the proficient level. By the 4th grade, 100 percent of students should be testing at or above basic skills level, but the latest NAEP reading test results showed that the state with the highest percentage (Connecticut) had only 78 percent of 4th grade students at or above that level. The results also suggested a downward trend: In 1998, 12th grade students performed more poorly in reading than in 1994.

It's no longer safe to assume that everything must be okay if your child continues to be promoted, as there is often an unpublicized "no-fail" policy in schools, where children are routinely advanced to the next grade when they have not achieved even a remedial level in the previous grade. The thinking was that "flunking" stigmatized a child and separated him from his peer group, and that the child would continue to do poorly and possibly end up not graduating. It was deemed preferable to put a child into the next grade and give additional academic support. Unfortunately, this support was not always available, but the policy was in place and the child would be passed along nonetheless. So how do you make sure that your child is on the right track—that he doesn't become a part of these bleak statistics?

You *can* identify specific learning problems by checking the results of whatever standardized test your child is required to take in school every year. But these tests vary from state to state, and not all teachers support the findings. Part of the problem is that America, unlike most advanced nations, does not have a national curriculum. The states' constitutional right to establish their own educational systems means that some schools have a wonderful school curriculum, but others leave much to be desired. It also means that students' annual standardized test scores might only reflect their performance on a regional level. The American Federation of Teachers (AFT) issued "Making Standards Matter 1996," an annual 50-state report on efforts to raise academic standards. Nearly every state is working to set common academic standards for its students, but the

AFT report makes it clear that most states have more work to do to strengthen their standards. For example, at this time, there are only 15 states with standards in all four core categories (English, Math, Science, and Social Studies) that are clear, specific, and well-grounded in content. For a report on an individual state, go online for the AFT state-by-state analysis. The URL is www.aft.org//index.htm.

Furthermore, school report cards only indicate your child's *overall* performance in reading, writing, and arithmetic. If you see a low grade in reading on your 2nd grader's report card, you only know that there's a problem—not what the problem is. You can, of course, schedule a conference with the teacher, but if the teacher is simply not conversant in phonics or reading levels, it will be difficult to isolate the problem.

But what if you could somehow figure out that your 2nd grader knows consonants and blends, but doesn't understand the difference between a long and a short vowel? This is what *How Well Does Your Child Read?* can help you do. Then, you can work with your child to remedy the problem—with workbooks, discussions, games, and exercises.

Why I wrote this book

As a parent, I had the same concerns you do. When my son was in the 1st grade, I began to suspect that he was not reading as well as he should have been. When my son's teacher was not able to provide much concrete information about why, I had him tested at the local Sylvan Learning Center.

The test was a simple, straightforward inventory of the basic skills involved in phonics and reading. I realized that something like this could be used by a parent to monitor a child's reading skills on an ongoing basis. As a linguist and the director of American Accent Training—a nationwide program to teach foreign-born students to speak standard American English—I had experience creating diagnostic speech analyses and grammar and accent tests. I used what I knew about linguistic development and created a phonics "inventory" to test my own son, as well as the children in the ACE (After Class Enrichment) Program I had founded at the local elementary school.

This became the foundation for *How Well Does Your Child Read?* and led me to write two more books featuring tests to help you assess your child's performance: *How Well Does Your Child Write?* and *How Well Does Your Child Do Math?*.

The material for my diagnostic tests has been garnered from a number of reliable sources. I studied the NAEP's assessments of American students' abilities in reading, mathematics, and writing. It has been conducting such tests since 1969, ranking the results of the tests by state and providing appropriate achievement goals for each age and grade. I also relied on books on test research; advice from the former director of Sylvan Learning Centers; and online information from the U.S. Department of Education, the American Federation of Teachers, Regional Educational Laboratories, and the ERIC Clearinghouses. Finally, my diagnostic tests went through a series of trial runs with children, in addition to being evaluated by experienced elementary school teachers and reviewed by an educational therapist.

How to use this book

How Well Does Your Child Read? contains a phonics and reading diagnostic/placement test for children in kindergarten through grade 5. It will help you determine to which grade level your child has mastered phonics and reading. You can use this assessment to target areas that may need additional work. Or if it shows that your child is performing at or above his grade level, this book can allay your doubts about your child's ability and help you guide him into the next level.

The book contains the following sections:

♦ A learning style pre-test to determine whether your child's learning style is primarily auditory (does your child acquire and retain information by what he hears?) or visual (does he acquire and retain information by what he sees?) (pages 23-24).

♦ A phonics assessment, testing knowledge of the alphabet (including upper and lower case); letter and sound correspondence (26 letters, 32 sounds); consonant blends (*st, tr, bl*); digraphs (*th, sh, ch, wh, ph*); long and short vowels; clusters (*str, spl*); double consonants; double vowels; word endings; and sight words (words that cannot be sounded out) (pages 29-52).

♦ A reading assessment, testing kindergartners on perception of story order and story sense (using pictures) and children in grades 1-5 on identification of the main idea and conclusion, finding details, and context (pages 53-84).

- Charts to help you track your child's progress (phonics chart on page 52; reading chart on pages 85-86).
- A chapter on grade level guidelines for kindergarten through 5th grade (pages 87-140).
- A reading reassessment (pages 141-172).
- An explanation of the NAEP's latest reading assessment, with a chart showing the performance of individual states (pages 175-177).
- Appendices containing listings of educational support centers and online resources (pages 179-186).
- A listing of 500 high-frequency words (pages 110 and 187-188).

The phonics assessment

For many years, teachers used the phonics method—in which rules governing the sound of a letter were used to sound out words—to teach reading, writing, and spelling. For example, *pet* has a short *e* sound because it is a one-syllable word ending in *t*. *Pete* has a long *e* sound because of the silent *e* at the end of the word. Phonics dealt with exceptions to these rules as *sight words*—words that don't look the way they sound, such as *laugh* or *thought*. Students learned these irregular words and memorized their spelling. But in recent years, educators came to prefer the whole language teaching method over phonics. The proponents of whole language felt that if children were exposed to literature, by being read to and having good books available, they would pick up the rules as they went along.

Some students *do* learn to read well with whole language. On the other hand, other students are faced with frustration and failure when they try to learn to read without the ability to break a word down into sounds and put them together for meaning. The study of phonics gives students "decoding" skills that enable them to sound words out.

Educators are now coming to the conclusion that the phonics and whole language debate is not a matter of "either/or." Phonics is the first logical step, followed by exposure to literature.

This, then, is how the diagnostic test in this book is organized—phonics first, reading second. Letter sounds need to be mastered—typically by the end of 1st grade—before your child can go on to the reading section. Therefore, each set of words in the phonics section requires an 80 percent accuracy rate. For example, if on a test page five sounds are tested, one mistake is acceptable, but two mistakes would mean your child had gotten only 60 percent correct. At this point, stop the test. Spend some time at home helping your child study the sounds on that page. You can try flash cards, letter games, or pointing out particular sounds when you read to your child. When you feel your child understands the information fully, you can give the test again.

The sound of a consonant (*b* or *t* or *m*) can be pronounced alone, but vowels need to be within the context of a word in order to distinguish between long and short vowels (for example, *mate* and *mat*). Therefore, in the phonics test, all vowel sounds are tested within words.

Most of the words used in the phonics test have been invented—for example, *wug* or *glav.* Invented words are helpful because your child will not have already memorized their pronunciations without first understanding the underlying rule—the way he might have with real words like *bag* or *glove*. Invented words can test whether your child really understands the rules or not. If a child sees *glav* and says "glav" with a short *a* sound, he has truly sounded out the word according to the rules of regular spelling. However, if he answers "glave" with a long *a* sound, you'll know he needs to practice the short *a* sound.

Scoring the phonics assessment

In the phonics assessment, mark a ✓ for correct answers and an ✘ for incorrect answers. Though it may seem quicker to mark only the incorrect answers, doing this might cause your child to react negatively and dispute your scoring, possibly slowing down the test.

As you give the phonics test, check the bottom of each page for the allowable number of ✘'s, which will vary between 1 and 5, depending on the number of items in the section. For example:

> 0 to 1 ✘ enter date in chart on page 52 and go to the next page; 2 or more ✘'s, stop test and go to Guidelines on page 87. Retest at a later date.

Do not go past the point where your child exceeds the allowable number of errors. Each time a particular test has been completed, note the date in the chart on page on page 52.

With each word your child has to pronounce in the phonics test, he may respond in one of four ways, which you would mark as follows:

Answers immediately and correctly	✓
Hesitates, then gives the correct answer	✗
Fails to respond	✗
Gives an incorrect response.	✗

Only the first type of response—an immediate and correct answer—will be considered the correct response.

If your child hesitates—that is, doesn't give the correct pronunciation *spontaneously*—you should write an ✗ in the corresponding box, even if your child does eventually give the right response. It is extremely important that your child answer immediately for the answer to be correct, because any hesitation means that he may be familiar with the sound or word, but has not mastered it.

It is also helpful for you to write down what your child actually said, as you can use this after the test to diagnose and practice vowels that your child has difficulty with.

Remember that a child can get the targeted sound (a vowel sound, for example) correct even if an untargeted sound (a consonant sound, for example) is wrong. From page 34 on, you are only listening for the targeted sound. For example, if you are targeting the long *a* sound in *later*, but your child immediately answers, "*tater*," the targeted vowel sound—a long *a*—is still correct. Mark a ✓ and write what your child actually said on the line. (This will be useful for diagnosing problems with certain consonants.) On the other hand, if your child answers *hopping* when the answer should have been *hoping*, he did not give the targeted sound—the long *o* sound—and you should mark an ✗.

There's no need to use a timer to measure how long your child pauses. Simply remember that a child needs to know phonics *cold*, and any hesitation means that a particular phonics skill has not been *mastered*. Because every child is different, you can define hesitation as when he breaks his own pace. If your child is stumped and doesn't respond, mark an ✖.

The reading assessment

After successful completion of the phonics section, give your child the reading test. If your child is a more advanced reader, you may be tempted to skip the phonics section and the early reading sections, but don't. Letting your child see just how much he already knows can be a great motivator. When your child starts to slow down or miss answers, he will have already gotten a sense of achievement.

For kindergartners, the reading test is made up of sets of pictures, rather than words, that tell a story. This section tests the kindergartner's grasp of story order by asking him to number four pictures in the order in which the scenes were most likely to have occurred. It will also test story sense, by presenting two pictures and then asking your child to point out which of two other scenes is most likely to happen next. At the kindergarten level, speed is not important—you are checking to see if the answer is correct.

The kindergarten pre-reading tests will tell you if your child needs work on logic, sequencing, or matching, as well as context and details.

For 1st grade through 5th grade, the reading section tests context and vocabulary, fact checking, finding the main idea, and drawing a conclusion. You will evaluate your child on the following four criteria:

1. **Fluency:** How smoothly did your child read? Was the reading choppy, halting, or disjointed? Was it smooth and flowing? Did the intonation reflect the punctuation and the meaning?

2. **Speed:** Did it take less than a minute or more than a minute?

3. **Vocabulary:** Were there more than three unknown words? Fewer than three?

4. **Response:** Was the response correct or incorrect?

Reading	❑ fluent	❑ halting
Speed	❑ less than 1 minute	❑ more than 1 minute
Vocabulary	❑ 0-3 unknown words	❑ 3+ unknown words
Response	❑ correct	❑ incorrect

In the reading assessment, it's okay for your child to look back over the text or picture for the answer. This part of the assessment is for comprehension, not memory.

An important distinction in assessing reading skills is the difference between *comprehension* and *fluency*. A child may read haltingly, but understand the material at the end, whereas another child may read beautifully, and have no idea of the content. The reading assessment will let you know what to work on.

During the reading main idea and conclusion assessments, mark the bottom of each page for your child's performance. These guidelines let you know your child's reading strengths and weaknesses. The first three categories—reading, speed, and vocabulary—are not critical for trying the next grade level. On the other hand, comprehension *is* critical. So if your child misses either a main idea or conclusion question, or goes beyond the acceptable number of errors for context or fact finding, the reading test should stop at that grade level.

Generally speaking, the more times a child reads a text, the more smoothly and fluently he will read. And once he is told the answer, he will remember it—independent of increased comprehension. Because of this, when you re-test the child, the reading selections must be taken from the back of the book and, unlike the phonics section, not simply repeated.

Is this an intelligence test?

No. It is extremely important to remember that early or late reading is not an indicator of intelligence. Phonics skills and the reading level will tell you the skill range or level a child has acquired *at that certain point*. Late readers can be given the tools and develop into great readers. Early readers may develop other, stronger interests. In either case, however, children need to be helped through the transition from phonics and basic comprehension, to enjoying and relating to literature and reading.

Before you begin

Before you plunge into the rest of this book, are you sure that no physical or learning impediments are hampering your child's ability to read? For example, has your child's eyesight been checked recently? If he has been displaying learning problems, have you ruled out the possibility of Attention Deficit Disorder (ADD) or dyslexia? Only after you've determined that your child is ready, willing, and *able* to learn should you give the diagnostic test to determine what your child's reading level is and what you may do to improve it.

How to give the test

Set aside 20 minutes alone with your child in a quiet room. Make sure there are no distractions—turn off the TV, and never try to give this test just before a big soccer match or gymnastics practice.

Tell your child this will only take a few minutes and that the results will help him enjoy reading more. Stress that there's no pressure, no punishment, no failing.

Depending on the age of your child, the two of you can sit side-by-side while you score and he answers the questions. Direct your child's attention to the words on the page, not the marks you're making. Some children can become anxious if they pay too much attention to your scoring.

Students in kindergarten through 2nd grade should be monitored closely because they cannot always read the instructions, and they will have a greater tendency to get sidetracked. Independent study starts in the 3rd grade, so children at the 3rd grade level or higher can have greater autonomy during the test. (Of course, the behavior of individual children can vary greatly, so there will be exceptions to this.)

For kindergartners, the test will take from one minute (because they don't know the alphabet well) to 20 minutes. I recommend a 20-minute limit to combat the "fatigue factor" as boredom or exasperation can lower children's scores even in subjects they know well. Children in 1st through 5th grade should finish the test within 20 minutes.

What if your child takes longer? Well, phonics skills need to be quick and accurate. If your child takes too much time on the phonics section, he doesn't know the material. At that point, the test should be stopped, and the previous lessons drilled. On the other hand, it's okay if your child goes over the allotted time with the reading selections as long as he is giving the correct responses. The critical factor in that section is comprehension, not speed.

What to do after the test

Once your child reaches the point in the test where the questions are beyond his grade level, you can end the test. Turn to the scoring section and determine the grade level that corresponds to your child's score. Once that has been determined, consult the chapter on standards for each grade level—kindergarten through 5th. Here you will find suggestions on helping your child with any areas of difficulty that have been identified in the assessment. These standards and guidelines can help you with remediation if your child scores below grade level. This chapter also introduces you to the next level or levels if your child is at or above grade level.

One of the primary functions of the test is to familiarize you with the materials that should be taught at each level. Once that familiarization has taken place, you can seek out appropriate materials for your child.

Children like to be read to from higher-level books, but when reading themselves, they need books that are interesting and challenging, not overwhelming. Also, it's okay if your child wants to read the same easy book over and over. That's an excellent way to reinforce the basics and build reading confidence and fluency.

Spelling and pronunciation drills can also become part of the remediation work you'll do with your child. You can use flash cards to reinforce your kindergartner's knowledge of sight words and of two- or three-letter, short vowel, phonetic words. This includes words such as *pat, sat, hat; it, bit, sit; in, tin,* and *fin.* For children in 1st grade and up, you can make lists of words on note cards for spelling drills. Call Matrix at 800-457-4255 to obtain the flash cards that are appropriate to your child's level.

Retesting

If you feel your child has made progress after the work you've done together, you can test him again. Or even if he performed at the appropriate level the first time around, you still may want to give the test periodically to monitor skills. In the first case, your child needs to be tested at the same level as before, but he may have memorized the answers, so use the reassessments in the back of the book. In the second scenario, you can just pick up at the point in the test where your child left off.

Each time you give the test, record the date so you can chart your child's progress. Continue monitoring until your child is at or above grade level.

How often should you retest your child? This depends upon the age of the child. A 5-year-old who is just learning his letters could be tested every four months, while a 7-year-old, who needs to master the concepts for school, could be tested every two months. Children who are on track could be tested at the beginning and end of each school year.

Now, if you're ready (and your child is ready), let's find out how well your child can read!

Learning Style
Pre-test

It is helpful for parents to understand a child's learning style. Some children's learning strength is *auditory*—they acquire and retain information by what they hear; others learn *visually*—by what they see; and some children learn the best in a *tactile* or *kinesthetic* way—by physically touching or manipulating the objects that they are counting.

This quick test will help determine if your child's learning style is markedly auditory or visual.

Auditory Sequential Memory

Tell your child the objects shown in each set at a rate of one every two seconds. Then ask her to repeat the list back. Keep adding a new object to the set until she makes a mistake.

1. 📫 ☎ ✂
2. ☎ 📖 🔔 ✒
3. 📖 ☎ ✒ 🕐 🔔
4. ☎ ✂ ✒ 📖 🕐 ★
5. 🔔 📫 ✂ ✒ 🕐 ★ 📖

Visual Sequential Memory

Show the set of objects to your child, allowing two seconds for each object in a set. Then remove or cover the paper and ask her to list the objects she saw. Keep adding a new set until she makes a mistake.

1. 🕐 ★ 🔔

2. ✈ ✂ ☺ ☎

3. 🔔 ★ 📬 📖 ✍

4. ✈ ✂ 🕐 🔔 ☺ ✎

5. 📖 ☎ ✂ ✎ 🕐 ★ 📬

Interpretation

Most people use a combination of learning styles, but usually one is dominant. If your child shows a marked preference for *visual memory*, she would benefit by practicing reading skills with flash cards and pictures.

If your child shows a marked preference for *auditory memory*, she would benefit by practicing out loud—chanting the alphabet, reciting simple word spellings, or listening to tapes.

A child with a marked preference for *kinesthetic memory* would benefit by practicing with manipulatives—blocks, word matching exercises, and making her own flash cards.

The main point is that not all approaches work for all children. Experiment with different approaches and see what works best for your child.

Test-taking Techniques

There are two elements to taking a test successfully. Most important, of course, is knowing the information. The other is knowing the test.

Tests are written according to basic standards and practices. This is why school tests are called *standardized*. It is very helpful for your child to be familiar with test standards and formats before starting a test, so that she can focus on the content, rather than on the test itself. Here are some basic guidelines:

First, look the whole test over. This includes noting how much time you have for the test, how long the test is, and what kind of test it is—multiple choice, fill-in-the-blank, essay, or a combination of the three. Many a 10-year-old has gotten to the end of a test with 10 minutes left to go, only to be dismayed to find two essay questions tucked away at the end of the test.

Next, put your pencil down and read the instructions. Then read them again.

After you read each instruction set, look for *key words* that tell you what kind of writing is needed (*describe, explain, persuade*), the specific facts you need (*who, what, where, when, why, how*), or the sequence of events (*first, then, next, at last, finally*). Notice if there are any negative words in the instructions (Which word is *not* a noun?) or if the question asks for *similarities* or *opposites*.

Make sure that you know exactly what you are supposed to be looking for in the text. If you are supposed to find the *main idea*, you have to read the entire passage and think about what the most important point was; whereas if you are looking for *details*, you can scan the passage to find the exact fact. Read all the questions before you read the passage—that way you'll know what you're looking for while you are reading. Be sure to underline the answers in the passage rather than trying to rely on your memory. Circle any words that you aren't sure of and try to figure them out by the context.

Following this, prioritize to determine if questions are equally weighted. If some questions are worth only 1 point and others are worth 10 points, spend more time and energy on the more heavily weighted problems.

If there are questions you just don't know the answer to, don't spend time agonizing over them. Move on to the questions you are familiar with, then go back to the ones you're less sure of.

One of the easiest techniques for a multiple choice test is the process of elimination. If there are four possibilities, chances are that one of them will be way off base, so first, eliminate the ridiculous. Another one will probably be fairly unlikely. Cross that one out, too. Of the two remaining, both will be possibilities, but since you've eliminated the clearly wrong answers, you can concentrate on finding the correct one of two, instead of the correct one of four. For example, here's a question from a typical 3rd grade standardized test:

Mark the answer with the correct punctuation.

Thanksgiving is always on a _____

❑ Thursday. ❑ Thursday?

❑ Thursday, ❑ Thursday

When you read it all together, "Thanksgiving is always on a Thursday," you can say that it is a complete sentence. Because it is a complete sentence, it needs an end mark. Hence, the last answer—*Thursday*—can be eliminated. From there, look at the sentence and ask yourself, "Is it a question? Is it the middle of a sentence?" This will eliminate *Thursday?* and *Thursday,* leaving *Thursday.*—which is the correct answer. Now that you've figured this question out, look for others that are similar to it.

When taking a multiple choice test, when you just don't know the answer, always take a guess from the answers you deem most likely to be correct. If you have four choices from which to choose, you have a 25 percent chance of getting the correct answer, and if you've narrowed those four choices down to two possible answers, then you have a 50 percent chance of getting the right answer.

On page 28 you will find a list of test-taking tips that you can keep handy for reviewing with your child, especially when she is preparing to take a test.

Test-taking tips

1. Look the whole test over.
2. Prioritize.
3. Read the instructions.
4. Read the instructions again.
5. Make sure that you have scratch paper for notes and outlines.
6. Look for key words.
7. Make sure that you know what you are looking for in the passage.
8. Make sure that you check all possible answers before you choose one. Don't choose the first one that looks likely.
9. Look for similar types of problems.
10. Review the test and complete any answers you may have skipped.

Phonics Assessment

Kindergarten and First Grade

Alphabet Upper Case   *Kindergarten*

Say each letter. Start with **Z** and work back to **A**.

	✓	✗	notes		✓	✗	notes
Z	☐	☐	____	M	☐	☐	____
Y	☐	☐	____	L	☐	☐	____
X	☐	☐	____	K	☐	☐	____
W	☐	☐	____	J	☐	☐	____
V	☐	☐	____	I	☐	☐	____
U	☐	☐	____	H	☐	☐	____
T	☐	☐	____	G	☐	☐	____
S	☐	☐	____	F	☐	☐	____
R	☐	☐	____	E	☐	☐	____
Q	☐	☐	____	D	☐	☐	____
P	☐	☐	____	C	☐	☐	____
O	☐	☐	____	B	☐	☐	____
N	☐	☐	____	A	☐	☐	____

✓ = immediate response   ✗ = slow or incorrect response
0 to 5 ✗'s enter date in chart on page 52 and go to the next
page; 6 or more ✗'s, stop test and go to Guidelines on page
87. Retest at a later date.

Alphabet Lower Case

Kindergarten

Say each letter. Start with **z** and work back to **a**.

	✓	✗	notes		✓	✗	notes
z	☐	☐	_____	m	☐	☐	_____
y	☐	☐	_____	l	☐	☐	_____
x	☐	☐	_____	k	☐	☐	_____
w	☐	☐	_____	j	☐	☐	_____
v	☐	☐	_____	i	☐	☐	_____
u	☐	☐	_____	h	☐	☐	_____
t	☐	☐	_____	g	☐	☐	_____
s	☐	☐	_____	f	☐	☐	_____
r	☐	☐	_____	e	☐	☐	_____
q	☐	☐	_____	d	☐	☐	_____
p	☐	☐	_____	c	☐	☐	_____
o	☐	☐	_____	b	☐	☐	_____
n	☐	☐	_____	a	☐	☐	_____

✓ = immediate response   ✗ = slow or incorrect response
0 to 5 ✗'s enter date in chart on page 52 and go to the next page; 6 or more ✗'s, stop test and go to Guidelines on page 87. Retest at a later date.

Consonants

First Grade

Make the **sound** of each letter below (not the *name*—for example, *buh*, not *bee*).

	✓	✗	notes		✓	✗	notes
b	☐	☐	_____	p	☐	☐	_____
c*	☐	☐	_____	q	☐	☐	_____
d	☐	☐	_____	r	☐	☐	_____
f	☐	☐	_____	s	☐	☐	_____
g*	☐	☐	_____	t	☐	☐	_____
h	☐	☐	_____	v	☐	☐	_____
j	☐	☐	_____	w	☐	☐	_____
k	☐	☐	_____	x	☐	☐	_____
l	☐	☐	_____	y	☐	☐	_____
m	☐	☐	_____	z	☐	☐	_____
n	☐	☐	_____				

*These letters have two sounds each. (See pp. 117)

✓ = immediate response   ✗ = slow or incorrect response
0 to 4 ✗'s enter date in chart on page 52 and go to the next page; 5 or more ✗'s, stop test and go to Guidelines on page 87. Retest at a later date.

Sight Words   *First Grade*

Read the following words.

	✓	✗	notes
a	☐	☐	_____
I	☐	☐	_____
is	☐	☐	_____
an	☐	☐	_____
and	☐	☐	_____
the	☐	☐	_____

✓ = immediate response   ✗ = slow or incorrect response
0 to 1 ✗ enter date in chart on page 52 and go to the next
page; 2 or more ✗'s, stop test and go to Guidelines on page
87. Retest at a later date.

Short Vowels   *First Grade*

The phonics words from this point on contain nonsense syllables, so you can accurately hear the changing vowels. From this page forward, you are only listening for the targeted vowel sound. If the consonant sound is wrong, but the vowel is correct, mark ✓. However, do write the actual word your child says on the line so you can determine which consonant sounds he has trouble with. Read the following words.

		✓	✗	notes
A	wag	☐	☐	_____
E	weg	☐	☐	_____
I	wig	☐	☐	_____
O	wog	☐	☐	_____
U	wug	☐	☐	_____

✓ = immediate response   ✗ = slow or incorrect response
0 to 1 ✗ enter date in chart on page 52 and go to the next page; 2 or more ✗'s, stop test and go to Guidelines on page 87. Retest at a later date.

Consonant Blends — *First Grade*

Here are **blends** at the beginning of a word. Read the following words.

		✓	✗	notes
BL	blan	☐	☐	_____
BR	brog	☐	☐	_____
PL	plep	☐	☐	_____
PR	prot	☐	☐	_____
CL	clin	☐	☐	_____
CR	cret	☐	☐	_____
DR	drid	☐	☐	_____
TR	trop	☐	☐	_____
ST	steg	☐	☐	_____

✓ = immediate response   ✗ = slow or incorrect response
0 to 2 ✗'s enter date in chart on page 52 and go to the next page; 3 or more ✗'s, stop test and go to Guidelines on page 87. Retest at a later date.

Sight Words *First Grade*

Read the following words.

	✓	✗	notes
to	☐	☐	_____
go	☐	☐	_____
do	☐	☐	_____
by	☐	☐	_____
or	☐	☐	_____
of	☐	☐	_____
as	☐	☐	_____
he	☐	☐	_____
she	☐	☐	_____
for	☐	☐	_____
say	☐	☐	_____
from	☐	☐	_____

✓ = immediate response   ✗ = slow or incorrect response
0 to 2 ✗'s enter date in chart on page 52 and go to the next page; 3 or more ✗'s, stop test and go to Guidelines on page 87. Retest at a later date.

Consonant Digraphs *First Grade*

There is an important distinction between a blend and a digraph. A blend can be *sounded out (bl)*, whereas a digraph uses two letters to form one new sound *(sh)*. In other words, you can't sound out a digraph. Here are consonant digraphs at the beginning of a word. Read the following words.

		✓	✗	notes
WH	whep	☐	☐	_____
TH	tham	☐	☐	_____
SH	shog	☐	☐	_____
CH	chun	☐	☐	_____
PH	pheb	☐	☐	_____

✓ = immediate response   ✗ = slow or incorrect response
0 to 1 ✗ enter date in chart on page 52 and go to the next page; 2 or more ✗'s, stop test and go to Guidelines on page 87. Retest at a later date.

Ending Digraphs *First Grade*

Here are consonant digraphs at the end of a word. Read the following words.

	✓	✗	notes
sith	☐	☐	_____
gach	☐	☐	_____
lish	☐	☐	_____
taph	☐	☐	_____

✓ = immediate response   ✗ = slow or incorrect response
0 to 1 ✗ enter date in chart on page 52 and go to the next
page; 2 or more ✗'s, stop test and go to Guidelines on page
87. Retest at a later date.

Long Vowels

First Grade

A silent *e* after the consonant makes a vowel long. Read
the following words.

	✓	✗	notes
vate	☐	☐	_____
rete	☐	☐	_____
fime	☐	☐	_____
pote	☐	☐	_____
kue	☐	☐	_____

✓ = immediate response   ✗ = slow or incorrect response
0 to 1 ✗ enter date in chart on page 52 and go to the next
page; 2 or more ✗'s, stop test and go to Guidelines on page
87. Retest at a later date.

Sight Words   *First Grade*

Read the following words.

	✓	✗	notes
what	☐	☐	_____
have	☐	☐	_____
saw	☐	☐	_____
was	☐	☐	_____
they	☐	☐	_____
there	☐	☐	_____
one	☐	☐	_____
some	☐	☐	_____
you	☐	☐	_____
your	☐	☐	_____
are	☐	☐	_____
does	☐	☐	_____
don't	☐	☐	_____
done	☐	☐	_____
gone	☐	☐	_____

> ✓ = immediate response   ✗ = slow or incorrect response
> 0 to 3 ✗'s enter date in chart on page 52 and go to the next
> page; 4 or more ✗'s, stop test and go to Guidelines on page
> 87. Retest at a later date.

Sight Words   *First Grade*

Read the following words.

	✓	✗	notes
good	☐	☐	_____
right	☐	☐	_____
often	☐	☐	_____
another	☐	☐	_____
why	☐	☐	_____
again	☐	☐	_____
every	☐	☐	_____
away	☐	☐	_____
along	☐	☐	_____
until	☐	☐	_____
going	☐	☐	_____
while	☐	☐	_____
both	☐	☐	_____
because	☐	☐	_____
few	☐	☐	_____

✓ = immediate response   ✗ = slow or incorrect response
0 to 3 ✗'s enter date in chart on page 52 and go to the next
page; 4 or more ✗'s, stop test and go to Guidelines on page
87. Retest at a later date.

Long Vowels   *First Grade*

In addition to the long vowels made by the silent *e* (for example, *not* becomes *note* with the silent *e*), there are other important long vowel sounds. Read the following words.

		✓	✗	notes
A	cray	☐	☐	_____
	dail	☐	☐	_____
E	neen	☐	☐	_____
	leat	☐	☐	_____
I	bly	☐	☐	_____
	snyle	☐	☐	_____
O	hoat	☐	☐	_____
	dold	☐	☐	_____
U	hoon	☐	☐	_____
	tew	☐	☐	_____

✓ = immediate response   ✗ = slow or incorrect response
0 to 2 ✗'s enter date in chart on page 52 and go to the next page; 3 or more ✗'s, stop test and go to Guidelines on page 87. Retest at a later date.

Sight Words   *First Grade*

Read the following words.

	✓	✗	notes
people	☐	☐	_____
heard	☐	☐	_____
heart	☐	☐	_____
sure	☐	☐	_____
honest	☐	☐	_____
beautiful	☐	☐	_____
busy	☐	☐	_____
cover	☐	☐	_____
move	☐	☐	_____
huge	☐	☐	_____

> ✓ = immediate response   ✗ = slow or incorrect response
> 0 to 2 ✗'s enter date in chart on page 52 and go to the next
> page; 3 or more ✗'s, stop test and go to Guidelines on page
> 87. Retest at a later date.

Ending Blends

First Grade

Read the following words.

	✓	✗	notes
moggle	☐	☐	_____
tepple	☐	☐	_____
lomble	☐	☐	_____
mardle	☐	☐	_____
riffle	☐	☐	_____
tottle	☐	☐	_____
beckle	☐	☐	_____
fengle	☐	☐	_____
sancle	☐	☐	_____
vample	☐	☐	_____

✓ = immediate response   ✗ = slow or incorrect response
0 to 2 ✗'s enter date in chart on page 52 and go to the next
page; 3 or more ✗'s, stop test and go to Guidelines on page
87. Retest at a later date.

Consonant Clusters   *First Grade*

After consonant blends, there are consonant clusters—three consonants together. Blends can occur at the beginning, middle, or end of a word. Clusters only occur at the beginning or middle of a word. They do not occur at the end. Read the following words.

		✓	✗	notes
THR	threm	☐	☐	_____
SHR	shrup	☐	☐	_____
CHR	chren	☐	☐	_____
SCR	scrim	☐	☐	_____
STR	strub	☐	☐	_____
SPR	spron	☐	☐	_____
SPL	splif	☐	☐	_____
SQU	squog	☐	☐	_____

> ✓ = immediate response   ✗ = slow or incorrect response
> 0 to 2 ✗'s enter date in chart on page 52 and go to the next page; 3 or more ✗'s, stop test and go to Guidelines on page 87. Retest at a later date.

Double Consonants   *First Grade*

Double consonants make a vowel short. Read the following words.

	✓	✗	notes
gatter	☐	☐	_____
tetter	☐	☐	_____
finner	☐	☐	_____
nopping	☐	☐	_____
lupper	☐	☐	_____

✓ = immediate response   ✗ = slow or incorrect response
0 to 1 ✗ enter date in chart on page 52 and go to the next
page; 2 or more ✗'s, stop test and go to Guidelines on page
87. Retest at a later date.

Short and Long Vowels   *First Grade*

This exercise contrasts words with and without a final *e*.
Read the following pairs of words.

	✓	✗	notes
dat	☐	☐	_____
date	☐	☐	_____
ret	☐	☐	_____
rete	☐	☐	_____
lin	☐	☐	_____
line	☐	☐	_____
nop	☐	☐	_____
nope	☐	☐	_____
ruk	☐	☐	_____
ruke	☐	☐	_____

> ✓ = immediate response   ✗ = slow or incorrect response
> 0 to 2 ✗'s enter date in chart on page 52 and go to the next
> page; 3 or more ✗'s, stop test and go to Guidelines on page
> 87. Retest at a later date.

Single and Double Consonants · *First Grade*

This exercise contrasts double and single consonants. Read the following pairs of words.

	✓	✗	notes
datter	☐	☐	_____
dater	☐	☐	_____
remmer	☐	☐	_____
remer	☐	☐	_____
finner	☐	☐	_____
finer	☐	☐	_____
topping	☐	☐	_____
toping	☐	☐	_____
bupper	☐	☐	_____
buper	☐	☐	_____

✓ = immediate response   ✗ = slow or incorrect response
0 to 2 ✗'s enter date in chart on page 52 and go to the next page; 3 or more ✗'s, stop test and go to Guidelines on page 87. Retest at a later date.

R-Controlled Vowels

First Grade

Here are different vowels in combination with the letter *R*. Read the following words.

	✓	✗	notes
mirt	☐	☐	_____
nurm	☐	☐	_____
lerg	☐	☐	_____
garp	☐	☐	_____
porf	☐	☐	_____

✓ = immediate response   ✗ = slow or incorrect response
0 to 1 ✗ enter date in chart on page 52 and go to the next page; 2 or more ✗'s, stop test and go to Guidelines on page 87. Retest at a later date.

Endings

These endings indicate consistent and accepted *changes in meaning*, such as the *-ed* ending for the past tense or *-er* for comparatives or to indicate a person who does something (e.g. *reader*). Read the following words.

	✓	✗	notes
wugged	☐	☐	_____
tudding	☐	☐	_____
lagger	☐	☐	_____
ribby	☐	☐	_____
ribbier	☐	☐	_____

These double consonant endings indicate the pronunciation of a short vowel sound. Read the following words.

	✓	✗	notes
nuck	☐	☐	_____
senk	☐	☐	_____
ting	☐	☐	_____
wint	☐	☐	_____
bolm	☐	☐	_____

✓ = immediate response   ✗ = slow or incorrect response
0 to 2 ✗'s enter date in chart on page 52 and go to the next page; 3 or more ✗'s, stop test and go to Guidelines on page 87. Retest at a later date.

Vowel Digraphs   *First Grade*

These are the vowel combinations that make a new sound. Read the following words.

	✓	✗	notes
toog	☐	☐	_____
maut	☐	☐	_____
gain	☐	☐	_____
lound	☐	☐	_____
thew	☐	☐	_____

> ✓ = immediate response   ✗ = slow or incorrect response
> 0 to 1 ✗ enter date in chart on page 52 and go to the next page; 2 or more ✗'s, stop test and go to Guidelines on page 87. Retest at a later date.

Phonics Record

As you give your child the phonics test, check the bottom of the page for the allowable number of errors. The goal is a minimum of 80 percent accuracy. Once your child has mastered a phonics skill, note the date in the chart below.

Date Passed	Phonics Skill	Level
	Alphabet Upper Case	Kindergarten
	Alphabet Lower Case	
	Consonant Sounds	Early 1st grade
	Sight Words	
	Short Vowels	
	Consonant Blends	
	Sight Words	Mid 1st grade
	Consonant Digraphs	
	Ending Digraphs	
	Long Vowels	
	Sight Words *(pages 40-41)*	
	Long Vowels	Late 1st grade
	Sight Words	
	Ending Blends	
	Consonant Clusters	
	Double Consonants	
	Short & Long Vowels (silent *e*)	
	Single & Double Consonants	
	R-Controlled Vowels	End 1st grade
	Endings	
	Vowel Digraphs	

Reading Assessment

Kindergarten through Fifth Grade

Matching Pictures   *Kindergarten*

Look at the picture on the left. Draw a circle around the matching picture in the box.

0-1 ✗, enter date in chart on page 85 and go to the next page; 2 or more ✗'s, go to Guidelines on page 87 and retest at a later date.

Matching Letters

Look at the letter on the left. Draw a circle around the matching letter in the box.

W | T   P   W

B | A   B   P

L | M   I   L

U | U   V   X

Z | B   Z   Y

0-1 ✗, enter date in chart on page 85 and go to the next page; 2 or more ✗'s, go to Guidelines on page 87 and retest at a later date.

Context

Circle the picture that best finishes each sentence.

The boy jumped into the

The cat chased the

The girl hugged her

0-1 **✗**, enter date in chart on page 85 and go to the next page; 2 or more **✗**'s, go to Guidelines on page 87 and retest at a later date.

Fact Finding

Look at the picture and tell if each sentence is TRUE or FALSE.

	True	**False**
1. The dog is jumping rope.	❑	❑
2. There are six animals in the picture.	❑	❑
3. There are more cats than dogs.	❑	❑

> 0-1 ✗, enter date in chart on page 85 and go to the next page; 2 or more ✗'s, go to Guidelines on page 87 and retest at a later date.

Story Order *Kindergarten*

Look at the four pictures. Decide what order they should be in to tell a story. Write numbers 1 to 4 in the little boxes to show the order.

Correct order, enter date in chart on page 85 and go to the next page; incorrect order, stop test and go to Guidelines on page 87. Restest at a later date.

Story Sense

Kindergarten

Look at the top pictures. Draw a circle around the bottom box that shows what is more likely to happen next.

Correct response, enter date in chart on page 85 and go to the next page; incorrect response, stop test and go to Guidelines on page 87. Restest at a later date.

Context

Choose the word that best finishes the sentence.

1. Every morning we get out of _____.

   ❑ far   ❑ bed   ❑ house

2. The dogs like to _____.

   ❑ bark   ❑ that   ❑ eats

3. Tomorrow is _____.

   ❑ Tuesday   ❑ July   ❑ hot

0-1 ✘, enter date in chart on page 85 and go on to the next page; 2 or more ✘'s, go to Guidelines on page 87 and retest at a later date.

Fact Finding

First Grade

Read the following paragraph and tell if each sentence is TRUE or FALSE.

> I am an animal. I have four legs. I have black and white stripes. I am a zebra. I live on the African plains.

	True	**False**
1. The animal has two legs.	❑	❑
2. The animal lives in the rain forest.	❑	❑
3. The animal is a zebra.	❑	❑

0-1 ✖, enter date in chart on page 85 and go on to the next page; 2 or more ✖'s, go to Guidelines on page 87 and retest at a later date.

Main Idea

First Grade

Read the following paragraph and answer the question that follows.

> Jenny looked out the window. It was snowing. She could not go out to play. Jenny said, "I wish it would stop snowing."

The main idea is:

❑ Jenny wanted the snow to stop.

❑ Jenny liked looking at the snow.

❑ Jenny made a wish.

Reading	❑ fluent	❑ halting
Speed	❑ less than 1 minute	❑ more than 1 minute
Vocabulary	❑ 0-3 unknown words	❑ 3+ unknown words
Response	❑ correct	❑ incorrect

Correct response, enter date in chart on page 85 and go to the next page; incorrect response go to Guidelines on page 87 and retest at a later date.

Conclusions   *First Grade*

Read the following paragraph and answer the question that follows.

> Bob got out of the car. He looked at all the kids playing at the new playground. He took his camera out of the case and adjusted the lens.

What did Bob do?

❑ Bob played at the playground.

❑ The kids played on the slide.

❑ Bob took a picture of the kids playing at the new playground.

Reading	❑ fluent	❑ halting
Speed	❑ less than 1 minute	❑ more than 1 minute
Vocabulary	❑ 0-3 unknown words	❑ 3+ unknown words
Response	❑ correct	❑ incorrect

Correct response, enter date in chart on page 85 and go to the next page; incorrect response go to Guidelines on page 87 and retest at a later date.

Context

Choose the word that best completes each sentence.

1. The puffer fish blows up like a balloon. It does this by taking in _____.

   ❏ trip   ❏ air   ❏ visitors

2. An elephant has a long trunk. It can _____ up to six feet long.

   ❏ fall   ❏ set   ❏ grow

3. In the olden days there were no books. Nobody knew how to _____.

   ❏ read   ❏ draw   ❏ see

4. Why don't you come to my _____?

   ❏ house   ❏ lunch   ❏ bag

5. I'm really _____ about the party.

   ❏ tired   ❏ hungry   ❏ excited

> 0-1 ✘, enter date in chart on page 85 and go to the next page; 2 or more ✘'s, go to Guidelines on page 87 and retest at a later date.

Fact Finding

Read the following paragraph and tell if each sentence is TRUE or FALSE.

> Sharks are a kind of fish. They live in the ocean. They are very good swimmers. A shark does not have bones. Its skeleton is made of cartilage. There are more than 250 kinds of sharks. The biggest sharks can grow over 50 feet long.

	True	False
1. Instead of bones, sharks have cartilage.	❑	❑
2. Most sharks live in lakes.	❑	❑
3. There are about 50 different kinds of sharks.	❑	❑
4. Sharks are good swimmers.	❑	❑

0-1 ✗, enter date in chart on page 85 and go to the next page; 2 or more ✗'s, go to Guidelines on page 87 and retest at a later date.

Main Idea   *Second Grade*

Read the following paragraph and answer the question that follows.

A Summer Story

It is hot in summer. The sun shines and birds sing. It is nice outdoors. Most kids like to play outdoors. Some kids like to rollerblade. Some kids swim. What do you do in summer?

What is the main idea?

- ❏ The sun shines in summer.
- ❏ In summer, there are many things to do outside.
- ❏ It doesn't rain in the summer.

Reading	❏ fluent	❏ halting
Speed	❏ less than 1 minute	❏ more than 1 minute
Vocabulary	❏ 0-3 unknown words	❏ 3+ unknown words
Response	❏ correct	❏ incorrect

Correct response, enter date in chart on page 85 and go to the next page; incorrect response go to Guidelines on page 87 and retest at a later date.

Conclusions   *Second Grade*

Read the following paragraph and answer the questions that follow.

How to Stop a Cat Fight

Sometimes cats fight. They make loud noises. They may scratch. Do not try to pull apart fighting cats. Turn on a hose and spray them with water. This will stop the fight.

When cats fight, they

☐ spray.
☐ scratch.
☐ turn on a hose.

Reading	☐ fluent	☐ halting
Speed	☐ less than 1 minute	☐ more than 1 minute
Vocabulary	☐ 0-3 unknown words	☐ 3+ unknown words
Response	☐ correct	☐ incorrect

Correct response, enter date in chart on page 85 and go to the next page; incorrect response go to Guidelines on page 87 and retest at a later date.

Context

Choose the words that best complete each sentence.

1. When a person is fasting, he does not eat. People don't _____ (a) while they are sleeping, so it is like they are fasting all night. When they get up in the morning, they 'break' the _____ (b) with breakfast.

> (a) ❑ food   ❑ sleep   ❑ eat
> (b) ❑ fast   ❑ lunch   ❑ slow

2. Spider monkeys are very quick and light. They can climb easily to escape other animals or to find _____ (a). They use their hands and feet to climb— and they also use their _____(b)!

> (a) ❑ deer   ❑ self   ❑ food
> (b) ❑ ears   ❑ tails   ❑ noses

3. It is very dangerous to pick wild mushrooms. Even though they might look tasty, they can be _____ (a). Many people get _____ (b) every year from picking wild mushrooms.

> (a) ❑ delicious   ❑ danger   ❑ poisonous
> (b) ❑ lost   ❑ died   ❑ sick

4. Some people believe that it's bad _____ (a) if a black cat crosses your path. Other people think that you'll have seven years' bad luck if you break a _____ (b). In order to get rid of bad luck, you can throw salt over your shoulder or you can knock on wood.

(a) ❑ luck   ❑ idea   ❑ beliefs
(b) ❑ legs   ❑ mirror   ❑ frame

5. If you are in an open field during a thunderstorm, you might want to look for _____ (a) under a tree. Don't do this. The lightning will be attracted to the tallest thing in the area—the tree! Lie _____ (b) on the ground, instead.

(a) ❑ danger   ❑ pressure   ❑ safety
(b) ❑ over   ❑ down   ❑ off

> 0-2 ✗'s, enter date in chart on page 85 and go on to the next page; 3 or more ✗'s, go to Guidelines on page 87 and retest at a later date.

Fact Finding

Third Grade

Read the paragraph below and answer the following TRUE or FALSE questions.

George Washington was the first president of the United States. He was born in 1732 and he died in 1799. He fought in the war against England from 1776 to 1781. This war was called the American Revolution. He became president in 1789, in New York.

There are many American cities named after George Washington. He is also on the one-dollar bill.

	True	False
1. There is only one city named after George Washington.	❑	❑
2. The American Revolutionary War was against England.	❑	❑
3. George Washington's face appears on a $10 bill.	❑	❑
4. The Revolutionary War ended after Washington became president.	❑	❑
5. George Washington was the president of England.	❑	❑

> 0-1 ✘, enter date in chart on page 85 and go on to the next page; 2 or more ✘'s, go to Guidelines on page 87 and retest at a later date.

Main Idea
Third Grade

Read the following paragraph and answer the question that follows.

How to Draw a Straight Line

Straight lines are hard to draw. Sometimes they go up on the end and sometimes they go down. Sometimes they go all over the place. To make a line straight, try using something that has a smooth edge. Lay it down on the paper and run a pencil along the side of it. Almost any smooth edge may be used, like the edge of a book, the smooth side of a comb, or even a coat hanger. As long as you hold it down while you are drawing, it will give you a straight line.

The main idea is:

❑ Anything smooth and straight can be used to make a straight line.

❑ Some lines go up on the end.

❑ Use a coat hanger to make a straight line.

Reading	❑ fluent	❑ halting
Speed	❑ less than 1 minute	❑ more than 1 minute
Vocabulary	❑ 0-3 unknown words	❑ 3+ unknown words
Response	❑ correct	❑ incorrect

Correct response, enter date in chart on page 85 and go to the next page; incorrect response go to Guidelines on page 87 and retest at a later date.

....

Conclusions

Third Grade

Read the following paragraph and answer the question that follows.

Brown Snakes in Guam

Guam is an island in the middle of the Pacific Ocean. About 150,000 people live there, but they are outnumbered by the brown tree snake. Forty years ago, there were no brown tree snakes in Guam at all. Today there are more than a million. Nobody knows where they came from or how to stop them from multiplying. They have killed and eaten thousands of birds. Many kinds of rare birds and one kind of bat are becoming extinct because of the brown snake.

Why are many kinds of rare birds becoming extinct in Guam?

❑ Because they are multiplying.
❑ Because they outnumber the brown tree snake.
❑ Because the brown snakes are eating them all.

Reading	❑ fluent	❑ halting
Speed	❑ less than 1 minute	❑ more than 1 minute
Vocabulary	❑ 0-3 unknown words	❑ 3+ unknown words
Response	❑ correct	❑ incorrect

Correct response, enter date in chart on page 85 and go to the next page; incorrect response go to Guidelines on page 87 and retest at a later date.

Context

Fourth Grade

Choose the words that best complete each sentence.

1. A whale is a mammal that _____ (a) through an opening in the top of its head. This opening is called a blowhole. It is similar to a nostril. Although whales can stay under _____(b) for long periods of time, they must eventually surface to breathe.

    (a) ❑ swims   ❑ sees   ❑ breathes

    (b) ❑ air   ❑ water   ❑ land

2. Hawaii is an island made up of three volcanic mountains in the Pacific _____(a). The only active _____ (b) in the United States, outside of Alaska, are found in Hawaii.

    (a) ❑ Ocean   ❑ Sea   ❑ Lake

    (b) ❑ volcanoes   ❑ mountains   ❑ islands

3. A diamond is a mineral. It is the hardest substance known. It is actually a form of carbon, just like coal! Coal is _____ (a), but _____ (b) are usually clear or transparent.

    (a) ❑ black   ❑ narrow   ❑ liquid

    (b) ❑ coal   ❑ gold   ❑ diamonds

4. The kangaroo is a hopping marsupial commonly found in Australia. _____(a) means it has a pouch to carry its babies. Kangaroos have powerful hind legs, short forelimbs, and long muscular tails. Male kangaroos are called boomers and females are _____ (b) flyers.

(a) ❏ Kangaroo ❏ Marsupial ❏ Pouch
(b) ❏ said ❏ called ❏ females

5. A fossil is the remains or imprints of plants or _____(a) preserved from prehistoric times. Fossils are found in rocks, coal, or amber. Fossils left by both vertebrate and _____ (b) animals are valuable to scientists who study prehistoric life.

(a) ❏ vehicles ❏ animals ❏ plants
(b) ❏ invertebrate ❏ vertebrate ❏ living

0-2 ✘'s, enter date in chart on page 85 and go on to the next page; 3 or more ✘'s, go to Guidelines on page 87 and retest at a later date.

Fact Finding

Fourth Grade

Read the following paragraphs and tell if each sentence is TRUE or FALSE.

The ear is an organ of hearing and balance. The human ear has three parts—outer, middle, and inner.

The outer ear is the part we can see. It includes the skin-covered cartilage called the auricle or pinna. The middle ear is separated from the outer ear by the eardrum. It has three small bones known as the hammer, anvil, and stirrup. They were given these names because of their individual shapes. The inner ear contains the sound-analyzing cells. It also contains semicircular canals that regulate balance and orientation.

	True	False
1. The only function of the ear is to hear.	☐	☐
2. The ear has three distinct parts.	☐	☐
3. The inner ear regulates balance.	☐	☐
4. The outer ear has a bone that resembles a hammer.	☐	☐
5. The eardrum separates the middle and inner ear.	☐	☐

0-1 ✘, enter date in chart on page 85 and go on to the next page; 2 or more ✘'s, go to Guidelines on page 87 and retest at a later date.

Main Idea   *Fourth Grade*

Read the following story and answer the question that follows.

> Bobby grew up in New York. He had been born there 11 years earlier and all of his friends were from his neighborhood.
>
> Now, Bobby sat next to his father as he drove the station wagon down the long highway. The engine was overheating, and they would have to stop soon to rest. In the back seat, Bobby's mother was holding the baby as they both slept.
>
> Although the Burnett family had left New York only three days before, it seemed like forever to Bobby. The long, boring ride made his legs feel like logs. His empty stomach was growling and he had a headache. Dad winked at Bobby as they rode along. "There's no turning back now," he said. Bobby tried to smile back at his father.

The main idea is:

- ❏ Moving to a new home is hard.
- ❏ Bobby grew up in New York.
- ❏ Traveling is exciting.

Reading	❏ fluent	❏ halting
Speed	❏ less than 1 minute	❏ more than 1 minute
Vocabulary	❏ 0-3 unknown words	❏ 3+ unknown words
Response	❏ correct	❏ incorrect

Correct response, enter date in chart on page 85 and go to the next page; incorrect response go to Guidelines on page 87 and retest at a later date.

Conclusions
Fourth Grade

Read the following story and answer the question that follows.

Stacey moved around her grandmother's stockroom whirling in graceful pirouettes. Her grandmother was typing at a nearby desk. Stacey's hair spun as she danced around.

Just then, Stacey heard her father calling her. She stopped dancing and hurried over to the cash register in the small market. "Your grandmother and I need some help in here," her father said. "Bring the bananas in from the loading dock. Then start mopping the floor so we'll be ready to open." As Stacey started down the stairs, she heard her father say, "Mom, I just don't know what to do about that girl. She's too busy dreaming about becoming a ballerina."

In a kind, gentle voice, her grandmother said to Stacey, "You have a special talent. You're going to be a great dancer. Someday your father will see that. So don't give up your dream."

This story shows that:
- ❏ Families should always stay together.
- ❏ Parents and children don't always agree.
- ❏ Parents and children are exactly alike.

Reading	❏ fluent	❏ halting
Speed	❏ less than 1 minute	❏ more than 1 minute
Vocabulary	❏ 0-3 unknown words	❏ 3+ unknown words
Response	❏ correct	❏ incorrect

Correct response, enter date in chart on page 85 and go to the next page; incorrect response go to Guidelines on page 87 and retest at a later date.

Context

Choose the words that best complete the sentences.

1. From the 9th to the 11th century, Scandinavian
_____ (a) called Vikings raided the coasts of
Europe, giving the _____ (b) the name the "Viking
Age." They were the best shipbuilders and sailors in the
world, and they traveled as far as Greenland and
Baghdad!

    (a) ❑ poets   ❑ warriors   ❑ weapons
    (b) ❑ period   ❑ traveling   ❑ prominent

2. Wolfgang Amadeus Mozart was an Austrian com-
poser. His music combines beautiful sound with classical
grace and technical perfection. A prodigy, he began
_____ (a) before he was five years old. During his
lifetime, he wrote works in almost every conceivable
_____ (b) of music.

    (a) ❑ driving   ❑ composing   ❑ recognizing
    (b) ❑ category   ❑ discussion   ❑ balance

3. Egypt of old is known as the Ancient Empire of the
Nile and was the site of one of the earliest civilizations.
Egypt was united about 3,200 BC and _____ (a) by
pharaohs (kings). Mummification and the building of
stone monuments began in the third _____ (b) ,
under the rule of the sun-worshippers—the religion of
the upper classes.

    (a) ❑ set   ❑ united   ❑ ruled
    (b) ❑ dynasty   ❑ minute   ❑ pyramid

4. The body contains three different vessels to carry blood. Arteries convey the blood away from the heart. The largest _____ (a) is called the aorta. Veins return the blood to the heart and lungs. The smallest are _____ (b) vessels called capillaries.

(a) ❑ aorta   ❑ artery   ❑ blood

(b) ❑ heart   ❑ vein   ❑ microscopic

5. The violin is a stringed musical instrument. It has a wooden body with a slightly convex back and front. The front is _____ (a) by two f-shaped resonance holes. It is played by _____ (b) a horsehair bow across the strings.

(a) ❑ pierced   ❑ covered   ❑ played

(b) ❑ throwing   ❑ delaying   ❑ drawing

0-2 ✗'s, enter date in chart on page 85 and go on to the next page; 3 or more ✗'s, go to Guidelines on page 87 and retest at a later date.

Fact Finding   *Fifth Grade*

Read the paragraph below and answer the following TRUE or FALSE questions.

> Amelia Earhart was an American aviator who lived from 1898 to 1937. In 1928, she became the first woman to cross the Atlantic by airplane, and in 1932, she was the first woman to make a solo flight across the Atlantic. She was the first person, man or woman, to fly alone from Honolulu to California.
>
> In 1937, she attempted to fly around the world, but her plane disappeared on the flight somewhere between New Guinea and Howland Island. To this day, her fate remains a mystery.

		True	False
1.	Amelia Earhart's goal was to fly around the world.	❑	❑
2.	Amelia Earhart was the first person to fly alone across the Atlantic Ocean.	❑	❑
3.	Amelia Earhart's plane disappeared when she was 39.	❑	❑
4.	Amelia Earhart's fate remains a mystery.	❑	❑
5.	Amelia Earhart's plane was found in Honolulu.	❑	❑

> 0-1 ✘, enter date in chart on page 85 and go on to the next page; 2 or more ✘'s, go to Guidelines on page 87 and retest at a later date.

Main Idea

Read the following story and answer the question that follows.

Southern Expeditions

For centuries, little was known about what was considered a distant, dangerous, frozen wasteland. Antarctica was the last continent to be discovered and was not sighted until the early 1800s. Since that time, many explorers have sailed south to visit the ice-covered land. In those days, their expeditions were as famous as those of the first astronauts.

Even before the land was discovered, stories were told about it. Centuries before anyone actually saw the continent, the ancient Greeks had thought that there was a continent at the bottom of the world. Over the years, tales of the undiscovered land grew. Some of the world's greatest sailors tried to find it. In 1772, the famous Captain James Cook undertook a grueling southern expedition.

Captain Cook was the first sailor to make it all the way to the ice cap that surrounds Antarctica in the winter. He sailed all the way around the continent but never actually saw it. Captain Cook went farther south than anyone had ever gone, and this record stood for 50 years.

In the 1820s, a different type of sailor was setting sail toward Antarctica—seal hunters and whale hunters such as a young American named

Palmer, who was probably the first person to see Antarctica. He and other adventurers were sailing through uncharted oceans in search of seals, and in doing so, became explorers as well as hunters. Nathaniel Palmer is believed to be the first person to see Antarctica.

The main idea is:

- ❑ Antarctica was not sighted until the early 1800s.
- ❑ Antarctica has been a source of fascination and intrigue for explorers for many centuries.
- ❑ Antarctica was the last continent to be discovered.

Reading	❑ fluent	❑ halting
Speed	❑ less than 1 minute	❑ more than 1 minute
Vocabulary	❑ 0-3 unknown words	❑ 3+ unknown words
Response	❑ correct	❑ incorrect

Correct response, enter date in chart on page 85 and go to the next page; incorrect response go to Guidelines on page 87 and retest at a later date.

Conclusions

Read the following story and answer the question that follows.

Seals

Seals are not fish. They're amphibious mammals that live both on the land and in the ocean. Some seals can stay at sea for months at a stretch—even sleeping in the water—but all seals need the land at some point. In order to avoid humans and other animals, they choose unpopulated areas to come onto the land.

Seals belong to a group of animals called "pinnipeds," or fin-footed, which includes the walrus, the sea lion, and the eared seal. Because of their fins, seals are excellent swimmers and divers. They have muscles in their noses that close their nostrils tightly when they dive. It is not unusual for them stay under water for as long as 30 minutes.

Being mammals, seals are warm-blooded animals that can adjust their bodies to various outside temperatures. They live in both warm and cold climates. Besides their fur, seals have a thick layer of fat called "blubber," which helps protect them against the cold. Unlike people, it is harder for seals to cool themselves off in hot weather and they can become ill or die if they get warm.

Answer the following questions about seals:

1. Based on the other words in the sentence, what is the correct definition for "*amphibious*"?
   - ❏ living on the land
   - ❏ living on land and in the sea
   - ❏ living in large groups

2. Based on the other words in the sentence, what is the correct definition for "*pinniped*"?
   - ❏ smart
   - ❏ excellent swimmer
   - ❏ fin-footed

3. Based on the other words in the sentence, what is the correct definition for "*mammal*"?
   - ❏ warm-blooded animal
   - ❏ cold-blooded animal
   - ❏ warm-blooded fish

4. Based on the other words in the sentence, what is the correct definition for "*blubber*"?
   - ❏ fur
   - ❏ fat
   - ❏ layer of skin

5. Based on what you've read, where do seals live?
   - ❏ tropical climates
   - ❏ cold climates
   - ❏ dry climates

Reading	❏ fluent	❏ halting
Speed	❏ less than 1 minute	❏ more than 1 minute
Vocabulary	❏ 0-3 unknown words	❏ 3+ unknown words
Response	❏ correct	❏ 2+ incorrect

0-1 ✖, enter date in chart on page 85 and go to the next page; 2 or more ✖'s, go to Guidelines on page 87 and retest at a later date.

Reading Record

Use this chart to keep a record of your child's reading progress. Once your child has successfully completed an assessment, enter the date in the chart. This will enable you to track your child's reading skills development as well as the pace at which he is making progress. If your child does not successfully complete a particular assessment, you may want to use the reassessment for that grade level and skill. See page 141 for reassessments for kindergarten through 5th grade.

Date Passed	Skill	Level
	Matching Pictures	Kindergarten
	Matching Letters	
	Context	
	Fact Finding	
	Story Order	
	Story Sense	
	Context	1st Grade
	Fact Finding	
	Main Idea	
	Conclusions	

Reading Record—*continued*

Date Passed	Skill	Level
	Context	2nd Grade
	Fact Finding	
	Main Idea	
	Conclusions	
	Context	3rd Grade
	Fact Finding	
	Main Idea	
	Conclusions	
	Context	4th Grade
	Fact Finding	
	Main Idea	
	Conclusion	
	Context	5th Grade
	Fact Finding	
	Main Idea	
	Conclusions	

Grade Level Guidelines

The first things a parent with a beginning reader wants to know are: Where do we start? What comes first? What is important?

One of the main problems with parents teaching reading is not that they don't know enough, but that they *know too much*. It's hard to go all the way back to the very beginning.

Starting Point

For children, reading encompasses learning the alphabet, putting all the letters in the right order, printing them neatly and correctly, sounding them out and understanding the meaning. For them, it's like trying to see the forest for the trees. Each element may be clear, but putting them all together for the big picture is extremely difficult. Parents on the other hand are generally literate, but have forgotten all the bits and pieces that go into the process of reading.

Fortunately, there is a comfortable sequence that enables children to learn phonics, and leads naturally into reading.

In terms of working with your own child, however, it is crucial to remember that there are stages of learning, types of memory, ways of learning, and internal time frames in which children learn. In general, children learn by doing. They are more successful with hands-on, concrete exercises, rather than more abstract, bookish exercises. For example, having your child rearrange letter cards to form a word will make a stronger, longer-lasting impression than if he just sits and looks at words on a page.

Some children are adroit psychological game players. They may pretend to forget large amounts of information, (*What? I didn't know that, really!*). If you feel yourself getting upset (*But you **know** this word!* or *We've been **over** this!* or *Are you paying attention?*), it's time to back off and make a fresh start later.

Reading is an enjoyable activity, not a punishment, and it should be taught playfully and lovingly. One day, reading will all make sense for your child. Your job, as a parent, is to keep practicing the fundamentals until that day comes.

Reading should be fun, not work

There will be a wide range in ability, interest, and performance among children at the beginning stages of reading. It may extend from an engaged interest to complete detachment and disinterest in books and reading. Almost all children, however, love to be read *to*. Don't be alarmed if at this early stage your child makes no connection between the spoken word and the printed word. This is natural because reading is a complex concept that takes time to be learned.

By reading to your child you will help him pick up the pre-basics: holding the book, turning the pages one at a time in the right direction, and following the pictures in a logical order. In time, with gentle encouragement, he will start to make the tenuous connection between letters printed on the page and actual spoken sounds, words, and ideas.

Reading *is* serious, but children need to be taught playfully. Two games that work well are variations on old standards—*Concentration* and *Go Fish*. For *Concentration*, start by using cards with matching pictures, then make cards with pictures that rhyme. Move on to cards with letters, rhyming words, and so on. In regular *Go Fish*, you use cards with numbers and players ask, for example, "Do you have a six?" In *Go Phish* (the phonics version), you use cards with letters or, later on, words. Players ask "Do you have a *T*?" or "Do you have a *Dog*?"

Books versus TV

There is a strong correlation between watching too much television and weak literacy. There is also a strong correlation between how much a family reads and the overall literacy of its members. The earlier you start reading to your child, the better, but it's never too late to pick up the habit. Read bedtime stories, take books along in the car—the parent not driving or an older sibling can read aloud, or the child can read on his own. This is a perfect setting for presenting your child with the idea of reading for fun, because generally there are no distractions from video games, television, and other attractions.

Take your child to the library to check out books of his choice and find out what programs your town's public library might have to encourage children to read.

Mostly, model the behavior you want your child to follow. Let your child see you reading and, when appropriate, talk to him about what you've read.

If you find it difficult to change your family's television viewing vs. reading habits, try a no-TV week for the entire household. This will be a great way for your child (and you) to discover the pleasure of reading.

Reading Prep

Spontaneous reading can and should happen any-where—while waiting in the car, at the doctor's office, in the park. However, it's good for your child to have a comfortable routine for reading. Here are some guidelines:

1. Find a quiet place for you and your child to read together uninterrupted for at least 10 minutes at a time.
2. Sit next to your child, so he can follow along with the words as you read.
3. Show your child the first page and how to open a book correctly.
4. Occasionally indicate words or phrases by pointing to them and moving your finger in a left to right direction as you read. For example, say, *"Oh, look, here's where it tells what the little bear said."* Indicate with your finger and follow the words as you read. *"My porridge is all gone! Someone has eaten all my porridge!"*
5. Review the story plot following the reading. Say, *"What did the little bear do when his chair was broken? What happened next?"* Three to four questions per story is enough.
6. When your child is familiar with the story, have him "read" it to you, using picture clues, while holding the book on his own lap.
7. As your child learns his letter names and sounds, show him selected words while reading. Say, *"See this word, it starts with the same letter 'b' as your name, Bobby. Can you find a letter in this line that says 'sss'?"*

Memorizing Words

In order to get a word firmly in your child's memory, it is helpful for him to really focus on it with the following sequence. This technique is not just for beginning readers. It can be used through college for memorizing new vocabulary, scientific terms, mathematical formulas, or foreign language vocabulary.

1. *Look* at the word.
2. *Say* the word.
3. *Cover* the word.
4. *Remember* what the word looks like.
5. *Write* the word from memory.
6. *Check* the word. Uncover it and check each letter carefully.

Reading is a habit, and it is your job as a parent to make sure that your child picks up this lifelong habit at an early age. Make books and other reading materials a part of your daily life. Have age-appropriate dictionaries handy for when a new word comes up. Mention items of interest in the newspaper. Point out that the television guide doesn't count as literature. Don't forget that habits have to be reinforced. As soon as your child can read on his own, set aside 10 minutes for daily reading. As he gets older, increase the time—15 minutes in 2nd grade, 20 minutes in 3rd grade, and so on. By the time your child is in 5th grade, he should feel comfortable choosing, reading, and using books on a wide range of topics and on a regular basis.

Following are the grade level guidelines for kindergarten through 5th grade, with the basic topics and common difficulties for each grade.

Phonics Definitions

Vowels. A, E, I, O, U and sometimes Y and W. Every word and syllable must have at least one vowel.

Consonants. Remaining letters and usually Y and W.

Consonant blends. Two or more *consonants* sounded together in such a way that *each* is heard—*black, train, cry, swim, fling*.

Consonant digraphs. Two *consonants* that together represent *one sound—when, thin, this, church, sheep, know, write, pack, thing*.

Consonant clusters. Three *consonants* that together represent *one sound—street, scrap, spring*.

Vowel digraphs. Two *vowels* that together represent *one sound*, for example, *school, book, bread, auto, yawn, eight*. Normally, with a double vowel, the first vowel stands for a long sound and the second is silent (*rain, jeep, heat, soap*) or the two vowels make a double sound—a diphthong (*coin or house*). With vowel digraphs, however, these rules are not followed.

Sight word. A word that does not follow the basic rules of spelling, and cannot be sounded out. For example, *pet* and *Pete* follow the rules, whereas *laughed* is pronounced *laft*. Sight words just need to be memorized or learned—by sight.

Syllable. A unit consisting of one vowel sound, with a consonant placed before or behind it. If you hear only one vowel sound in a word (*joke, miles*), it's a one-syllable word and cannot be divided. If you hear two vowel sounds (*basket, people*), it's a two-syllable word.

Kindergarten

Basic Skills

Most kindergartners should know how to say or sing the alphabet. They should be able to recognize their own names in print. Some may know how to print the alphabet, both upper and lower case, but this depends on their fine motor skills. They should know the positions—right, left, top, and bottom. This will help them know how to put their name on their papers in the proper position, how to follow the text from left to right and top to bottom, and how to open the book at the front, rather than the back. They need to know that there are *letters* in the alphabet and the association between each letter and its sound. They should also know that when you put the sounds together, they make *words*.

In texts appropriate for kindergartners, there should be a picture for every sentence, so that they can *see* the idea and then back it up with words.

Adults tend to take for granted that a story has a particular order, probably chronological. Children need to have this reinforced. You can do this by using daily examples such as putting on shoes and socks. Ask your child questions like, *"Which do you put on first? Why?"* She will naturally know the answer. But, having to stop, think about it and explain it will help develop logic sequencing. As a parent and adult, you have to remember that concepts that you take for granted need to be pointed out to your child, using concrete examples.

Story order exercises help a child see a story develop and, at the same time, tell stories himself. This storytelling precedes the written word and will get your child thinking in a certain way.

Furthermore, children need to have logical consequences pointed out and reinforced. Discuss how the first
picture leads into the second one, and then have your
child choose the logical third and explain why this choice
makes sense. A kindergartner should be able to finish a
story in a logical way, as well as predict the outcome.

Kindergartners are now ready for *Go Fish* and *Concentration* games with easy words, such as *cat, pet,* and
dog.

Another way to develop your child's readiness for
reading is to have her make flash cards. Participation
will encourage your child to use the cards, and the actual writing will be a memory aid.

Common Difficulties

At each age and at each stage there are particular
trouble spots that show up:

1. **Awareness of the Alphabet.**
   When a pre-reader starts to understand that
   there is a relationship between those little
   marks on a page and the sounds that come
   out of our mouths, she is on her way to
   reading. This is a highly abstract concept for
   a 5-year-old, but the sooner you start with an
   awareness of the alphabet, the longer your
   child will have to internalize the 26 symbols
   and the sounds they represent.

2. **Name and Sound of the Letter.**
   Another level of difficulty in the English
   alphabet is that there is a difference between
   the "name" of the letter and the "sound" of the

letter. For example, the name of the letter *S* is *ess*, but the sound of the letter is *sss*. This is an important distinction for your child to make, because it helps immediately with sounding out short words. Later on, it is used to clarify long and short vowels and to distinguish between hard and soft consonants (*C* as in *cat* or as in *nice*).

3. **Similar Letter Shapes.**

It is common to see children confused by the *four corners* letters:

b	d
p	q

One solution is to choose the key letter—*b*— and make sure that your child understands it. Use several approaches. Trace the *b* on your child's back and say *bee*. Take a <u>b</u>asketball and a <u>b</u>at and use them to form the letter *b*. She can see the spatial relationship of the ball and the bat, so the ball is where the *loop* goes and the bat is the *stick*. Talk about the ball being on the right side and the bat being on the left. Move the ball and have your child put the ball to the right of the bat. Then have her copy the pattern by writing *b*'s on paper.

Once she solidly knows **b**, she can go on to **d**, then **p** and finally **q**.

Another approach is that **d** and **q** are really the same as **a**, but **d** has a taller stick going up, and **q** has a tail going down.

4. **Socialization and Manners.**
In addition to these concrete methods that you can use to help your child learn the alphabet, there are also some more intangible ways that are equally important. The presence or absence of a child's social skills will be a large factor in the ease or difficulty with which she succeeds. According to the U.S. Department of Education, "The single best childhood predictor of adult adaptation is *not* IQ, *not* school grades, and *not* classroom behavior, but rather the adequacy with which the child gets along with other children." (Hartup, 1992) Children need to go to school prepared to get along with others, share books and toys, and take turns playing, listening, and helping.

More Kindergarten Skills

Letter Patterns. Recognizing *letter patterns* is very important for developing the pre-reading skills. Have your child find and circle the same letter groups from a list of similar ones. For example:

To give your child a grasp of a word (c-u-p, for example), use exercises that give the first and last consonant, and have your child fill in the blank with one of the suggested vowels. Make sure that you use pictures and that you say the word repeatedly, both as a word *(cup)*, and as individual sounds *(kuh-uh-puh)*. It is very important to keep the "uh" part of "kuh" or "puh" almost silent. Your goal is only the consonant sound. An over-pronounced "uh" will lead to difficulties with syllables later on.

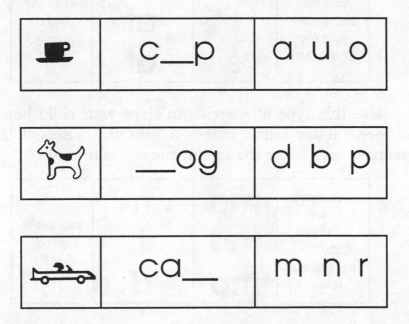

Hint: When you are helping a kindergartner with this type of exercise, cover up everything except the row you are working on. The whole exercise may look too "busy" to a child's eye.

Word Families. Play with rhyming word cards and point out the tiny differences that change the sound of the word—for example, by changing just one letter the word *cat* becomes *mat*, then *hat*, and so on. The example shown below should give you a good start at this. Rearranging the cards and saying the words provide visual, tactile, and auditory reinforcement. Remember that each of these "modalities" is good, but exercises that combine two or three are much more effective.

These are minimal changes— just the first letter.	c r s	at at at	*at is the word family.*

Use this type of exercise to show your child how a different letter sound makes a new word. Repeat this exercise with letter changes at the end of a word:

These are more minimal changes— just the last letter.	ma ma ma	n t d	*ma is the word family.*

and in the middle of a word:

These are still more minimal changes— just the middle letter.	c c c	a u o	p p p

First Grade

Basic Skills

Children learn to sound out words and begin basic reading in the 1st grade. The basic rules of phonics, from the alphabet to long vowels, are learned at this age. First graders should be able to read age-appropriate texts, sound out words they haven't seen before, and figure out simple meanings from the context.

By the end of 1st grade, children should be able to identify the *syllables* in a word, using them to distinguish between the base word and the various endings (lo**g**, log**s**, logg**ed**, logg**er**, logg**ing**).

Also, by the end of the year, students should be familiar with the *mechanics* of reading—the rules of pronunciation (including consonants, consonant blends, short vowels, and long vowels), and the lists of sight words and high frequency words.

It is not unusual to see a child still reversing words and letters at this stage—*d* for *b* and *no* for *on*, etc. This is not a cause for worry or a panic about dyslexia. If you suspect, however, that there is an actual reading problem, do not hesitate to discuss this with the school principal or the eye doctor. There are educational measures that can be taken to ease the way for a child with reading or vision difficulties.

Children will also track their reading with their fingers at this age. This is not an impediment. The eye muscles have not yet developed sufficiently to track back and forth, and the comprehension level is not high enough to keep place without a physical marker.

Moving on from the actual mechanics of reading, 1st graders should be able to say what the main point or main idea of a story is, in general terms. Furthermore, they should draw simple conclusions and explain why certain characters behaved the way they did. They should also have opinions about what happened in a story.

In terms of reading aloud, encourage your 1st grader to start using punctuation as a guide to how sentences sound. A statement—ending in a period—should sound different from a question—ending in a question mark.

When you and your child are reading, you will often be asked about a word—its meaning, pronunciation, why it is spelled a certain way. This is an excellent habit to encourage. Immediately say the word back to him. If a child can see a word and then hear it immediately after, it will reinforce the connection between print and sound. When he makes a mistake, don't make a big deal about it; mistakes are a natural part of life.

When a child can figure a word out from the context, he is really starting to read. He is putting all the pieces together—phonics, vocabulary, and comprehension. In order to help with this, read the same books over and over, pausing at his favorite spots, so he can fill in the gaps. For a 5- or 6-year-old, it is quite common to memorize a whole story without being able to read yet. There are many benefits to this. He learns how to tell a story, what the rhythms and patterns of the language are, and new vocabulary in the story. By repetition and pictures, he is able to make sense of it. Later, as he comes to understand the sound-letter relationship, the underlying structure will support his learning.

Once children have a good grasp of one-syllable words, they can use that same skill to move on to longer words. Being able to find the small word within a big word is a great advantage to an early reader. For example, *fantastic* is a *big* word to a 1st grader, but *fan* can be sounded out, as can *tas* and *tic*. When they put them all together as *fan•tas•tic*, they've sounded out a big word.

Reading and Being Read to

It is generally accepted wisdom that reading to a child will help produce a reader. The more you read aloud to your child, the more familiar he will be with the idea of books, the idea of getting pleasure and information from books, the recognition of letters on the printed page, and the correlation of printed words and information.

However, a child's reading skills will lag far behind his spoken language abilities for the first six to 10 years of his life. Talking and listening are effortless, but reading and writing take work. So, a child who is used to listening to advanced books may become bored and frustrated when he is only able to read a beginning book.

Other children, to the despair of their parents, will just read the same "baby books" over and over again. This gives a child an immediate sense of success. It gives him the idea that *"I can read."* Through the 1st grade, rereading familiar material reinforces the basics of reading, trains the eye coordination for consistent reading, satisfies the child's needs for the familiar and the comfortable, and allows the child himself to figure out new word based on their context.

Parents are well aware of the importance of reading and the enormous effect it will have on their child's future. Every parent wants his or her child to read, to read well, and to read often. There are not many guarantees in life, but if you sit patiently with your child night after night and read interesting stories, explain the rules of reading, reinforce this understanding with his own reading, and finally, read a lot yourself, you will have a child who reads. Naturally, there will be voracious readers, who devour every printed surface in the house and there will be more informational readers, who read to get what they want. But if you go through the steps, you will achieve 100 percent literacy in your home.

Common Difficulties

For each grade level, there are certain challenges that arise. In 1st grade, the following are common.

1. **Confusion between *long* and *short* vowels.**
   While a 1st grader should know the short vowels (*bat, bet, bit, hot, but*), he may not distinguish between *mat* and *mate*. You might hear the second word read as *mat*, *matee, ma-teh*. Explain the *silent E* rule, and that E "has a job to do." The final E makes the vowel say its name, but the E itself is completely silent. Similarly, when they are in the early writing stages, they may just put the first letter (I l t p → I like to play) or write the consonants, leaving the vowels out (picture → pkchr).

2. **Different learning styles.**
   Some children wiggle around and concentrate less, while others sit more quietly and grasp concepts more quickly. But there is more than one way of learning. It is important to use all of the senses in order to find the ones that work for the particular student: Visual (*shapes*), auditory (*sounds*), kinesthetic (*touching* and *feeling*).

3. **Frustration with exceptions.**
   Once a child has mastered a rule, exceptions
   to the rule can be intensely frustrating.
   Explain that some words don't follow the
   rules and that they can't be sounded out.

4. **Understanding the *phonics*, but not
   integrating them into *reading*.**
   It's a big leap to go from looking at letters on
   a page to making them tell a story. If a child
   gets stuck on a word, you can fill in the
   blanks for him. If you notice a pattern of
   missing words, it could be a gap in
   understanding of the rules. It helps to have
   your child say the rule back to you.

5. **Forgetting words they "knew" well.**
   Kids learn in stages. Sometimes something
   committed to short-term memory will just
   slip out the back door. Relax and go over it
   again. Don't get frustrated or your child will
   shut down and be afraid to try.

6. **Leaving the word out.**
   Some children simply skip over words they
   don't know. If your child skips a word,
   backtrack and repeat the entire phrase. This
   puts the word in context for him, letting him
   hear the flow of the entire sentence with the
   word in place.

7. **Mumbling difficult words.**
   Language is originally and primarily an oral
   communication system. Often, when a child is
   telling a story, he can mumble a detail he's
   not quite sure of and keep going, as long as it
   doesn't break the rhythm of the story. In

reading, too, difficult words will be mumbled over. If this happens too frequently, the entire meaning can be lost. Children get nervous reading, and not knowing a word can be embarrassing. Clarify the pronunciation for your child. If it follows a phonetic rule, have your child sound it out. If it is a sight word, quickly explain both the pronunciation and meaning. Try not to disrupt the flow of the reading. Also, a child can sound loud in his own head, not realizing how quietly the words are coming out. Try telling him to "shout" it out once or twice so he can feel what louder speech sounds like.

8. **Making up words.**
Frequently younger children will just look at the first letter and say a word that starts with that same letter. Of course, all meaning is lost. If this happens, ask if the sentence makes sense with the words used. Have him reread it slowly, sounding out the words. Talk about the meaning of the sentence in particular and the story in general.

9. **Over-pronouncing the T.**
At some point, readers will come up against a quirk of American English, which is that *T* and *D* sound the same, as in *latter* and *ladder*. In reading, encourage them to make the leap from the over-pronounced *let-ter* to the word that they know and use, *letter*. Also, the *T* at the end of a word is hardly pronounced in speech. But is highly visible, so children get confused and want to put a big *T* sound at the end of a word.

10. Getting stuck on the first letter and stopping.
Because the first letter, generally a consonant, is introduced early and often to the new reader, it seems children can get stuck there. They will look at a word such as *car*, and say k-k-k-k-, without going on the next sound. Or, if they do go on, they get confused and stop making sense. Ask what word would make *sense* at that point. For example, if the sentence is *The bear is walking in the woods* and the child is having trouble with the word *woods*, talk about bears, where they live, and what that particular bear might be doing.

More First Grade Skills

As your child is learning to read and grasp the concepts of phonics and how letters make words, here are guidelines to help your child learn to read.

1. Pay close attention to the **order in which you introduce the letters** and **how you relate each letter to its sound**. Keep it simple. Too much information is overwhelming. For example, the letter A has six different pronunciations, but a beginning reader should only learn the short A of *cat*.*

2. Children should practice **reading to themselves** rather than reading out loud. The reason for this is to develop the eye coordination to track side to side and line to

line, as children read more quickly to themselves than they can out loud.

3. Focus on **upper case letters** in the beginning, then move to lower case. In kindergarten and early 1st grade, most children use all capital letters to write words, including their names. In 1st grade, children learn to distinguish between the two cases and to use them appropriately. Do *not* introduce them at the same time (i.e. **A a**).

4. Practice sounding out words that **follow the rules**, such as *cat, late*, etc.

5. Words that can't be sounded out should be learned as **sight words**, such as *laugh, mother, have*, etc.

6. Whenever your child sounds a word out, make sure that he knows the **meaning**.

7. Fairly advanced words such as *Christmas* or *Reebok* might be absorbed as sight words early on, due to the great exposure to them that children experience.

8. When the beginning reader is first learning to sound words out, practice **word families** *(bat, cat, sat, mat, hat)*. Point out that only the first letter changes, and that all the words rhyme.

9. Let your child **track the words** across the page with his finger, or have him use an index card to keep each line separate. Immature eyes will "stand" on each word, and not flow over to the next words on a line. Additionally, it is very easy for a child to lose

track from line to line. A card or ruler to guide the eye will help.

10. Have your child write as well as read, (a daily journal, the shopping list, letters, etc.).

*The Six 'A' Sounds: *pack, pace, park, final, parent, war.*

High-Frequency Words. Not all words are used equally. Researchers have actually counted which words are used most, and consequently, *should be known best by students.* Here are the first 100 of those words. The other 400 are at the back. Have your child practice flying through these words. Use flashcards. And, of course, use Dr. Seuss. This way, your child can practice these common function words, both in and out of context. Generally speaking, their recognition and reading will be better in context.

The First 100

the	of	and	a	to	in	is
you	that	it	he	for	was	on
are	as	with	his	they	at	be
this	from	I	have	or	by	one
had	not	but	what	all	where	
when	we	there	can	an	your	
their	said	if	do	will	each	
about	how	up	no	out	them	
then	she	many	some	so	these	
would	other	into	has	more	her	
two	like	him	see	time	could	
make	than	first	been	its	who	
now	people	my	made	over	did	
down	only	way	find	use	may	
after	long	little	very	after	words	
called	just	where	most	know	which	

Consonant Blends. Blends don't seem like they should be difficult, but they often are hard for children to put together. This is because they learn the individual consonants first (B *buh* and L *luh*), so when they try to form even a simple word such as *blue*, it comes out as *buh-luh-oo*. It only gets more complicated with **clusters**, with *suh-tuh-er-eet* instead of *street*.

At this point, you have to get your child to make the connection between words that he already knows and the sounds that he's trying to create from the printed page. He can say *street*, so that's half the battle. Work on isolating the sound, *str*, and practice saying it out loud. *Street, str, str-eet, str, street*. Then, go back to the printed word, cover up the back end, and correlate the sound and the letters. Once the spoken *str* matches the written one, uncover the back end and let the whole word come out, *street*.

Word Endings. It takes time for a child to realize that a word can have parts to it. He might think *walked* looks like a two-syllable word (*wal-ked*) and not be able to figure it out. But when he understands that it is *walk* plus an *-ed* ending, reading becomes easier.

When your child has trouble with one of these words, cover up the ending, so the child can read the easy part (a word he may already be familiar with), then uncover the suffix and let him add it on (for the big word). His grammar skills will take over, and he will say *walk<u>ed</u>* instead of *wal-ked*, and later will know to spell it as *walked* instead of *walkt*.

Spelling and Pronunciation. In the 1st grade, children learn to spell according to certain rules. Spelling changes in order to maintain pronunciation. In a nutshell, the main rules are:

1. The *e* reaches over and makes the vowel say its name.
   rat → *rate*   *not* → *note*   *fin* → *fine*

2. When two vowels go a-walking,
   The first one does the talking.
   bed → *bead*   *got* → *goat*   *ran* → *rain*

Adding an ending (*ing, ed, er, est*) can cause changes. The rules are:

1. For short vowels, double the consonant.
   hop →   *hopping   hopped   hopper*

2. Long vowels lose the silent *e* and keep the single consonant.
   hope →   *hoping   hoped   hoper*

Even with the rules introduced, there will be vestigial phonetic sounding out. Your child may write things that sound like they should be there, but really aren't, such as *gowing* for *going*. To remedy this, review the ending with other words (*ask+ing*, *show+ing*) so the child can see and understand the pattern.

Reading is made up of several discrete skills. Two of the most distinct are reading and spelling. Good readers are not necessarily good spellers, and some excellent spellers never pick up a book. To illustrate this, if you read the imaginary word *feen*, there is only one way to pronounce it. However, if you are asked to spell a word that sounds like *feen*, you could come up with *feen, fene, fean,* or *phean*. This is because there are different spelling rules that can apply to the long E sound as well as the F sound. If a child knows the spelling rules, reading will be easy. Spelling words still need to be addressed on a case by case basis.

More Spelling Rules. Here are a few rules that will help your child with spelling and pronunciation.

Short Vowel Rule: If a word or syllable has only one vowel and it comes at the beginning or between two consonants, the vowel usually stands for a short sound—*am, is, bag, fox.*

Long Vowel Rule 1: Silent *e* rule. If a one-syllable word ends in an E, the vowel is long—*make, time, more, Pete, rule.*

Long Vowel Rule 2: Two vowels walking rule. If a one-part word or syllable has two vowels, the first vowel usually stands for a long sound and the second is silent—*rain, jeep, heat, soap.*

Long Vowel Rule 3: Final vowel rule. If a word or syllable has one vowel and it comes at the end of the word or syllable, the vowel usually stands for a long sound. For example: *we, go, cupid, pony.*

***Y* as a Vowel Rules.** If Y is the only vowel at the end of a one-syllable word, Y sounds like long I: *fly, try, by.* If Y is the only vowel at the end of a word of more than one syllable, Y usually has a sound like: *silly, funny, baby.*

Soft *C* and *G* Rule. When C or G are followed by E, I, or Y, a soft sound is produced: *ice, city, range, gym.*

Double Vowels. One of the most difficult areas for young children is the wide variety in vowel combinations and the subsequent pronunciation. There are both regular and irregular double vowels. The boxed words follow Long Vowel Rule 2, but the rest are exceptions. This aspect of reading, sight words, just requires *practice.*

ou	house, mouse, douse, louse

but   soup, four, touch, through,
though, rough, cough, courage,
furious

ea	seat, meat, treat, neat

but   head *or* hear *or* heard *or* heart *or*
great *or* idea *or* create *or*
beautiful *or* theatre *or* theatrical
or bureau

ow	how, now, brown, cow

but   show, low, throw

ie	tried, lied, fried

but   friend *or* fiend *or* diet *or* icier *or*
orient *or* derriere

oa	soap, boat, toast, goat

but   broad

oo	tooth, booth, choose, loose

but   took, good, look

The regular double vowels are EA, EE, AI, OA, IE, AY and OW. Irregular double vowels are very difficult for new readers because there are so many exceptions. Even adults have to check back in certain circumstances. Remember this old poem?

Have You Heard the Word?

Beware of *heard*, a dreadful *word*,
That looks like *beard* and sounds like *bird*,
And *dead*: It's said like *bed* not *bead* —
For goodness sakes, don't call it *deed*.
Watch out for *meat* and *great* and *threat*,
(They rhyme with *suite* and *straight* and *debt*.)

Believe it or not, irregular words are in the minority in terms of the words in the English language. More than 80 percent of the words in the dictionary are regular—but the problem is that in everyday language, we don't use the dictionary words. We use common terms that we've worn down and gotten used to over the centuries. These have come out to be irregular though this daily use.

The good news is that once the new reader gets past the familiar, but highly irregular words of colloquial speech, he will find that the longer, more sophisticated, Latin- and Greek-based words of literature will seem simple by comparison and simple to sound out.

R-Controlled Vowels. An R-controlled vowel means that an R can change the pronunciation of the previous vowel—the short *o* of *hot* turns into the long *o* of *horn*. It helps to remember two of the early sight words *or* and *for* have a long *o*. Another tricky thing about R is that sometimes the vowel in front of it is pronounced, *here*, and sometimes it isn't, *her*.

Children first learn *R* as a single consonant—*run* or *red*. Later, *R* is incorporated into a blend or cluster—*trip* or *shrill*. Next, they learn the *-er* ending—*runner* or *later*. And finally, there are the R-controlled vowels—*more*, *care* or *fire*.

Vowel Combo	Basic Rule	Final *E* Rule	Silent Vowel Before *R*	Sight Words
ar	car	care	dollar	arrive
ir	spirit	fire	first	siren
er	very	here	herd	her
or	for	more	color	word
ur	fur	cure	fur	bury

The problem with the consonant *R* and the R-controlled vowels is that they are two different *R*'s. The consonant *R* is regular whereas R-controlled vowels are not. When a child first comes across a word like *faster*, he may read it as *fast•air* or *fast•eer* and spell it as *fastr*. The word *first* may be read as *feerst* or *fyrst,* and spelled as *frst*. This situation necessitates the introduction of the *-er* ending. Once they have *-er* drilled into them, however, it can become the only option, with *ferst, hert, werst,* and *coler* showing up in spelling before *feerst* disappears from reading.

It helps to pare down the options. Primarily, *-er* is an ending. It is not common in the beginning of a word, except for *where*, *here* and *there*. Fortunately, *-ar* and *-or* are clearly pronounced, so for an R-controlled vowel, the real distinction is between *-ir* and *-ur*, as in *fir* and *fur*.

L-Controlled Vowels. An L-controlled vowel means that an L can change the pronunciation of the previous vowel. There are a couple of little things to help an early reader. First, 'ol' has a long *o*. It's easy for 1st graders to remember by starting with the word *old* and building up from there. You ask the child, *"Can you find the little word in the big word?"* Whenever you have an *-old* base, cover up the first letter so your child can read *old*, then move your finger and he can add on. **c** + *old*, **g** + *old*, **t** + *old*. *Colt* and *bolt* can coattail on this.

-old	told, fold, hold, bold, sold, cold, gold, mold
-all	cal, tall, stall, hall, ball, fall, wall
-oll	doll, follow
-alk	talk, walk, chalk
-ald	cold, bolt, bald, scald

Call may be read as *cal* for a while, but since *all* is learned early, use the same technique. **c** + *all*, **b** + *all*, **t** + *all*. *Bald* can coattail, but *walk* and *talk* are sight words (with a silent L!).

Soft Consonants. Children learn early that vowels have different pronunciations, but they generally learn consonants as having a single sound. At this stage, they need to learn that when a *C* is followed by *a, o,* or *u*, the letter *c* usually sounds like *k*. But when it is followed by an *e* or an *i*, it takes the soft *s* sound.

Hard C = K

ca-	cat, call, catch, can, cave, car
co-	come, copy, cough, cost
cu-	cut, customer, cub, cup

Soft C = S

ci-	city, circus, circuit, cinnamon
ce-	certain, center, celebrate, certificate
-ice	nice, police, Janice, lattice
-uce	truce, lettuce, spruce, deuce
-ace	race, place, trace, face, lace
-ece	piece, niece, fleece

Similarly, there are two *g* sounds. When *g* is followed by an *a*, *o* or *u*, it takes the hard *g* sound. *Gi* and *ge* can also sometimes be the hard *g*. When a *g* is followed by an *e*, it takes the soft *j* sound. There are a few exceptions such as *get*. Sometimes a *gi* or *gy* will sound like *j*.

Hard G = G

ga-	gas, gap, gave, gain, gallop
go-	go, gone, got, goat
gu-	gum, guppy, gullible, gustatory
ge-	get, gecko, gear, geyser
gi-	girl, gift

Soft G = J

ge-	gentle, George, general, gem
gi-	giant, ginger, giraffe, gin
gy-	gym, Gypsy, biology
-age	cage, stage, garage, page
-uge	huge, gauge, gouge, refuge

Hint: Sometimes E has two jobs. There is the old job of making the vowel say its name, and a new one of turning the *G* into *J*, or turning *C* into *S*.

That Tricky Y. Sometimes the letter Y sounds like a long I and sometimes like a long E. The trick is to remember an easy one-syllable word, like *my*, and then add on the correlated ones. Once that is secure, go on to the two-syllable words, making a big distinction for the different ending sound.

One Syllable = I
fly, fry, spy, try, my, shy, by, cry

Two Syllables = E
pretty, silly, funny, happy, party
any, many, penny, money, honey

I and Y are actually closely related, with Y being the Greek I, as they call it in French. You can see the transition from Y to I in *penny* to *penniless*, *lady* to *ladies*, *easy* to *easily*, etc.

Second Grade

Basic Skills

Second graders should have the basic reading skills. Sounding out should be second nature and the child should start reading in longer and longer phrases, rather than word by word.

Reading should consist of stories with fewer pictures than before, and the child should be able to follow a simple story line. Second graders start reading chapter books.

Every child should sit and read for at least 15 minutes a day. He can be with a parent or on his own, reading out loud or silently to himself. Choosing the book himself will give him greater incentive to read. Although the book may seem too easy to the parent, or it may be that he has read the book 900 times, let your child choose the book for the 15 minute reading. Your job is to make certain that the child sits still and reads. This means checking to make sure that his eyes are moving back and forth on the page. Encourage him to ask both how to pronounce a word and what it means.

After mastering phonics, the child starts working towards the *bigger picture* of reading. This raises the *point* of reading—is it to entertain oneself, to gather information, to integrate one's experience with that of the world, to understand a multicultural perspective? It is any or all of these, depending on the child, and his needs and motivations.

In order to arrive at any of these points, however, he will need to start using the following four tools. These are not limited to 2nd grade reading and there are more that will be introduced in the higher grades, but these will hold any reader in good stead through college and beyond. The earlier children learn these skills, and the more adroit they become at implementing them, the more satisfying their reading will be on a personal level, and the more effective their reading and writing will be on academic and professional levels.

Common Difficulties

1. **Main Idea.** This is *big-picture* understanding as opposed to noticing the *details*. This skill lets a child step back and think about the whole story. For a 2nd grader, the main idea is generally in the first sentence. The *main idea sentence* tells about the whole story, using all the details to add up to the entirety. A question that elicits main point understanding is, *"What is this story mostly about?"*

2. **Fantasy vs. Reality.** By the 2nd-grade stage, when a child is talking to someone, there is a fairly clear distinction between something that actually happened, and something that is imaginary, pretend, possible, or untrue. A large part of this understanding comes from the presentation of the information—an awareness of the real context, the speaker's attitude or tone of voice, etc. In reading, however, (as they are generally still at the monotone stage), they tend to miss some of the clues that would indicate whether something actually happened or not. In order to help the child distinguish, ask questions about what happened. Then, if you notice the child going astray, you can point

out the references that support either reality or fantasy. Ask, *"What would have happened if...?"* or *"Could he really fly?"* or *"How could...?"* Use starter questions to get your child thinking creatively, rather than answering questions about who did what to whom, and when.

3. **Drawing Conclusions.** In a story, the writer doesn't spell out every last detail—there are things that a reader will need to figure out or guess at. Conclusions are drawn from information given, (*He did it again!*—The word *again* allows the reader to conclude that something has happened before.) The type of question that enable a child to draw logical conclusions is *"What do you think would happen from that? Why?"* or *"What can you tell from the story?"* or *"From the story, what do you know about ...?"* or *"How do you think this person (character) would feel? Why?"*

    A good conclusion exercise is to give the child specific information and have him come up with the situation. For example, *"You see bats, balls and gloves. You hear, 'Strike One!' You smell hot dogs. Where are you?"*

4. **Getting the Facts.** When teachers ask the class to *get the facts* of a story, they are really looking for the details. The first thing a reader does is to get the main idea. Then, he goes on and finds the facts that support the main idea. The type of questions that elicit an awareness and understanding of the details might ask about what someone looked like, what they said or did, and when things happened. This is

where the journalistic 5 W's come into play,
and their correlating responses:

Who?	He. She. It.
What?	The tree.
Where?	Here. There. Everywhere.
When?	Yesterday, tomorrow, Monday.
Why?	Because...
How?	By doing...

More Second Grade Skills

Syllables. This is a good place to start working with syllables. Initially, *suh-tuh-er-eet* for *street*, has four syllables. After the blend idea is understood and the second part of the word has been revealed, the child can hear that there is only one sound present, *street*.

Second graders start to come across longer words in their reading, so it is helpful to teach them how to break up a word into components, or *syllables*.

Syllables are extremely helpful in sounding out words. A long word can be too daunting for a beginning reader, causing him to give up, whereas knowing the syllables lets him see the *smaller parts* that make up the whole.

You can see how words grow and become more complex by adding more syllables:

fact; per•fect; per•fec•tion; per•fec•tion•ist; per•fec•tion•ism.

Compound Words. Compound words are important because they are a cultural shorthand in English. They encapsulate whole ideas into two words. Exercises where the child takes two pictures and uses them to form a single word are helpful in getting him to see the breakdown of a word, as well as its origin. With a strong foundation in both suffixes and compound words, a child will make fewer reading and spelling mistakes such as *neckless* for *necklace*.

Prefixes. Children learn word endings in the 1st grade for grammatical changes—plurals (*-s*), past tense (*-ed*), continuous (*-ing*), etc. In the 2nd grade, they learn how to put two words together to form a third word with compound nouns. Then, once the idea of breaking up a word is clear, the advancing reader can learn a category for vocabulary, such as the prefix *pre-*, rather than learning case by case.

un-	un•happy, un•usual, un•known
dis-	dis•like, dis•honest, dis•appear
ad-	ad•monish, ad•vocate
re-	re•port, re•read, re•play

Suffixes. Earlier, children learned the grammatical endings. There is another category of endings called suffixes, which are the opposite of prefixes. Whereas the suffixes are common, the actual meanings are abstract, so the child can forego learning the meaning at this point.

-ment	excite•ment, apart•ment
-ish	baby•ish, green•ish, self•ish
-tion	condi•tion, situa•tion, inven•tion
-tain	cap•tain, moun•tain, foun•tain

Contractions. When a 2nd grader speaks, contractions come quite naturally, but they can give pause to even an advancing reader. Children often wonder what letter is left out and where the apostrophe goes. The main rule is quite simple: The two words are joined and the apostrophe replaces the letter(s) that has been removed.

With *negatives*, leave out the O in *not = n't*.

is not	isn't	are not	aren't
was not	wasn't	were not	weren't
do not	don't	does not	doesn't
did not	didn't	will not	won't
has not	hasn't	have not	haven't

Positives:

you are	you're	they are	they're
we are	we're	I am	I'm
he is	he's	it is	it's
I have	I've	I had	I'd
I will	I'll	I would	I'd

Homonyms. An area of confusion for many young readers is *homonyms*, where two words that sound the same and are spelled the same have two completely different and unrelated meanings. However, 2nd graders should be becoming proficient at understanding confusing homonyms by the context. Here are some common homonyms:

bear	to carry; the animal (grizzly bear)
suit	to be agreeable to; clothing
bat	a flying animal, a baseball bat

Third Grade

Basic Skills

A 3rd grader can be expected to read a designated 3rd grade text fluently and with expression—using the voice to indicate the *meaning* of the text (emotion and contrast), as well as the *grammatical* indications (question or statement, beginnings or endings, listing, commas and exclamation marks).

Expression and Meaning. Reading with *expression* is relating feeling, emphasis and meaning, based on both vocabulary and pronunciation. It is typical of a 2nd grader to read on regardless of punctuation, and this is perfectly acceptable at that level.

A 3rd grader should read with expression that fully reflects the punctuation.

Help your child read the following sentences:

1	**Statement**	It's here.
2	**Question**	It's here?
3	**Exclamation**	It's here!
4	**Beginning/End**	As I said, it's still here.
5	**Listing**	It's here, there, and everywhere.
6	**Quotes**	"It's here!" said Bob.

Phrasing and Comprehension

Word-by-word reading is so choppy that it is hard to understand the meaning of it. If you teach your child to read in phrases, not only will it make his reading clearer to the listener, but his own comprehension will improve. The first step to reading in phrases is to use the punctuation. Pause at a comma, and stop at a period.

He came, he saw, he conquered.

For a child first learning to read, there is the technique of finding the small words within a longer word—*fan•tas•tic*. You can use a similar technique to find the small phrases in a longer sentence. Start each phrase within a sentence with a preposition (in, at, for, by, to, with, etc.).

I drove <u>to the store</u> <u>in a red car</u> <u>on Friday morning</u>.

Understanding the Context

Reflecting the expanding vocabulary of the typical eight-year-old, the reader should be able to go through a text and figure out any new words through the context. For example, if he sees the sentence, *"After the rain, the hill was so muddy and **wuggy** that the hikers all slid to the bottom,"* he should figure out that the nonsense word *wuggy* could mean *slippery* or *wet* or *crumbly*. The clues would be *rain, muddy* and *slid*.

Main Idea

A third-grader should be able to read a whole chapter book (rather than just a paragraph or short story) and talk about the main ideas in it. At this level, there are longer, more difficult words and longer, more difficult sentences. There are more details and more complex ideas to absorb.

If, at any point, you discover that your child is having trouble grasping the main idea of what he reads, use examples such as figuring out the moral of each of the Aesop's Fables or other familiar stories.

"Why did the fox say that the grapes were sour?"

"What happened when the boy cried 'wolf' too many times? Has anything like this ever happened to you?"

"What would a wolf in sheep's clothing be in real life?"

"What was the point of the dog in the manger? What did the dog want? What did the cow want? Who was fair or unfair?"

Another way to clearly determine the main idea of a text is to change the statement to a question. If the answer is *yes*, you have found the main idea. For example, suppose you are trying to choose between the following two main idea choices.

Dogs are greedy.

It's wrong not to share something that you can't use yourself.

Convert each one to a question and see which works.

Are dogs greedy? No, not particularly.

Is it wrong not to share something that you can't use yourself? Yes.

If both sentences are true, choose the larger, more important truth.

It's wrong not to share something that you can't use yourself. *(True, and to the point.)*

Drawing Conclusions

Conclusions become more developed and are based on subtler cues in the language. Texts from which conclusions can be drawn include chapter books, simple newspaper articles, instruction sheets, and children's magazines. A typical conclusion statement by a child is, "You can tell that..." For example, upon reading the following: *The petting zoo was broken into and three animals were missing. Later that week, the animal control officers found a chicken, a duck, and a rabbit from the petting zoo.* The conclusion can be drawn that all three animals were found. A child could say, "*You can tell that they found all three of them because they listed three animals at the end.*"

Making Inferences

Bobby was furious. He was holding his crumpled test paper in his hand. "I studied hard," he yelled. "Look at this test!" Knowing what the reader knows about studying and taking tests, plus what the story tells, what must have happened? It would be an informed guess to say that Bobby had not done well on the test. Perhaps earlier in the book, however, the reader had learned that Bobby was a perfectionist, so he could be that upset about missing only one question.

Sequencing

This is a very important skill in terms of using sequential or chronological logic to create order in events. A child with clarity of thought will have an easier time with both reading and writing, not to mention math and history. Third graders can be expected to understand flashbacks, stories told in different orders by different characters and the thread of a story related through a series of letters or newspaper articles. It helps a child to practice articulating this skill with everyday situations, such as a movie or typical school day (including subjects, recess, sports, and what the teacher did, and when.) They say, "Start at the beginning," but the beginning is frequently the hardest part to determine. Practice with, "What happens first?"

Projecting an Outcome

After hearing or reading of a series of events, a third-grader should be able to predict what migh happen next. This is not only a type of inference, but a good indicator of how well a child understands sequencing, the main idea, and the facts of the story up to that point.

Getting the Facts

This is an extension of a 2nd grade skill. It should include the five W's in more depth, with more adjectives and descriptive vocabulary, as well as numbers, dates, personal and place names, and both figurative and literal information (*He felt the logs* vs. *His legs felt like logs*).

Self-correction

It's vital to reread and cross-check for facts and ideas. At this age, children are reluctant to go back over something they have completed once, but by doing so they will pick up important facts that they missed, as well as garner a clearer understanding of the main idea. This is also the point where children need to look up any unknown words that they can't figure out from the context. One 3rd grader, who enjoyed stories about England tried to figure out *knickers* from the context. Since people were always putting them on before they went out, he figured they were boots—until he came across a reference to a plaid pair! Then he figured he'd better look the word up in a dictionary.

Writing

In addition to getting the facts and ideas from reading, it is at the 3rd grade level that writing starts to gain sophistication. Of course, children will have been putting various forms of ideas on paper since kindergarten, but from this level on, the output is expected to increase and improve. They need to come up with their own facts, main ideas, conclusions and inferences.

The more a child reads, the more familiar he will be with the conventions of printed materials, including paragraphs, punctuation, capitalization, indenting and spelling.

Fourth Grade

Basic Skills

A 4th grader should be able to identify a piece as nonfiction, fiction, drama, or poetry. The prefixes *ex-*, *mis-*, *dis-*, *uni-*, *bi-*, and *tri-*, and the suffixes *-ous*, *-ship*, and *-ness*, should be recognized easily. They should know the difference between a fact and a simile (a simile is a phrase using like or as, such as he is as hungry as a horse or she ran like the wind). Young readers should be able to read visual presentations, such as diagrams, charts, and maps to categorize and understand information. They should know where a topic sentence generally occurs and how key words relate to the topic. Hand in hand with their writing skills, they should recognize the three main types of writing—informative, descriptive, and persuasive. They need to recognize and understand recurring themes in fiction, such as friendship, honor, death, dealing with adversity, etc.

There is a big dividing line between 3rd and 4th grades—through 3rd grade a child is learning to read, whereas from the 4th grade on, a child is reading to learn. This means that children have learned the basics, and are ready to take on the reading tasks of analysis, synthesis, summary, restating, contrast and comparison. They need to use context to find information that isn't expressly stated in the text, such as time and place.

Main Idea and Getting the Facts

A 4th grader should be able to read a text and summarize the most important points, without getting tangled in the details. He also needs to recognize and extract the facts.

135

Drawing Conclusions

In a story, the writer doesn't spell out every last detail. There are things that a reader will need to figure out or guess at. Earlier, we saw only **conclusions**, which are drawn from information given.

He did it again!

The word *again* allows you to conclude that something has happened before. Conclusions are logical deductions, based on evidence. It is necessary that the author has provided all the required information. A common syllogism is:

All men are mortal.
Socrates is a man.
Therefore, Socrates is mortal.

Making Inferences

Inferences, on the other hand, are *educated guesses* that the reader makes based on what the writer says *plus* what the reader knows.

A child comes home from school. He goes up the walk and into the house. "Hey! Dad! I'm hungry!"

The writer doesn't say that he went into his own house, but the reader can figure out that he did. Nor does he say that the father was home, but you can guess that he was.

Analysis and Evaluation

This is a more advanced skill. Children are called upon to make higher level distinctions. Earlier, child distinguished between fantasy and reality. At this stage, they determine the degree to which the plot is realistic. This is a good place for a child to bring in this own experience. An older person might read a story about teenagers and find it perfectly plausible, whereas a young person, with his own perspective and relativity to the age group, might be able to point out aspects that don't ring true.

Furthermore, readers can begin to analyze the author's word choice and topic. Does the author use positive words for a group of people or disparage a group of people? What references to age, gender, occupation, race, intelligence, or feelings are made and what is implied by them? Some authors bring up images of nature, whereas others have more urban settings. Newspapers are a good place to examine bias through the presentation of information. What is brought up first? What is buried at the end of the article? How do the photographs shape the words that accompany them? And so on.

Word Roots

Students can start expanding their vocabularies, improving their comprehension, and understanding spelling changes by knowing a few basic Latin root words and their prefixes.

With this knowledge, readers can make educated guesses at the meaning of a word based on its origins. This will supplement the information derived from the context. They will also have a better understanding of some of the spelling shifts that take place. For example, B/P and C/G/Q shift back and forth (*describe* to *descriptive; second* to *sequence* to *segue; distinct* to *distinguish*). Prefixes shift toward alliteration (*un•legal* is *illegal*, *ad•similate* is *assimilate*, *con•port* is *comport*, *sub•ceptible* is *susceptible*). I and Y trade off frequently (*pony* to *ponies*, *easy* to *easily*).

Fifth Grade

Basic Skills

A 5th grade reader should be familiar with common genres of literature such as mysteries, biographies, folk tales, fantasy, science fiction and nonfiction, and recognize how each one shapes the stories or information presented in them.

In terms of *comprehension*, 5th-graders are in a position to state the main idea of a passage from a 5th-grade reading book, extracting the pertinent details and weeding out the irrelevant ones. Additionally, they should be able to talk *about* the story, as well as retell it in their own words.

They should figure out the meaning of new and difficult words by the *context*, and correct their own mistakes by using the context.

They should be able to identify *cause* and *effect* in either fiction or nonfiction works.

By looking even beyond the main idea, they should be able to tell what the *author's purpose* was—why he wrote that particular book, told that particular story and used those particular words to do it.

Based on their own lives, they should also be capable of seeing relationships between their own experiences and those depicted in the work, thus deriving a deeper understanding of what the author was trying to say.

They should easily identify the setting by location and relationship to the characters. They can think about how the story would have changed if it had been moved from one place in the world to another.

They should be able to tell if the plot is realistic or not, and whether a character could be a real person or not, based on the reasons for a character's actions, taking into account the situation and motivation of the person portrayed. It should be clear whether it is a stereotypical representation of a person or a fully developed and characterized individual. The characters should be identified by name, occupation, appearance, age, temperament, etc. With this understanding of the character, readers should be able to take on a character's perspective and explain his point of view.

Students need to recognize how the structure supports a story. If it is an epistolary novel, how do the letters contribute to the understanding of the book? If it is told in flashbacks, how does this build up to a complete understanding of the plot? Are there metaphors or similes?

Readers should be developing favorite authors, as well as opinions on the works they have read. With these authors, they should be able to identify themes within each book, as well as from book to book. They should be able to compare and contrast books by the same author, along with books from different authors.

Finally, they should be familiar with the major genres, and recognize how this shapes the materials presented in them.

Reference Skills

Reference skills should include outlining and note taking; recognizing fiction and nonfiction; using reference texts such as the dictionary, thesaurus, encyclopedia, world almanac, and telephone book; and using the card catalogue, as well as various book sections of the library. They should recognize and use the reference sections within a book such as the table of contents, index, glossary, and bibliography.

Reading Reassessments

Kindergarten through Fifth Grade

Matching Pictures

Look at the picture on the left. Draw a circle around the matching picture in the box.

0-1 ✗, enter date in chart on page 85 and go to the next page; 2 or more ✗'s, stop test and go to Guidelines on page 87. Retest at a later date.

Matching Letters   *Kindergarten*

Look at the letter on the left. Draw a circle around the matching letter in the box.

D	B	D	W

K	A	N	K

J	J	I	L

X	R	Y	X

F	E	F	Y

0-1 ✗, enter date in chart on page 85 and go to the next page; 2 or more ✗'s, stop test and go to Guidelines on page 87. Retest at a later date.

Context

Circle the picture that best finishes each sentence.

We took a trip in the

I was reading a good

The teacher ate her

 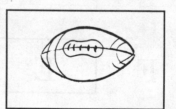

> 0-1 ✖, enter date in chart on page 85 and go to the next page; 2 or more ✖'s, stop test and go to Guidelines on page 87. Retest at a later date.

Fact Finding

Look at the picture and tell if each sentence is TRUE or FALSE.

	True	**False**
1. The dog is playing with his friends.	❑	❑
2. The dog is bouncing a ball.	❑	❑
3. The dog is taller than the bush.	❑	❑

0-1 ✖, enter date in chart on page 85 and go on to the next page; 2 or more ✖'s, stop test and go to Guidelines on page 87. Retest at a later date.

Story Order

Look at the four pictures. Decide what order they should be in to tell a story. Write numbers in the little boxes to show the order the pictures belong in.

Correct order, enter date in chart on page 85 and go to the next page; incorrect order, stop test and go to Guidelines on page 87. Retest at a later date.

Story Sense

Kindergarten

Look at the top pictures. Draw a circle around the bottom picture that shows what is more likely to happen next.

Correct response, enter date in chart on page 85 and go to the next page; incorrect response, stop test and go to Guidelines on page 87. Retest at a later date.

Context

Choose the word that best finishes the sentence.

1. We put jam on the _____.

     ❑ bread   ❑ air   ❑ lots

2. Selma took a _____.

     ❑ next   ❑ funny   ❑ bath

3. The story was very _____.

     ❑ good   ❑ does   ❑ tall

0-1 ✖, enter date in chart on page 85 and go to the next page; 2 or more ✖'s, stop test and go to Guidelines on page 87. Retest at a later date.

Fact Finding
First Grade

Read the paragraph and tell if each sentence below is TRUE or FALSE.

> I am a toy. I am big and round. I can bounce. I am made of rubber. I am a ball.

	True	**False**
1. The toy is square.	❏	❏
2. The toy is big.	❏	❏
3. The toy is a car.	❏	❏

0-1 ✖, enter date in chart on page 85 and go to the next page; 2 or more ✖'s, stop test and go to Guidelines on page 87. Retest at a later date.

Main Idea

First Grade

Read the following paragraph to your child and have her answer the question that follows.

Susan looked in the cookie jar. It was empty. She had really wanted a chocolate chip cookie. Susan was disappointed. She had a bowl of corn flakes instead.

What is the main idea?

❑ Susan was disappointed.

❑ Susan wanted a cookie.

❑ Susan had corn flakes.

Reading	❑ fluent	❑ halting
Speed	❑ less than 1 minute	❑ more than 1 minute
Vocabulary	❑ 0-3 unknown wds.	❑ 3+ unknown words
Response	❑ correct	❑ incorrect

Correct response, enter date in chart on page 85 and go to the next page; incorrect response, stop test and go to Guidelines on page 87. Retest at a later date.

Conclusions   *First Grade*

Read the following paragraph to your child and have her answer the question that follows.

> Sally has always wanted to visit a farm. Today she finally got a chance to visit one. While she was there, she got to ride a horse and see cows, pigs, and ducks. Sally said, "I wish I could live on a farm."

Which sentence describes Sally?

❏ Sally has dark curly hair.

❏ Sally has a pet duck.

❏ Sally likes the farm.

Reading	❏ fluent	❏ halting
Speed	❏ less than 1 minute	❏ more than 1 minute
Vocabulary	❏ 0-3 unknown words	❏ 3+ unknown words
Response	❏ correct	❏ incorrect

Correct response, enter date in chart on page 85 and go to the next page; incorrect response, stop test and go to Guidelines on page 87. Retest at a later date.

Context   *Second Grade*

Choose the word that best completes each sentence.

1. The cheetah can run much faster than a person. It is known for its _____.

    ❑ speed   ❑ teeth   ❑ height

2. In Japan, they do not always cook their fish. They like to eat it _____.

    ❑ today   ❑ outdoors   ❑ raw

3. When you are sleepy, it is hard to keep your _____ open.

    ❑ eyes   ❑ door   ❑ window

4. When will the snow _____?

    ❑ white   ❑ fall   ❑ spill

5. I want to go to the beach and _____.

    ❑ tree   ❑ swim   ❑ visit

> 0-1 ✘, enter date in chart on page 85 and go to the next page; 2 or more ✘'s, stop test and go to Guidelines on page 87. Retest at a later date.

Fact Finding

Read the following paragraph and tell if each sentence is TRUE or FALSE.

> Spiders have eight legs. Did you know that they also have eight eyes? Many people are afraid of spiders, but spiders are helpful to us. Without spiders there would be too many bugs. Spiders are also known as arachnids.

	True	False
1. Spiders have more legs than eyes.	❑	❑
2. Spiders can be helpful to people.	❑	❑
3. Without spiders, there would be lots of bugs.	❑	❑
4. Spiders are also known as amphibians.	❑	❑

0-1 ✗, enter date in chart on page 85 and go to the next page; 2 or more ✗'s, stop test and go to Guidelines on page 87. Retest at a later date.

Main Idea

Read the following story and tell what the main idea is.

Sports

Many kids like to play team sports. When you play on a team, you have to work with other people. Some people try to score points alone. They think it will be their point. Points made in team sports are team points. If you don't want to share the points you make then you should play golf.

The main idea is:

❑ Any point made is for the whole team.

❑ Some players score their own points.

❑ Golf is fun.

Reading	❑ fluent	❑ halting
Speed	❑ less than 1 minute	❑ more than 1 minute
Vocabulary	❑ 0-3 unknown wds.	❑ 3+ unknown wds.
Response	❑ correct	❑ incorrect

Correct response, enter date in chart on page 85 and go to the next page; incorrect response, stop test and go to Guidelines on page 87. Retest at a later date.

Conclusions   *Second Grade*

Read the following story and answer the questions that follow.

Dolphins

Dolphins do not sleep like we do. They take many short naps. Like us, dolphins breathe air. But dolphins live in the sea. Dolphins can talk under water.

How are dolphins and people the same?

- ❏ They sleep like we do.
- ❏ They breathe air.
- ❏ They live in the sea.

Reading	❏ fluent	❏ halting
Speed	❏ less than 1 minute	❏ more than 1 minute
Vocabulary	❏ 0-3 unknown wds.	❏ 3+ unknown wds.
Responses	❏ correct	❏ incorrect

Correct response, enter date in chart on page 85 and go to the next page; incorrect response, stop test and go to Guidelines on page 87. Retest at a later date.

....

Context

Third Grade

Choose the words that best complete the sentences.

1. Have you ever wondered how a fly can walk on the
_____ (a) ? It is because it has _____ (b)
hairs on its feet that keep it from falling.

    (a) ❑ heat   ❑ ceiling   ❑ third
    (b) ❑ wall   ❑ one   ❑ sticky

2. When you look at an iceberg, you can only see the
tip. An iceberg is nine _____ (a) bigger than the
part you can see. Most of it is under _____ (b) .

    (a) ❑ times   ❑ lives   ❑ more
    (b) ❑ air   ❑ water   ❑ land

3. In America, it is very common to shake hands
when you meet _____ (a). In Japan, it is more
usual to bow to a person. There may be differences,
but good _____ (b) are very important in both
countries.

    (a) ❑ something ❑ new   ❑ someone
    (b) ❑ food   ❑ manners   ❑ handshake

4.   Anteaters don't only eat ants. They also eat termites and other _____ (a). Anteaters have no teeth but have a long, sticky _____ (b) that can be up to two feet long!

   (a) ❑ rugs   ❑ insects   ❑ anteaters
   (b) ❑ tongue   ❑ anthill   ❑ eye

5. Bears hibernate all winter. They sleep in a _____ (a) and don't eat for several months. They live off of their body fat. It stands to _____ (b) that when they finally wake up they are hungry and grouchy!

   (a) ❑ rock   ❑ cave   ❑ winter
   (b) ❑ eat   ❑ wake   ❑ reason

0-2 ✘'s, enter date in chart on page 85 and go to the next page; 3 or more ✘'s, stop test and go to Guidelines on page 87. Retest at a later date.

Fact Finding   *Third Grade*

Read the following paragraph and tell if each sentence is TRUE or FALSE.

Nowadays, people use many machines every day. One of the earliest machines was a very simple one. Let's see if you can guess what it was. It was not invented until the Bronze Age in Europe.

At first, it was made of round, wooden disks. In 2700 BC, spokes were added. That was almost 5,000 years ago. Do you know what this simple machine is? It is the wheel!

		True	False
1.	The earliest wheel was made with spokes.	❑	❑
2.	The wheel was invented 2,700 years ago.	❑	❑
3.	The wheel is not a machine.	❑	❑
4.	The first wheel was made of bronze.	❑	❑
5.	The wheel was invented in Europe.	❑	❑

> 0-1 ✘, enter date in chart on page 85 and go to the next page; 2 or more ✘'s, stop test and go to Guidelines on page 87. Retest at a later date.

Main Idea

Third Grade

Read the following paragraphs and tell what the main idea is.

Trees

Trees are not just the huge plants you see growing in a forest. A large part of the tree grows under the ground. This part is called the roots. If the tree is big and really old, the roots may reach down 100 feet!

The roots hold the tree into the ground. Without roots, trees would fall over! The roots do another important job for the tree. They gather minerals and water from the soil to feed the tree so it will grow. Most land plants could not live without roots to support them and to feed them.

The main idea is:

❑ The roots of the tree are underground.

❑ The roots do important jobs for the tree.

❑ Roots can grow to be 100 feet long.

Reading	❑ fluent	❑ halting
Speed	❑ less than 1 minute	❑ more than 1 minute
Vocabulary	❑ 0-3 unknown wds.	❑ 3+ unknown wds.
Response	❑ correct	❑ incorrect

Correct response, enter date in chart on page 85 and go to the next page; incorrect response, stop test and go to Guidelines on page 87. Retest at a later date.

Conclusions   *Third Grade*

Read the following paragraphs and answer the question that follows.

Pet Grasshoppers

Believe it or not, some people keep grasshoppers as pets. It's important to always keep two of them together. Otherwise, the grasshoppers would get lonely!

People keep grasshoppers in a jar filled with dirt. The dirt helps grasshoppers feel like they are at home. They need a screen over the jar to let air in. The screen also keeps the grasshoppers in! Instead of a screen, some people use a small net or a cheesecloth. They make sure there is room under the screen for the grasshoppers to hop! Grasshoppers are clean, quiet pets.

When you have a pet grasshopper, it is important to

- ❑ Keep it quiet.
- ❑ Provide it with all the things it needs.
- ❑ Use a cheesecloth.

Reading	❑ fluent	❑ halting
Speed	❑ less than 1 minute	❑ more than 1 minute
Vocabulary	❑ 0-3 unknown wds.	❑ 3+ unknown wds.
Response	❑ correct	❑ incorrect

Correct response, enter date in chart on page 85 and go to the next page; incorrect response, stop test and go to Guidelines on page 87. Retest at a later date.

Context

Fourth Grade

Choose the words that best complete the sentences.

1. The giraffe is the tallest animal. A _____ (a) giraffe can be up to 18 feet tall. They browse in treetops at heights that other animals can't reach. They can _____ (b) most of their enemies and have been known to kill lions with a single powerful kick.

(a) ❏ few   ❏ another   ❏ male
(b) ❏ follow   ❏ outrun   ❏ play

2. Table tennis is a game, usually played indoors, by two or four _____ (a) . It is like a miniature game of tennis. It is also called Ping-Pong. The regulation game is played on a table that measures 9 feet by 5 feet, and is 2.5 feet high. A 6-inch net _____ (b) the table in two.

(a) ❏ referees   ❏ players   ❏ games
(b) ❏ includes   ❏ falls   ❏ divides

3. The carnivorous fish called the piranha is _____ (a) to the catfish. Piranha are found in Africa and the Amazon. They have powerful jaws and _____ (b) sharp triangular teeth, capable of killing humans and cattle.

(a) ❏ known   ❏ related   ❏ fiercer
(b) ❏ razor   ❏ round   ❏ heavy

4. In the ancient Roman religion, Neptune was the god of water. In later times, he was _____ (a) with the Greek god of the sea, Poseidon. The 8th _____ (b) from the sun is named after him.

(a) ❑ identified   ❑ exclaimed   ❑ divided

(b) ❑ star   ❑ planet   ❑ moon

5. World War I began in 1914 and was touched off by the _____ (a) of Archduke Ferdinand of Austria. The Allies (Great Britain, France, Russia, Serbia, Belgium, Italy, Portugal, Romania and America) _____ (b) the Central Powers (Germany, Austria-Hungary and Bulgaria). The Allies finally won in 1918.

(a) ❑ invention   ❑ President   ❑ assassination

(b) ❑ discussed   ❑ fought   ❑ introduced

0-2 ✘'s, enter date in chart on page 85 and go to the next page; 3 or more ✘'s, stop test and go to Guidelines on page 87. Retest at a later date.

Fact Finding   *Fourth Grade*

Read the following paragraph and tell if each sentence is TRUE or FALSE.

Confucius was an ancient Chinese philosopher. He was born around 500 BC in Lu, a former feudal state in China.

He was upset by the constant fighting between the Chinese states and the corruption and greed of the rulers, so he supported a moral system that would preserve peace and give the people a stable, fair government.

After this death, his philosophy became a religion called Confucianism, which had ideas similar to the Golden Rule. He believed that people should be treated they way they themselves would like to be treated.

		True	**False**
1.	Confucius changed his name to Lu.	❑	❑
2.	Before Confucius was a philosopher, he was a warrior.	❑	❑
3.	Confucius' philosophy is quite different from the Golden Rule.	❑	❑
4.	Confucius thought that rulers were corrupt.	❑	❑
5.	During his lifetime, Confucius turned his philosophy into a religion.	❑	❑

0-1 ✘, enter date in chart on page 85 and go to the next page; 2 or more ✘'s, stop test and go to Guidelines on page 87. Retest at a later date.

Main Idea   *Fourth Grade*

Read the following story and tell what the main idea is.

One day, a rabbit met a lion in the woods. The lion was hungry and irritable. He said, "Don't move! I'm going to eat you up." While he was talking, the lion backed the rabbit up against a rock. The rabbit realized she couldn't run away. "I'll have to use my brain instead of my legs," she thought.

Aloud to the lion, the rabbit said calmly, "I would have made a good lunch for you last month. But I've had eight babies since then. I have to look for food all day long in order to feed them." "Stop!" the lion interrupted. "I don't care how many children you have. I'm going to eat you right now." The lion stepped closer to the rabbit.

"Wait!" yelled the rabbit. "Look how thin I am. I ran off all my fat looking for food for my children. But I know where you can find something delicious!" The lion sat back to hear what the rabbit had to say. "There's an old well not far from here. There's a big piece of cheese in the bottom of it. Come on, I'll show you."

The lion followed closely after the rabbit, making sure she couldn't run away. "See," said the rabbit when they got to the well. Inside the well was what looked like a round, yellow piece of cheese. It was really the reflection of the moon, but the lion didn't know this. The lion leaned over the well, wondering how to get the cheese. The rabbit jumped up and quickly pushed the lion in. "I am a clever little thing," the rabbit thought as she hopped home to her children.

The main idea is:

❑ The rabbit was trapped, but used her brains to trick the lion and escape.

❑ The lion was irritable and wanted to eat.

❑ The moon's reflection looks like a piece of cheese.

Reading	❑ fluent	❑ halting
Speed	❑ less than 1 minute	❑ more than 1 minute
Vocabulary	❑ 0-3 unknown wds.	❑ 3+ unknown wds.
Response	❑ correct	❑ incorrect

Correct response, enter date in chart on page 85 and go to the next page; incorrect response, stop test and go to Guidelines on page 87. Retest at a later date.

Conclusions   *Fourth Grade*

Read the following story and tell what the conclusion is.

One day, the hare and the tortoise were talking. Actually, the hare was bragging and the tortoise was listening. "I run faster than the wind," boasted the hare. "I pity you because you are the slowest thing I've ever seen!"

"Oh, really?" asked the tortoise with a smile. "Let's race to the other side of the meadow."

"Ha!" laughed the hare. "You must be joking! You'll lose! Well, if you insist, let's race."

"I'm on my way," the tortoise said, and started walking slowly and steadily across the meadow. The hare stood there and laughed. "How sad! That slowpoke wants to compete with me!" he said. "I'll take a little nap while that poor old tortoise plods along. When I wake up, he'll still only be halfway there." Some time later, the hare woke up. He saw that while he had been sleeping, the tortoise had won the race.

The best way to get reach a goal is
- ❑ By working hard and not giving up.
- ❑ By sleeping first to get some rest.
- ❑ By thinking you're better than others.

Reading	❑ fluent	❑ halting
Speed	❑ less than 1 minute	❑ more than 1 minute
Vocabulary	❑ 0-3 unknown wds.	❑ 3+ unknown wds.
Response	❑ correct	❑ incorrect

Correct response, enter date in chart on page 85 and go to the next page; incorrect response, stop test and go to Guidelines on page 87. Retest at a later date.

Context
Fifth Grade

Choose the words that best complete the sentences.

1. Tidal waves are seismic sea waves or tsunami. They are catastrophic ocean waves generated by submarine movements such as earthquakes, volcanic _____ (a) or landslides beneath the ocean. Tsunamis can travel at speeds up to 450 miles per hour. When they approach _____ (b) water, their height can rise to as high as 100 feet.

   (a) ❏ volcanoes   ❏ speeds   ❏ eruptions

   (b) ❏ dry   ❏ shallow   ❏ tsunami

2. Hummingbirds feed on insects and the nectar of flowers, for which their long, _____ (a) bills are especially adapted. They are usually seen hovering or darting as they feed in flight. Their wingbeats are so rapid (50-75 beats per second) that their wings appear _____ (b) .

   (a) ❏ slender   ❏ invisible   ❏ expensive

   (b) ❏ falling   ❏ old   ❏ blurred

3. Alfred Nobel invented dynamite. He was, however, a pacifist who regretted the _____ (a) power that he had created. He _____ (b) the Nobel Prize as an award for outstanding achievement in physics, chemistry, medicine, peace, literature, and economics.

   (a) ❏ kind   ❏ sweet   ❏ destructive

   (b) ❏ established ❏ said   ❏ blamed

4. In 1943, Jacques Cousteau invented the _____ (a), also known as a self-contained underwater breathing apparatus (scuba). He also founded the French navy's undersea research group. He made many _____ (b) films about his work before his death in 1997.

(a) ❑ aqualung   ❑ fertilizer   ❑ shark cage
(b) ❑ automobile   ❑ documentary   ❑ music

5. The New York City Ballet is one of the _____ (a) American dance companies of the 20th century. It was founded by Lincoln Kirstein and George Balanchine in 1946. The company developed a distinctly American style of dancing by combining Italian, French, and Russian _____ (b) with a unique musical flair.

(a) ❑ foremost   ❑ American   ❑ ballet
(b) ❑ engineers   ❑ columns   ❑ traditions

> 0-2 ✗'s, enter date in chart on page 85 and go to the next page; 3 or more ✗'s, stop test and go to Guidelines on page 87. Retest at a later date.

Fact Finding

Fifth Grade

Read the following paragraph and tell if each sentence is
TRUE or FALSE.

Dr. Martin Luther King was a preacher and
civil rights leader. He was born in 1929 and died
in 1968. He led a boycott against the city bus
lines because of their segregation policy.

Because of his philosophy of nonviolent
resistance, he was arrested several times in the
1950s and 1960s. In 1963, he organized the
March on Washington, which brought more than
200,000 people together. In 1964, he was
awarded the Nobel Peace Prize.

In 1968, he was shot and killed by an
assassin's bullet on the balcony of the motel
where he was staying. James Earl Ray was
convicted of his murder.

	True	**False**
1. Martin Luther King led a bus boycott because of the poor service.	❏	❏
2. Dr. King was a civil rights leader, preacher, and Nobel prize winner.	❏	❏
3. Dr. King assassinated James Earl Ray.	❏	❏
4. Dr. King believed that violence was not an effective way to accomplish goals.	❏	❏
5. Dr. King could not get anyone to march on Washington.	❏	❏

> 0-1 ✖, enter date in chart on page 85 and go to the next
> page; 2 or more ✖'s, stop test and go to Guidelines on
> page 87. Retest at a later date.

Main Idea   *Fifth Grade*

Read the following story and tell what the main idea is.

As long as there have been people, they have wanted to move from one place to the next. Until the wheel was invented, they had to walk or ride horses. In some parts of the world, wealthy people had other people carry them around in palanquins. With the invention of the wheel, however, the possibilities for transportation multiplied. When railroads became the major means of transportation, they replaced earlier types of travel such as the stagecoach and horse drawn wagon. Railroads were the main form of transportation in America for a hundred years, but starting in the early 1900s, they have had to deal with competition from other forms of transportation.

These days, millions of people own cars. Buses are an inexpensive mode of travel and readily accessible. Eighteen-wheel trucks are used for transporting merchandise. Airplanes offer fast transportation over long distances. Due to these alternatives, there has been a steep decline in the use of trains.

Almost all railroads have serious problems that could push them out of business. On the other hand, railroads provide low-cost, fuel-saving transportation that will always be important.

The main idea is:

- ❏ When railroads became the main form of transportation, they took the place of other means of travel.
- ❏ Starting in the early 1900s, railroads have dealt with competition from other forms of transportation.
- ❏ Even though there are many modes of transportation available today, trains continue to be very useful and valuable.

Reading	❏ fluent	❏ halting
Speed	❏ less than 1 minute	❏ more than 1 minute
Vocabulary	❏ 0-3 unknown wds.	❏ 3+ unknown wds.
Response	❏ correct	❏ incorrect

Correct response, enter date in chart on page 85 and go to the next page; incorrect response, stop test and go to Guidelines on page 87. Retest at a later date.

Conclusions
Fifth Grade

Read the following story and answer the question.

For many years in the late 1800s, strong men gave their lives to the railroad tracks that crisscross the United States. They worked and sweat to lay thousands of miles of track that carried passengers and freight from one coast to the other. The strongest of these men was the hammerman John Henry. He could drive steel and lay track faster, better, and straighter than any other man alive.

Around 1870, the steam drill was invented. One day, another company on the far side of a mountain decided to dig a tunnel using the steam drill. John Henry was matched against the best man from that company to see who would reach the middle of the mountain first. To make a long story short, John Henry beat the steam drill by four feet! That night, he said, "I was a steel driving man." Then he lay down and closed his eyes forever.

How did John Henry feel the night he won the contest?

❑ Excited that he'd won a valuable prize.
❑ Like he had accomplished his goal.
❑ Ready for another contest soon.

Reading	❑ fluent	❑ halting
Speed	❑ less than 1 minute	❑ more than 1 minute
Vocabulary	❑ 0-3 unknown wds.	❑ 3+ unknown wds.
Response	❑ correct	❑ incorrect

Correct response, enter date in chart on page 85 and go to the next page; incorrect response, stop test and go to Guidelines on page 87. Retest at a later date.

Answer Key

Assessments

page

60	1. bed 2. bark 3. Tuesday
61	1. false 2. false 3. true
62	Jenny wanted the snow to stop.
63	Bob took a picture of the children playing at the new playground.
64	1. air 2. grow 3. read 4. house 5. excited
65	1. true 2. false 3. false 4. true
66	In summer, there are many things to do outside.
67	scratch
68-69	1. (a) eat, (b) fast 4. (a) luck, (b) mirror 2. (a) food, (b) tails 5. (a) safety, (b) down 3. (a) poisonous, (b) sick
70	1. false 2. true 3. false 4. false 5. false
71	Anything smooth and straight can be used to make a straight line.
72	Because the brown snakes are eating them all.
73-74	1. (a) breathes, (b) water 4. (a) Marsupial, (b) called 2. (a) Ocean, (b) volcanoes 5. (a) animals, (b) invertebrate 3. (a) black, (b) diamonds
75	1. false 2. true 3. true 4. false 5. false
76	Moving to a new home is hard.
77	Parents and children don't always agree.
78-79	1. (a) warriors, (b) period 4. (a) artery, (b) microscopic 2. (a) composing, (b) category 5. (a) pierced (b) drawing 3. (a) ruled, (b) dynasty
80	1. true 2. false 3. true 4. true 5. false

81-82   Antarctica has been a source of fascination...
83-84   1. living on land and in the sea
        2. fin-footed
        3. warm-blooded animal
        4. fat
        5. cold climates

Reassessments

page

148   1. bread   2. bath   3. good
148   1. false   2. true   3. false
150   Susan was disappointed.
151   Sally likes the farm.
152   1. speed   2. raw   3. eyes   4. fall   5. swim
153   1. false   2. true   3. true   4. false
154   Any point made is for the whole team.
155   They breathe air
156-57 1. (a) ceiling, (b) sticky   4. (a) insects, (b) tongue
        2. (a) times, (b) water   5. (a) cave, (b) reason
        3. (a) someone, (b) manners
158   1. false   2. false   3. false   4. false   5. true
159   The roots do important jobs for trees.
160   Provide it with all the things it needs.
161-62 1. (a) male, (b) outrun   4. (a) identified, (b) planet
        2. (a) players, (b) divides   5. (a) assassination, (b) fought
        3. (a) related, (b) razor
163   1. false   2. false   3. false   4. true   5. false
165   The rabbit was trapped, but used her brains to escape.
166   By working hard and not giving up.
167-68 1. (a) eruptions, (b) shallow
        2. (a) slender, (b) blurred
        3. (a) destructive, (b) established
        4. (a) aqualung, (b) documentary
        5. (a) foremost, (b) traditions
169   1. false   2. true   3. false   4. true   5. false
171   Even though there are many modes of transportation
      available today, trains continue to be useful and valuable.
172   Like he had accomplished his goal.

174

NAEP Reading Achievement Standards

The National Assessment of Educational Progress (NAEP), an arm of the U.S. Department of Education, serves the vital function of reporting to educators, parents, policy makers, and the general public how well our students are achieving in the area of reading proficiency.

The 1994 NAEP Reading Assessment was administered to national samples of 4th-, 8th, and 12th-grade students attending public and nonpublic schools, and to samples of fourth graders in the 44 jurisdictions that participated in the 1994 Trial State Assessment. Nearly 140,000 students were assessed in the national and jurisdiction samples. Students' reading performance is described on a proficiency scale ranging from 0 to 500, and in relation to three reading achievement levels: *Basic, Proficient,* and *Advanced.* The assessment results are reported based on the performance of students at each of the three grades and within specific subgroups of the population. For each grade, the definitions are cumulative from *Basic* through *Advanced*. One level builds on the previous level. That is, knowledge at the *Proficient* level presumes mastery of the *Basic* level, and knowledge at the *Advanced* level presumes mastery of both the *Basic* and *Proficient* levels.

Fourth Grade Reading Achievement Levels

Fourth-grade students performing at the *Basic* level should demonstrate an understanding of the overall meaning of what they read. When reading text appropriate for 4th graders, they should be able to make relatively obvious connections between the text and their own experiences, and extend the ideas in the text by making simple inferences.

Fourth-grade students performing at the *Proficient* level should be able to demonstrate an overall understanding of the text, providing inferential as well as literal information. When reading text appropriate to 4th grade, they should be able to extend the ideas in the text by making inferences, drawing conclusions, and making connections to their own experiences. The connection between the text and what the student infers should be clear.

Fourth grade students performing at the *Advanced* level should be able to generalize about topics in the reading selection and demonstrate an awareness of how authors compose and use literary devices. When reading text appropriate to 4th grade, they should be able to judge texts critically and, in general, give thorough answers that indicate careful thought.

Grade 4: NAEP Trial State Assessments in Reading
1998 Assessment, Public Schools Only

State	At or Above Basic	Below Basic
Alabama	56%	44%
Arizona	53%	47%
Arkansas	55%	45%
California	48%	52%
Colorado	69%	31%
Connecticut	78%	22%
Delaware	57%	43%
Florida	54%	46%
Georgia	55%	45%
Hawaii	45%	55%
Indiana†	66%	34%
Iowa	70%	30%
Kentucky	63%	37%
Louisiana	48%	52%
Maine	73%	27%
Maryland	61%	39%
Massachusetts	73%	27%
Michigan	63%	37%
Minnesota	69%	31%
Mississippi	48%	52%
Missouri	63%	37%
Montana	73%	27%
Nebraska†	66%	34%
Nevada	53%	47%
New Hampshire	75%	25%
New Jersey†	65%	35%
New Mexico	52%	48%
New York	62%	38%
North Carolina	62%	38%
North Dakota†	73%	27%
Oregon	61%	39%
Pennsylvania†	61%	39%
Rhode Island	65%	35%
South Carolina	55%	45%
Tennessee	58%	42%
Texas	63%	37%
Utah	62%	38%
Virginia	64%	36%
Washington	63%	37%
West Virginia	62%	38%
Wisconsin	72%	28%
Wyoming	65%	35%

† Not represented in 1998; reflects 1994 data
* NAEP 1998 Reading Report Card for the Nation and the States, U.S. Dept. of Ed.,
Office of Educational Research and Improvement

More High-Frequency Words

The First 100 listed on page 110

The Second 100

get	through	back	much	go	good	new
write	our	me	man	too	any	day
same	between	right	look	think	around	also
another	came	come	work	three	must	here
because	does	part	even	place	well	such
take	why	help	put	different	away	again
off	went	old	number	great	tell	men
say	small	every	found	still	name	should
home	big	give	air	line	set	own
under	read	last	never	us	left	end
along	while	might	next	sound	below	saw
something	thought	both	few	those	always	show
large	often	together	asked	house	don't	world
going	want	school	until	important	form	food
keep	children					

The Third 100

feet	land	side	without	boy	once	kind
animals	life	enough	took	four	head	above
began	almost	live	page	got	earth	need

far	hand	high	year	mother	light	country
father	let	night	picture	being	study	second
soon	story	since	white	ever	paper	hard
near	sentence	better	best	across	during	today
however	sure	knew	it's	try	told	young
sun	thing	whole	hear	example	heard	several
change	answer	room	sea	against	top	turned
learn	point	city	play	toward	five	himself
usually	money	seen	didn't	morning	car	I'm
body	upon	family	later	turn	move	face
door	cut	done	group	true	half	red
fish	plants					

The Fourth 100

living	black	eat	short	united	run	book
gave	order	open	ground	cold	really	table
remember	tree	course	front	American	space	inside
ago	sad	early	I'll	learned	brought	close
nothing	though	idea	before	lived	became	add
become	grow	draw	yet	less	wind	behind
cannot	letter	among	able	dog	shown	mean
English	rest	perhaps	certain	six	feel	fire
ready	green	yes	built	special	ran	full
town	complete	oh	person	anything	hot	hold
state	list	stood	hundred	ten	fast	felt
kept	notice	can't	strong	voice	probably	area
horse	matter	stand	box	start	that's	class
piece	surface	river	common	stop	am	talk
whether	fine					

The Fifth 100

round	dark	past	ball	girl	road	blue
instead	either	held	already	warm	gone	finally
summer	understand	moon	animal	mind	outside	power
problem	longer	winter	deep	heavy	carefully	follow
beautiful	everyone	leave	game	system	bring	watch
shall	dry	fact	within	floor	ice	ship
themselves	begin	third	quite	everything	carry	sat
distance	although	possible	heart	real	simple	snow
rain	suddenly	leaves	easy	lay	size	wild
weather	miss	pattern	sky	waked	main	center
someone	field	stay	itself	boat	question	wide
least	tiny	hour	happened	foot	care	low
else	gold	build	glass	rock	tall	alone
bottom	walk	check	fall	poor	map	friend
language	job					

Index

How Well Does Your Child Write?

A Step-by-Step Assessment of Your Child's Writing Skills and Techniques to Develop Them

For Nate

Special thanks to Susan Greenberg, Vicki Spandel,
Heidi Goodrich, Carol Jago, Linda Lewin
and Larry Kaltveldt.

Contents

Introduction

You've probably noticed that times have changed since you were in school. The work your child brings home seems quite different from what *you* were learning at that age. Children today are expected to know more and possess more advanced skills at an earlier age. You're left to wonder: "What is normal for a child in my child's grade?" or "What are the national standards in writing?"

You may also begin to worry that report cards and scores on standardized tests aren't telling you enough about how your child is *really* performing academically. After all, news reports are assaulting you with discouraging statistics about American education. In 1996, the National Assessment of Educational Progress (NAEP), an arm of the U.S. Department of Education that monitors academic achievement through periodic testing of 4th, 8th, and 12th graders, found that 80 percent of 4th graders' informative essays, more than 60 percent of their narrative essays, and more than 40 percent of their persuasive essays were minimally developed.

It's no longer safe to assume that everything must be okay if your child continues to be promoted, as there is often an unpublicized "no-fail" policy in schools, where children are routinely advanced to the next grade when they have not achieved even a remedial level in the previous grade. The thinking was that "flunking" stigmatized children and separated them from their peer group, and that the child would continue to do poorly and possibly end up not graduating. It was deemed preferable to put a child into the next grade and give additional academic support. Unfortunately, this support was not always available, but the policy was in place and the child would be passed along nonetheless. So how do you make sure that your child is on the right track—that she doesn't become a part of these bleak statistics?

You *can* identify specific learning problems by checking the results of whatever standardized test your child is required to take in school every year. However, these tests vary from state to state, and not all teachers support their findings. Part of the problem is that America, unlike most advanced nations, does not have a national curriculum. The states' constitutional right to establish their own educational systems means that some schools have a wonderful school curriculum, but others leave much to be desired. It also means that students' annual standardized test scores might only reflect their performance on a regional level. The American Federation of Teachers (AFT) issued "Making Standards Matter 1996," an annual 50-state report on efforts to raise academic standards. Nearly every state is working to set common academic standards for their students, but the AFT report makes it clear that most states have more work to do to strengthen their standards. For example, at this time, there are only 15 states with standards in all four core categories (English, Math, Science, Social Studies) that are clear, specific, and well-grounded in content. For a report on an individual state, go online for the AFT state-by-state analysis. The URL is: www.aft.org//index.htm.

Furthermore, school report cards only indicate your child's *overall* performance. If you see a low grade in English composition on your 5th grader's report card, you only know that there's a problem—not what the problem is. You can, of course, schedule a conference with the teacher, but as many teachers have not been specifically trained in assessing writing skills, it would be difficult to isolate the problem.

But what if you could figure out that your 5th grader has a well developed vocabulary and knows how to use punctuation correctly, but can't construct an introduction or conclusion for an essay? This is what *How Well Does Your Child Write?* can help you do. With this knowledge, you can work with your child to remediate the problem—with workbooks, discussions, games, and writing exercises.

Why I wrote this book

As a parent, I had the same concerns you do. When my son was in the 1st grade, he was having trouble with reading in a whole language program. I began researching elementary education and assessment and wrote *How Well Does Your Child Read?* and later, *How Well Does Your Child Do Math?* By the time my son was in the 3rd grade, he read well, but I noticed that there were not many writing assignments. The children wrote in their journals, but those were kept in the classroom, and the homework called for minimal, fill-in-the-blank type answers. I was dissatisfied with the results these exercises were producing, so I did research to develop a system for teaching my son key writing skills at home. Out of that came the inventory of skills and abilities that went into *How Well Does Your Child Write?*

The test is a simple, straightforward inventory of the basic skills involved in writing. It can also be used as a writing portfolio for children. As a linguist and the director of American Accent Training—a nationwide program to teach foreign-born students to speak standard American English—I had experience creating diagnostic speech analyses and grammar and accent tests. As an author, I used what I knew about writing and created a writing "inventory" to test my own son, as well as the children in the ACE (After Class Enrichment) Program I had founded at the local elementary school.

The material for my diagnostic tests has been garnered from a number of reliable sources. I studied the NAEP assessments of American students' abilities in reading, mathematics, and writing. NAEP has been conducting such tests since 1969, ranking the results of the tests by state and providing appropriate achievement goals for each age and grade. I also relied on books on test research, and online information about state standards. Finally, my diagnostic tests went through a series of trial runs with children, in addition to being evaluated by experienced elementary school teachers and reviewed by an educational therapist.

How to use this book

How Well Does Your Child Write? contains a writing diagnostic/placement test for children in kindergarten through 5th grade. It will help you determine if your child can write coherently and whether your child can write appropriately to a specific audience. You can use this assessment to target areas that may need additional work. Or if it shows that your child is performing at or above her grade level, this book can allay your doubts about your child's ability and help you guide her to the next level.

The book contains the following sections:

♦ Six different writing assessments (one per grade level, kindergarten through 5th grade). Each includes up to three writing samples (informative, descriptive, persuasive); concrete and imaginary idea flow; vocabulary; and conventions (penmanship, spelling, punctuation, and grammar).

♦ A scoring section at the end of each assessment.

♦ Grade level guidelines: a review and explanation of the components of writing, including conventions, outlines, vocabulary, and style as well as the most common difficulties at each grade level, with recommendations on overcoming them.

♦ Appendices containing listings of educational support centers and online resources.

There are several things to be gained from having your child take this test. Initially, you will see the areas in which your child excels or is competent, as well as the areas that require further development. Also, you will see the scope and level of work expected at each grade level, along with the criteria by which it is graded. An other main purpose is to familiarize you with the variety of components that go into writing—divided mainly into conventions and idea flow. (Although a printing or cursive sample is included at each level, it is important to note that penmanship is not a component of writing. It is only assessed here to let you know what the standards are.) Finally, these tests will acquaint you with both your child's aptitudes and knowledge.

Aptitudes and *knowledge* are two distinct aspects of every individual. Aptitudes are natural talents—special abilities for doing or learning to do certain types of things. There are always some skills that come naturally, while others are a constant struggle—one person can take a radio apart and put it back together, whereas someone else may have a natural ability to play a musical instrument. Knowledge, on the other hand, is acquired—from parents, teachers, books, experience, and so on. Aptitudes suggest a general direction, and knowledge is gained to follow that direction. You can't acquire an aptitude, but you can increase your knowledge. This is why the idea flow measurements will probably remain fairly stable over the years, while vocabulary, grammar, and punctuation should change.

The elements of good writing

There are two distinct parts to writing at the elementary level: how it looks and what it says. These are *presentation* and *content*. Presentation consists of penmanship, straight margins, good spacing, proper format (title, heading, etc.), appropriate punctuation, correct spelling, standard grammar, and an outlined structure.

Content includes ideas and idea flow, vocabulary, style, clarity of thought, and the use of language in a creative, unique, telling, or memorable way.

Writing involves various skills that are not necessarily cumulative or dependent upon each other. For example, in math, a person needs to know how to add and subtract in order to multiply and divide, and division leads directly into fractions. Writing does not follow this type of pattern. Even if a person does not know the exact definitions of a noun and a verb, or how a comma differs from a semicolon, she can be a clear and understandable writer.

Generally speaking, in the lower elementary grades, (kindergarten through 2nd) the presentation skills are highlighted. In 3rd grade, with presentation skills acquired and in use, starts the transition to content.

The difficulty lies in reconciling the two. Assessing presentation skills is quite straightforward—spelling, punctuation, format, and grammar have clearly defined rules. Assessing content is subjective—there is a range for creativity, vocabulary, idea flow, and imagination. You can say that *potatoe* is spelled wrong and *potato* is spelled right, but can you say that *exquisite* is a "better" word than *lovely*? No, it depends on the context and the situation.

While presentation can be tinkered with—by correcting spelling, using the right punctuation, rewriting, and printing neatly—substance is both more difficult for a child to develop and harder to measure objectively. Thus, this book will help you answer such questions as: Are my child's essays organized? Do her ideas flow logically? Does he have a broad vocabulary and does he use words properly? Does he have a distinct style?

Scoring the writing assessments

As you may already realize, the evaluation of writing is a tricky task—it's subjective, flexible, and conditional. Many people feel that while reading and math can be tested easily, it's difficult to evaluate writing in a systematic way.

Practically speaking, however, there are certain guidelines that will allow you to determine both the grade level and the caliber of your child's writing. In writing assessment, scoring guidelines are called a *rubric*. A good rubric will lay out the components to be evaluated and will give a range against which you can measure your child's performance in a particular writing sample. These tests use rubrics with a range of three categories: exceptional, competent, and developing. In kindergarten and 1st grade, the developing category is called "prewriting."

Be sure to let your child know what the standards are before he starts on a writing sample—when your expectations are clear and familiar, he will be much more successful in meeting them and more capable of judging her own work. A good rubric is also a starting point for discussing assessment of your child's written classwork with the teacher.

The idea flow assessments (thought completion, synonyms, homonyms, concrete and imaginary possibilities) measure the rate of flow of ideas. Children who are full of thoughts, ideas, plans, and projects will score high on this category. Other children may ultimately come up with as many ideas, but not as quickly. It is important to note that an idea flow assessment is not measuring the quality of the ideas, only how fast they flow. It measures how many ideas the child comes up with, not whether they are sensible or creative. This is why you need to allow the child to come up with anything, and not judge or weed out ideas that you may think are 'silly' or irrelevant.

There are two different scoring sheets for these tests. The first is for the *individual skills*, such as printing, grammar, and idea flow. These are tested separately because skills can vary if they are taken in context of the assessment of the skill itself (mistakes on a spelling test) or in context of another skill (spelling errors while concentrating on a first draft of an essay). The individual skills are scored and recorded on a single page at the end of every grade level, and have specific guidelines for each particular test.

The *writing sample* scoring has one page for recording the score and one for the rubric from which the score is drawn. When you assess the writing samples at the kindergarten and first grade levels, you are primarily scoring the printing. Generally speaking, 5- and 6-year-olds haven't yet acquired sufficient skills to actually write a story.

If you would like a percentage for the error rate in spelling, Here's a simple formula you can use: Count the number of errors and put that over the total number of words in the sample. Then multiply the errors by 100 and divide by the total words. This will give you the percentage of errors and works regardless of the length of the piece. For example, a 1st grader who wrote 13 words and misspelled 5 of them would have a 38 percent error rate (5 x 100 = 500; 500 ÷ 13 = 38). A 5th grader who wrote 175 words with 5 misspellings would have an error rate of 2.8 percent (5 x 100 = 500; 500 ÷ 175 = 2.8).

At the kindergarten through 2nd grade levels, the conventions and presentation skills are primary, but from 3rd grade on, you should also start judging the entire passage for structure, vocabulary, and content. Third grade is the transition level between *presentation* (K-2nd) and *content* (4th-5th). Presentation and conventions will always be important, but there will be more emphasis on organization, vocabulary, and content.

Because there are fewer tests in the 1st grade than in the 5th, there are fewer individual skills rubrics. The individual skills rubrics, however, contain the same elements from kindergarten through 5th grade, but the range is tailored to each level.

Before you begin

Before you plunge into the rest of this book, are you sure that no physical or learning impediments are hampering your child's ability to write? For example, has her eyesight been checked recently? If she has been displaying learning problems, have you ruled out the possibility of Attention Deficit Disorder (ADD) or dyslexia? Only after you've determined that your child is ready, willing, and *able* to learn should you give the diagnostic test to determine what her writing level is and what you may do to improve it.

How to give the test

Set aside 20 minutes alone with your child in a quiet room. Make sure there are no distractions—turn off the TV, and never try to give the test just before a big soccer match or gymnastics practice. Tell your child this will only take a few minutes and that the results will help her enjoy writing more. Stress that there's no pressure, no punishment, no failing.

Students in kindergarten though 2nd grade should be monitored closely because they have a greater tendency to get sidetracked. Sit with your child, explain each task and watch to make sure she has accomplished it. Have her complete only one or two tests (in any order within the appropriate grade level) at a time in order to limit the "fatigue factor."

Independent study starts in the 3rd grade, so children at that level can have greater autonomy during the test and, if willing, write for more than 20 minutes. Students in 4th or 5th grade should be able to concentrate for up to an hour.

Writing takes time, but a good rule of thumb is that each individual skills assessment should not take more than 5 minutes, whereas each writing sample can take as long as the child is willing to put into it.

Once the child has completed the assessment for her grade level, score the completed section on the page noted at the bottom of the test page. Then turn to the grade level guidelines on page 113 for standards and common difficulties at that grade level. Because writing is cumulative, it is a good idea to read the guidelines for every grade, so no points are overlooked. These standards and guidelines can help you with remediation if your child has trouble with certain concepts and will introduce you to the next level if your child is at or above grade level.

One of the primary functions of these tests and guidelines is to familiarize you with the topics that should be taught at each level. Once that familiarization has taken place, you can offer your child extra support in the areas where she needs further development. For example, work on problem areas by using spelling drills, encouraging your child to write stories for fun, and asking questions about events or stories to practice logical thought. Use these methods to support your child's classroom work. It also goes without saying that the more your child reads, the better writer she will become.

In addition to the writing samples in the book, keep a journal of your child's writing—a representative sample once a month, so you can track development and improvement over the years.

Retesting

After the first assessment, you will know which areas to work on with your child—whether they include sentence structure, idea flow, or printing. Continue working on the weaker areas until your child is at or above grade level. At the same time, support the stronger areas that were revealed by the assessment.

If you feel your child has made progress after the work you've done together, whether remediation, grade level or advanced, test her periodically to monitor how the concepts are being applied.

Writing is a slower, more gradual process than math or reading. Advances are made in several areas at a time, so while you may keep weekly or monthly records in your portfolio, actual testing only need be done every 4 to 6 months. Each time you give the test, record the date so you can chart your child's progress.

Now, if you and your child are ready, let's find out how well your child can write!

NAEP Writing Achievement Standards

The National Assessment of Educational Progress (NAEP), an arm of the U.S. Department of Education, serves the vital function of reporting to educators, parents, policy makers, and the general public how well American students are performing.

The "Writing Report Card" describes the writing performance of American school children based on a survey conducted in 1996 by the NAEP. It considers such questions as, How well do American students write? How much emphasis do schools place on writing instruction? and What approaches are being used to teach writing?

To evaluate the writing abilities of American students, NAEP asked nationally representative samples of 4th-, 8th-, and 12th-grade students attending public and private schools—approximately 30,000 in all—to respond to a variety of writing tasks in three categories: *informative, persuasive,* and *narrative.*

Informative writing focuses primarily on the subject matter element in communication and is used to share knowledge and to convey ideas.

Persuasive writing focuses on the reader, with the primary aim of influencing others to take some action or bring about change.

Narrative or **Descriptive** writing encourages students to incorporate their imagination and creativity into the production of stories or personal essays.

Students' responses to each writing task were evaluated by trained raters who used a modified primary-trait analysis. The scoring guidelines defined six successive levels of task accomplishment:

---

6 Extensively elaborated Students create a well developed, detailed, and well written response to the task. They show a high degree of control over the various elements of writing. These responses may be similar to "5" responses, but they are better organized, more clearly written, and less flawed.

5 Elaborated Students write a well developed and detailed response to the task. They may go beyond the requirements of the task.

4 Developed Students provide a response to the task that contains necessary elements. However, these papers may be unevenly developed.

3 Minimally developed Students provide a response to the task that is brief, vague, or somewhat confusing.

2 Undeveloped response to task. Students begin to respond to the task, but they do so in a very abbreviated, confusing, or disjointed manner.

1 Response to topic Students respond to some aspect of the topic, but do not appear to have fully understood the task. Or, they recopy text from the prompt.

0 Not rated Blank, totally off task, indecipherable, illegible, and "I don't know."

Source: NAEP, U.S. Department of Education

Terms You Should Know

Parts of speech

Noun A noun is a person, place, or thing.
mother, playground, tree

Verb A verb is an action word (or the verb *to be*).
run, jump, sit, have, be (is, are)

Pronoun A pronoun replaces a noun.
he, she, it, we, they, him, her, us, them, someone, something, somewhere

Adjective An adjective describes a noun.
funny, little, purple

Adverb An adverb describes a verb, adverb, or adjective. It typically ends in *ly*.
really, quickly, fast

Conjunction A conjunction joins words or phrases.
and, so, but, because, when, though

Preposition A preposition tells location or direction.
in, at, for, by, over, toward

Exclamation An exclamation is a short remark or yell.
Well, Hey! No! Help!

Punctuation marks

Period Indicates a full stop. Used at the end of a sentence and after abbreviations.

> *Mr. Smith has a car.*

Comma Indicates a separation of ideas or of elements within a sentence.

> *They had apples, oranges, and bananas.*
> *We planned to leave early, but we got up late.*

Question mark Indicates a direct question.

> *Where are you going?*

Exclamation mark Indicates an exclamation.

> *Wow! That was great!*

Apostrophe Indicates the omission of a letter or letters from a word, or the possessive case.

> *We can't use Bob's car today.*

Quotation marks Indicates the beginning and end of a quoted passage. Single marks are used for a quotation within a quotation.

> *"Where is the car?" asked Linda.*

Parentheses Indicates a digression from the theme.

> *The five characters (Meg, Jo, Beth, Amy, and Marmee) play vital roles in Louisa May Alcott's novel* Little Women.

Hyphen Determines the relationship between words and parts of words. Used between the syllables of a word when a word is divided at the end of a line of text.

> *She was feeling self-righteous as she antici-pated the outcome.*

Dash Used to set off ideas much like parentheses.

> *The five characters—Meg, Jo, Beth, Amy, and Marmee—play vital roles in Louisa May Alcott's novel* Little Women.

Colon Indicates that a quotation, an explanation, an example, or a series is to follow. Used after the greeting in a business letter. Also used in time (*2:30*) and ratios (*1:2*).

> *Please bring the following: scissors, glue, and construction paper.*

Semi-colon Works like a weak period or a strong comma. It connects independent clauses and indicates a closer relationship between the clauses than a period does.

> *I would prefer to stay home; however, I must go to the ball game.*
>
> *We visited Long Island, New York; Chicago, Illinois; and Los Angeles, California among other major cities.*

Kindergarten Assessment

Printing

Have your child print the alphabet.

Upper case

_____

- - - - - - - - - - - - - - - -

_____

- - - - - - - - - - - - - - - -

_____

- - - - - - - - - - - - - - - -

_____

Lower case

_____

- - - - - - - - - - - - - - - -

_____

- - - - - - - - - - - - - - - -

_____

- - - - - - - - - - - - - - - -

_____

Date: _____   Go to scoring on page 216.

Drawing Sample

Have your child draw a self-portrait.

Date: _____   Go to scoring on page 216.

Idea Flow

Thought completion

Have your child dictate an ending to each of the following sentences.

1. The dog was barking because_____

    _____

    _____

    _____

2. The kids wanted to play, but_____

    _____

    _____

    _____

3. I was hungry, so_____

    _____

    _____

    _____

Date: _____   Go to scoring on page 216.

Idea Flow

Categories

Have your child dictate as many in each category as possible.

animals

_____   _____

_____   _____

_____   _____

_____   _____

_____   _____

_____   _____

colors

_____   _____

_____   _____

_____   _____

_____   _____

_____   _____

Date: _____   Go to scoring on page 216.

Idea Flow

Concrete

Have your child tell you of as many things as possible that he or she could do with a **piece of paper**.

1. _____

2. _____

3. _____

4. _____

5. _____

6. _____

7. _____

8. _____

9. _____

10. _____

11. _____

12. _____

13. _____

14. _____

15. _____

Date: _____ Go to scoring on page 216.

Writing Sample

Have your child print his or her **name** and **age**.

Date: _____ Go to scoring on page 217.

Writing Sample

Descriptive

Have your child write what animal is pictured below and what it is doing.

Date: _____ Go to scoring on page 217.

Verbal Narrative

Have your child tell a story about the picture below. Use
a tape recorder or take notes.

_____

_____

_____

_____

_____

_____

_____

_____

_____

_____

_____

_____

Date: _____ Go to scoring on page 217.

Kindergarten Individual Skills Record

Circle the category that applies to the work on the corresponding page.

3 Exceptional	2 Competent	1 Pre-Writing

Printing page 208

Knows all of the letters of the alphabet, upper & lower.	Knows most of the letters of the alphabet.	Knows few or none of the letters of the alphabet.
Prints left to right and top to bottom.	Prints left to right and top to bottom.	Does not print left to right or letters not written in a top to bottom order.
Uses upper and lower cases.	Uses all upper or all lower cases.	Mixes upper and lower cases randomly.
Letters well formed, evenly spaced.	Letters clear and legible; some variety in spacing.	Letters are barely legible or scribbled; spacing is irregular.
Lines are followed.	Lines are generally followed.	Lines are not followed.

Drawing page 209

Detailed, with facial features, fingers, shoes, clothes.	Upper and lower body, limbs with hands and feet, facial features.	Stick figure; no details.

Idea Flow—Thought completion page 210

Makes sense; gives some supporting details.	Makes sense.	Doesn't make sense.

Idea Flow—Categories page 211

19+	10-18	0-9

Idea Flow—Concrete page 212

6+	3-5	0-2

Kindergarten Writing Record

Circle the category that applies to the work on the corresponding page.

3 Exceptional	2 Competent	1 Pre-Writing

Informative writing page 213

Prints first and last name correctly.	Prints first name correctly.	Prints the first letter or letters of first name.
Writes age number correctly.	Writes age number correctly.	Doesn't write age number correctly.
Prints left to right and top to bottom.	Prints left to right and top to bottom.	Doesn't print left to right or write from top to bottom.
Uses upper and lower cases.	Uses all upper or all lower cases.	Mixes upper & lower cases randomly.
Letters well formed, evenly spaced.	Letters clear and legible; some variety in spacing.	Letters are barely legible or scribbled; spacing is irregular.
Lines are followed.	Lines are generally followed.	Lines are not followed.

Circle the category that applies within each writing sample. Use the chart on the following page for guidelines.

Descriptive writing page 214

Printing	3	2	1
Spelling	3	2	1
Grammar	3	2	1
Vocabulary	3	2	1
Structure	3	2	1
Idea Flow	3	2	1

Verbal narrative page 215

Grammar	3	2	1
Vocabulary	3	2	1
Structure	3	2	1
Idea Flow	3	2	1

Kindergarten Scoring Guidelines

3 Exceptional	2 Competent	1 Pre-Writing
Printing		
Writes all of the letters of the alphabet, upper & lower case; letters are well formed, evenly spaced and follow the lines.	Writes most of the letters of the alphabet; letters are clear & legible; some variety in spacing; lines are generally followed.	Knows few or none of the letters of the alphabet; letters are barely legible or scribbled; spacing is irregular; lines are not followed.
Spelling		
Almost all familiar or phonetic words spelled correctly.	Some phonetic words (**hat, dog**) are spelled correctly.	Exclusively inventive spelling or random letters.
Grammar		
Few grammatical errors.	Some errors in verb tense, noun/verb agreement, irregular past tense (**runned**), or word order.	Confusing word order; many tense errors, little or no correlation of verbs with time references. (**I go tomorrow.**)
Vocabulary		
Good variety of vocabulary; descriptive words.	Some variety of vocabulary; daily words.	Very basic, limited vocabulary; no description.
Structure		
Addresses the topic; includes details; meaning is clear.	Addresses the topic; some details; makes sense.	Does not address the topic or follow the prompt; **OR** does not make sense.
Idea Flow		
Uses two or more ideas; piques reader's interest.	Uses one strong idea; holds reader's attention.	Uses one weak idea; hard to follow.

First Grade
Assessment

Printing

Print the following. Remember the importance of good spacing and punctuation and to print neatly.

We played many fun games at camp today.

_____

- - - - - - - - - - - - - - -

_____

- - - - - - - - - - - - - - -

_____

- - - - - - - - - - - - - - -

_____

- - - - - - - - - - - - - - -

_____

- - - - - - - - - - - - - - -

_____

- - - - - - - - - - - - - - -

_____

Date: _____   Go to scoring on page 228.

Spelling

Cross out any words that are spelled wrong and write the correct spelling on the line below.

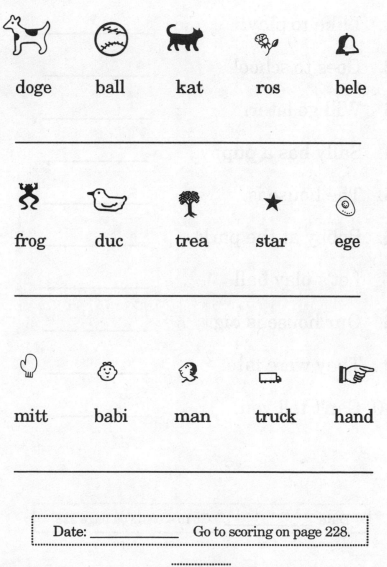

doge   ball   kat   ros   bele

_____

frog   duc   trea   star   ege

_____

mitt   babi   man   truck   hand

_____

Date: _____   Go to scoring on page 228.

Grammar

Complete sentences

Read the following groups of words. Then determine if each group forms a complete sentence or not. Write **Y** for yes and **N** for no.

1. I like to play.   _____

2. Goes to school.   _____

3. Will go later.   _____

4. Sally has a puppy.   _____

5. The house is.   _____

6. Bobby at the park.   _____

7. Let's play ball.   _____

8. Our house is big.   _____

9. They were late.   _____

10. Can't tell you.   _____

Date: _____   Go to scoring on page 228.

Idea Flow

Thought completion

Write an ending to each of the following sentences.

1. The children were running because_____

   _____

   _____

   _____

   _____

2. There was a huge crash, and then_____

   _____

   _____

   _____

   _____

3. Eddie's mom saw the boys playing high in the

   tree and_____

   _____

   _____

   _____

   _____

Date: _____   Go to scoring on page 228.

Idea Flow

Categories

List as many items in each category as possible.

games and toys

_____   _____

_____   _____

_____   _____

_____   _____

_____   _____

_____   _____

shapes

_____   _____

_____   _____

_____   _____

_____   _____

_____   _____

_____   _____

Date: _____   Go to scoring on page 228.

Idea Flow

Concrete

List as many things as possible that you could do with a **stick**.

1. _____

2. _____

3. _____

4. _____

5. _____

6. _____

7. _____

8. _____

9. _____

10. _____

11. _____

12. _____

13. _____

14. _____

15. _____

Date: _____   Go to scoring on page 228.

Writing Samples

Informative

Print your **name** and **age**, **telephone number**, and **address**.

_____

– –

_____
_____

– –

_____

– –

_____
_____

– –

_____

– –

_____
_____

– –

_____
_____

– –

_____

Date: _____   Go to scoring on page 229.

Writing Sample
Descriptive

Write a story about the picture shown below using as much detail and description as possible.

_____

_____

_____

_____

_____

_____

_____

_____

Date: _____   Go to scoring on page 229.

First Grade Individual Skills Record

Circle the category that applies to the work on the corresponding page.

3 Exceptional	2 Competent	1 Pre-Writing

Printing page 220

Knows all of the letters of the alphabet, upper & lower.	Knows most of the letters of the alphabet.	Knows few or none of the letters of the alphabet.
Prints left to right and top to bottom.	Prints left to right and top to bottom.	Does not print left to right or letters written from bottom to top.
Uses upper and lower case letters	Uses all upper or all lower case.	Mixes upper and lower case randomly.
Letters well formed, evenly spaced.	Letters clear & legible, some variety in spacing.	Letters are barely legible or scribbled, spacing is irregular.
Lines are followed.	Lines are generally followed.	Lines are not followed.

Spelling page 221

13–16	7–12	0–6

Grammar page 222

8–10	5–7	0–4

Idea Flow—Thought Completion page 223

Logical and detailed.	Makes sense.	Doesn't make sense.

Idea Flow—Categories page 224

15+	7–14	0–6

Idea Flow—Concrete page 225

8+	4–7	0–3

First Grade Writing Record

Circle the category that applies within each writing sample. Use the chart on the following page for guidelines.

3 Exceptional	2 Competent	1 Pre-Writing

Informative writing page 226

3	2	1
Prints first and last name correctly.	Prints first name correctly.	Prints the first letter or letters of first name.
Writes age number correctly.	Writes age number correctly.	Doesn't write age number correctly.
Prints left to right and top to bottom.	Prints left to right and top to bottom.	Doesn't print left to right or write from top to bottom.
Uses upper and lower cases.	Uses all upper or all lower cases.	Mixes upper & lower cases randomly.
Letters well formed, evenly spaced.	Letters clear and legible; some variety in spacing.	Letters are barely legible or scribbled; spacing is irregular.
Lines are followed.	Lines are generally followed.	Lines are not followed.

Descriptive Writing page 227

	3	2	1
Printing	3	2	1
Spelling	3	2	1
Grammar	3	2	1
Vocabulary	3	2	1
Structure	3	2	1
Idea Flow	3	2	1

First Grade Scoring Guidelines

3 Exceptional	2 Competent	1 Pre-Writing
Printing		
Writes the alphabet, upper & lower case; letters very well formed, evenly spaced and follow the lines.	Writes the alphabet; letters are clear and legible; some variety in spacing; lines are generally followed.	Writes most of alphabet; letters barely legible; spacing is irregular; lines not followed.
Spelling		
Correct spelling. Harder sight words (**thought**) may be spelled incorrectly.	Phonetic words (**bat, dog**) spelled correctly; some inventive spelling (**tol** for **tall**).	Exclusively inventive spelling or random letters.
Punctuation		
Correct use of capitals and periods.	Some errors in use of capitals and periods.	Random or no capitals or periods.
Grammar		
Few grammatical errors; appropriate use of conjunctions to avoid choppiness and run-on sentences.	Some errors in verb tense, noun/verb agreement, irregular tense (**gots**); run-on sentences.	Confusing word order; many tense errors, little or no correlation of verbs with time references (**I ran tomorrow**).
Vocabulary		
Good variety of colorful vocabulary; descriptive words.	Some variety of vocabulary; daily words.	Very basic, limited vocabulary; no description.
Structure		
Addresses the topic; includes details; clea and organized.	Addresses topic; some details; makes sense; some organization.	Does not address the topic; **OR** does not make sense.
Idea Flow		
Two or more ideas; holds reader's interest.	One strong idea; keeps reader's attention.	Uses one weak idea; hard to follow.

Second Grade
Assessment

Printing

Print the following sentences. Remember the importance of paying attention to spacing and punctuation and to print neatly.

It is fun to go to the park with my family. We go there every Saturday.

Date: _____   Go to scoring on page 242.

Spelling

Underline and correct any spelling errors in the following sentences.

1. Bob was in the truk.

2. She laffed at the joke.

3. Hector wolked to the park.

4. The dogs ar in the howse.

5. Peter sed that he is hapy.

6. Lucy fell, but she was fain.

7. Do yu know hwo is in the car?

> See the Answer Key to determine number of accurate corrections.
> 1 point for correctly underlining; 1 point for correctly spelling; minus 1 point for each incorrect underlining or spelling.
>
> Date: _____ Go to scoring on page 242.

Punctuation and Capitalization

Add the correct punctuation and capitalization to the following words and sentences.

1. bob gomez

2. i am hungry

3. where are you

4. he saw tim in the yard

5. dont you like to play ball

6. jump

7. sam cant tell time

See the Answer Key to determine number of accurate corrections. Deduct from that any errors in corrections for the total score.

Date: _____ Go to scoring on page 242.

Contractions

Write the contraction for each of the following.

1. I am   _____

2. do not   _____

3. you are   _____

4. he is   _____

5. we are   _____

6. is not   _____

7. they are   _____

8. have not   _____

9. can not   _____

10. would not   _____

Date: _____   Go to scoring on page 242.

Grammar

Complete sentences

Read the following groups of words. Then determine if each group forms a complete sentence or not. Write **Y** for yes and **N** for no.

1. He bought a new car. _____

2. Like it a lot. _____

3. But we forgot. _____

4. Help me! _____

5. We liked it, but. _____

6. Let's play. _____

7. Can help me now? _____

8. The big, white house. _____

9. The play was good. _____

10. Mom, Dad, and me. _____

Date: _____ Go to scoring on page 242.

Idea Flow

Thought completion

Write an ending to each of the following sentences.

1. Julia was supposed to be home at five. She was

   hurrying because_____

   _____

   _____

2. The room was getting really crowded, so_____

   _____

   _____

   _____

3. Kevin's brother wanted to know why_____

   _____

   _____

   _____

Date: _____ Go to scoring on page 242.

Idea Flow

Synonyms

Synonyms are words with similar meanings such as *funny, amusing, comical, makes me laugh*. List as many synonyms for each word as possible.

good

_____   _____

_____   _____

_____   _____

_____   _____

mad

_____   _____

_____   _____

_____   _____

big

_____   _____

_____   _____

_____   _____

_____   _____

Date: _____   Go to scoring on page 242.

Idea Flow

Concrete

List as many things as possible that you could do with a
cottonball.

1. _____

2. _____

3. _____

4. _____

5. _____

6. _____

7. _____

8. _____

9. _____

10. _____

11. _____

12. _____

13. _____

14. _____

15. _____

Date: _____ Go to scoring on page 242.

Writing Sample

Informative

Write as much as possible about your family.

_____

- - - - - - - - - - - - - - - - - - - -

_____

- - - - - - - - - - - - - - - - - - - -

_____

- - - - - - - - - - - - - - - - - - - -

_____

- - - - - - - - - - - - - - - - - - - -

_____

- - - - - - - - - - - - - - - - - - - -

_____

- - - - - - - - - - - - - - - - - - - -

_____

- - - - - - - - - - - - - - - - - - - -

Date: _____ Go to scoring on page 243.

Writing Sample

Descriptive

Write a story about the picture shown below.

_____

_ _ _ _ _ _ _ _ _ _ _ _ _ _ _ _ _ _ _

_____

_ _ _ _ _ _ _ _ _ _ _ _ _ _ _ _ _ _ _

_____

_ _ _ _ _ _ _ _ _ _ _ _ _ _ _ _ _ _ _

_____

_ _ _ _ _ _ _ _ _ _ _ _ _ _ _

_____

_ _ _ _ _ _ _ _ _ _ _ _ _

_____

_ _ _ _ _ _ _ _ _ _ _ _ _

_____

_ _ _ _ _ _ _ _ _ _ _ _ _

Date: _____   Go to scoring on page 243.

Second Grade Individual Skills Record

Circle the category that applies to the work on the corresponding page.

3 Exceptional	2 Competent	1 Developing

Printing page 232

3	2	1
Letters are very well formed, evenly spaced.	Letters are clear and legible; little variety in spacing.	Letters are difficult to read, various sizes; irregular spacing.
Ascenders/descenders clearly distinguished.	Ascenders/descenders not clearly distinguished.	Ascenders/descenders undistinguished.
Uniform slant.	Generally uniform slant.	Random direction.
Lines are followed.	Lines are generally followed.	Lines not followed well.

Spelling page 233

18–20	9–17	0–8

Punctuation and Capitalization page 234

15–17	9–14	0–8

Contractions page 235

9–10	6–8	0–5

Grammar page 236

9–10	6–8	0–5

Idea Flow—Thought Completion page 237

Logical and detailed.	Makes sense.	Doesn't make sense.

Idea Flow—Synonyms page 238

9+	4–8	0–3

Idea Flow—Concrete page 239

9+	4–8	0–3

Second Grade Writing Record

Circle the category that applies within each writing sample. Use the chart that follows for guidelines.

Level	3 Exceptional	2 Competent	1 Developing

Informative Writing page 240

	3	2	1
Printing	3	2	1
Spelling	3	2	1
Punctuation	3	2	1
Grammar	3	2	1
Vocabulary	3	2	1
Structure	3	2	1
Idea Flow	3	2	1

Descriptive Writing page 241

	3	2	1
Printing	3	2	1
Spelling	3	2	1
Punctuation	3	2	1
Grammar	3	2	1
Vocabulary	3	2	1
Structure	3	2	1
Idea Flow	3	2	1

Second Grade Scoring Guidelines

3 Exceptional	2 Competent	1 Developing

Printing

Letters very well formed, evenly spaced; ascenders/descenders clearly distinguished; uniform slant; follows the lines.	Letters are clear and legible; little variety in spacing; some ascenders/descenders irregular; lines well followed.	Letters are difficult to read and of various shapes and sizes; irregular spacing; lines are not followed well.

Spelling

Few or no spelling errors.	All phonetic words (**dog**) are spelled correctly; harder sight words (**laugh**) may be spelled incorrectly.	Extensive inventive spelling of sight words, and occasionally of phonetic words.

Punctuation

Correct use of capitals and end marks.	Some errors in use of capitals and end marks.	Random or no use of capitals or end marks.

Grammar

Few or no grammatical errors; appropriate use of conjunctions to avoid both choppiness and run-on sentences.	A few errors in verb tense, noun/verb agreement, irregular tense (**putted**) or word order; run-on sentences.	Confusing word order; some words omitted; some tense errors; little support of verbs with time references.

Vocabulary

Good variety of vocabulary; specific nouns and descriptive modifiers used (**huge dragon**).	Some variety of vocabulary; some descriptive modifiers.	Very basic, limited vocabulary; no description or modifiers.

Structure

Addresses the topic, shows organization and detail; variety of sentence structure; creative use of language.	Addresses the topic, some organization, sufficient detail; at least two types of sentence structure; concrete use of language.	Does not address the topic or follow the prompt; no structure or detail; limited or no variety of sentence structure.

Idea Flow

Introduces & weaves into the narrative several different and interesting concepts & perspectives; imaginative use of abstract words and ideas.	Introduces some ideas, mainly connected to the narrative; single perspective, day-to-day use of concrete words and ideas.	Only one or two, ideas, loosely connected to the narrative; single perspective, basic words and ideas.

Third Grade Assessment

Cursive

Write the following in cursive. Pay attention to spacing and punctuation. Write neatly.

Dinosaurs roamed the earth 70 million years ago. Some scientists say that dinosaurs were cold-blooded. Other scientists say that they were warm-blooded. What do you think?

Date: _____   Go to scoring on page 257.

Spelling

Underline and correct any misspelled words in the following paragraph.

My Family

I hav too brothers and one sister.
My sister haz brown hair and
grene eyes and livs far awey. Her
name is Maryann. She has for
childrin. The twinz are still babys.
My brothers are vary tal. My older
brother is namd Henry, and my
younger brother is Paul. Thay are
nise too me. How meny brothers
an sisters do yoo hav?

> See the Answer Key to determine the number of
> accurate corrections. Deduct from that any errors
> in correction for the total score.
>
> Date: _____   Go to scoring on page 257.

Punctuation and Capitalization

Add the correct punctuation and capitalization to the following sentences.

1. i live in portland oregon

2. why are you going with mr smith

3. we like cars trains boats and bikes

4. go away

See the Answer Key to determine the number of accurate corrections. Deduct from that the number of errors in corrections for the total score.

Date: _____ Go to scoring on page 257.

Grammatical Errors

There are grammatical errors in this paragraph. Correct as many as you can, including nouns, pronouns, verb tenses, run-on sentences, and sentence fragments.

Zelda and her cat was playing.

Like to play. Oops! The kitty bited

her on the finger and it very

hurted and Zelda runned and told

her mother what the cats had did

and her mother put a bandage on

Zelda finger and putted the cat

outside. The cat sat down and.

See the Answer Key to determine the number of accurate corrections. Deduct from that the number of errors in corrections for the total score.

Date: _____ Go to scoring on page 257.

Grammatical Terms

Circle each noun. Underline each verb. Put a square around each adjective.

Jordan and Jaime walked home

from school. It was just a short

distance. The boys were happy

because they had finished a very

difficult test. Their mother was

glad to see them and said she was

going to buy them some ice cream.

The ice cream was delicious.

See the Answer Key to determine the number of correctly labeled terms. Deduct from that the number of incorrectly labeled terms for the total score.

Date: _____   Go to scoring on page 257.

Idea Flow

Thought completion

Write an ending to each of the following sentences.

1. The school principal said that if_____

   _____

   _____

   _____

   _____

2. When Jorge opened the door, _____

   _____

   _____

   _____

   _____

3. Samantha waited until_____

   _____

   _____

   _____

   _____

Date: _____ Go to scoring on page 257.

Idea Flow

Synonyms are words with similar meanings such as *funny, amusing, comical, makes me laugh*. List as many synonyms for each word as possible.

pretty

_____   _____

_____   _____

_____   _____

_____   _____

tough

_____   _____

_____   _____

_____   _____

_____   _____

happy

_____   _____

_____   _____

_____   _____

_____   _____

Date: _____   Go to scoring on page 257.

Idea Flow

Concrete

List as many things as possible that you could do with a **piece of string.**

1. _____

2. _____

3. _____

4. _____

5. _____

6. _____

7. _____

8. _____

9. _____

10. _____

11. _____

12. _____

13. _____

14. _____

15. _____

Date: _____ Go to scoring on page 257.

Idea Flow   *Imaginary*

If 3rd graders ruled the world, how would things be different? List as many things as possible.

1. _____

2. _____

3. _____

4. _____

5. _____

6. _____

7. _____

8. _____

9. _____

10. _____

11. _____

12. _____

13. _____

14. _____

15. _____

Date: _____   Go to scoring on page 257.

Writing Sample

Write about the type of dinosaur that you think is the most interesting, and explain why. Use additional paper if necessary.

Date: _____ Go to scoring on page 258.

Writing Sample

Descriptive

Write a complete story about the picture. Use additional paper if necessary.

Date: _____   Go to scoring on page 258.

Third Grade Individual Skills Record

Circle the category that applies to the work on the corresponding page.

3 Exceptional	2 Competent	1 Developing

Cursive page 246

3	2	1
Letters are very well formed, evenly spaced. Capitals distinguished from lower case. All letters connected within a word. Ascenders/descenders clearly above and below body letters. Uniform slant. Lines followed.	Letters clear and legible; little variety in spacing. Some capitals printed. Some breaks within words, some printing. Ascenders/descenders not clearly above and below body letters. Generally uniform slant. Lines generally followed.	Letters difficult to read, various sizes; irregular spacing. Capitals not distinguished. Irregular connections or only printing. Ascenders/descenders same height as body letters. Random direction. Lines not followed well.

Spelling page 247

35–40	17–34	0–16

Punctuation and Capitalization page 248

19–21	9–18	0–8

Grammatical Errors page 249

11–13	7–10	0–6

Grammatical Terms page 250

23–26	15–22	0–14

Idea Flow—Thought Completion page 251

Logical and detailed.	Makes sense.	Doesn't make sense.

Idea Flow—Synonyms page 252

10+	6–9	0–5

Idea Flow—Concrete page 253

11+	6–10	0–5

Idea Flow—Imaginary page 254

11+	6–10	0–5

Third Grade Writing Record

Circle the category that applies within each writing sample. Use the chart on the following page for guidelines.

Level	3 Exceptional	2 Competent	1 Developing

Informative Writing page 255

	3	2	1
Cursive	3	2	1
Spelling	3	2	1
Punctuation	3	2	1
Grammar	3	2	1
Vocabulary	3	2	1
Structure	3	2	1
Idea Flow	3	2	1

Descriptive Writing page 256

	3	2	1
Cursive	3	2	1
Spelling	3	2	1
Punctuation	3	2	1
Grammar	3	2	1
Vocabulary	3	2	1
Structure	3	2	1
Idea Flow	3	2	1

Third Grade Scoring Guidelines

3 Exceptional	2 Competent	1 Developing

Cursive

Letters are very well formed, evenly spaced. Capitals distinguished from lower case. All letters connected within a word. Ascenders/descenders clearly above and below body letters. Uniform slant. Lines followed.	Letters clear and legible; little variety in spacing. Some capitals printed. Some breaks within words, some printing. Ascenders/descenders not clearly above and below body letters. Generally uniform slant. Lines generally followed.	Letters difficult to read, various sizes; irregular spacing. Capitals not distinguished. Irregular connections or only printing. Ascenders/descenders same height as body letters. Random direction. Lines not followed well.

Spelling

Few or no spelling errors after self-editing.	All phonetic and most sight words are spelled correctly; homonyms (**hair, hare**) may be confused. Silent letters (**know**) difficult.	All phonetic and some sight words spelled correctly; homonyms frequently used randomly. Silent letters omitted.

Punctuation

Correct use of capitals, end marks and commas.	Some errors in use of capitals, end marks and commas.	Random or no use of capitals, end marks and commas.

Grammar

Few or no grammatical errors; good use of conjunctions (**but, however**); little choppiness and few run-on sentences.	A few errors in verb tense, noun/verb agreement, irregular tense (**holded, if he was**) or word order; run-on sentences.	Confusing word order; omitted words; some tense errors; little support of verbs with time references.

Vocabulary

Good variety of vocabulary; specific nouns and descriptive modifiers used appropriately (**a rotten temper** vs **mad**).	Some variety of vocabulary—mostly one or two syllable words; some descriptive modifiers.	Very basic, limited vocabulary; no description or modifiers.

Structure

Has a beginning, middle and conclusion; addresses the topic, shows organization and detail; variety of sentence structure; creative use of language.	One sentence intro, no conclusion; addresses the topic, some organization, sufficient detail; at least two types of sentence structure; concrete use of language.	No introduction or conclusion, little structure or detail; limited or no variety of sentence structure; limited use of language **OR** does not follow prompt or address the topic.

Idea Flow

Introduces and weaves into the narrative four or more different and interesting concepts and perspectives; imaginative use of abstract words and ideas.	Introduces at least three ideas, and connects them within the narrative; single perspective, day-to day use of concrete words and ideas.	Introduces one to two ideas, loosely connected to the narrative; single perspective, basic words and ideas.

Fourth Grade
Assessment

Cursive

Write the following in cursive. Pay attention to spacing and punctuation. Write neatly.

There are many ways of measuring things. You can use a cup, a scale, a ruler, or a thermometer. How do you measure little things, like bacteria, though?

A recent invention called the germo-meter (jer•MAH•meder) is a digital wand that indicates the presence or absence of germs.

The only problem is that even a germometer doesn't tell you if it's good bacteria or bad bacteria!

_____

_____

_____

_____

_____

_____

_____

_____

_____

_____

Date: _____   Go to scoring on page 275.

Spelling

Underline and correct any spelling errors.

It's hard to beleive what some peeple tell you. My freind's dad told her that he wood be comeing for Chrismas, but diden't. She thuoght that he had forgoten. It turned out that he had colled and canselled, but she hadn't gottin the messige. In the beggining, she was upset, but than he said, "It's you're lucky day, kid. I'll be their tommorow and I'm taking you on a trip to Texas!" She was delihgted, and he was, to.

> See the Answer Key to determine the number of accurate corrections.
> 1 point for correct underlining; 1 point for correct spelling; minus 1 point for incorrect underlining or spelling.
>
> Date: _____   Go to scoring on page 275.

Punctuation and Capitalization

Add the correct punctuation and capitalization to the following sentences.

bobby is a little boy he has a brother

named irwin and a dog called harry

they all live in sheboygan wisconsin

one day bobby irwin and harry fell in

a well they yelled help they couldnt

get out on their own do you think

anyone will find them lets hope so

See the Answer Key to determine the number of accurate corrections. Deduct from that any errors in corrections for the total score.

Date: _____   Go to scoring on page 275.

Grammatical Errors

There are grammatical errors in this paragraph. Correct as many as you can, including nouns, pronouns, conjunctions, verb tenses, run-on sentences, sentence fragments, and word order.

In order to build a bicycles, it is importance to follow the instructions, which is included with every kits. But the difficulty of build bikes has increase since the past ten years. A bicycle built well, it will be guaranteed to work. If you will start early in the morning, you will finish it in a day if you works real careful. Before you put the bike together. Make sure you have all of the pieces. No matter how long it takes to build it, though, do a good job by it. Because it is worth it.

See the Answer Key to determine the number of accurate corrections. Deduct from that any errors in corrections for the total score.

Date: _____ Go to scoring on page 275.

Grammatical Terms

In the box below, list all the appropriate words in each category. Not every word in the paragraph will be used. Don't repeat words that are used more than once.

Ellie and Zack ran quickly around the dark, dusty room, looking for the silver key. Ellie wanted to find it so she could unlock the door and everyone could escape. It had all started out with the rusty gate. Zack had known they weren't supposed to go inside, because there was a *No Trespassing* sign, but it was so different from the drab little town.

Noun	Pronoun	Verb	Adjective	Conjunction

Date: _____   Go to scoring on page 275.

Idea Flow

Thought completion

Write a beginning to each of the following sentences.

1. _____

_____

_____

_____

_____ but Elmer kept on running.

2. _____

_____

_____

_____ she really couldn't believe her luck.

3. _____

_____

_____

so now he understood why timing was so important.

Date: _____   Go to scoring on page 275.

Idea Flow

Synonyms

Synonyms are words with similar meanings such as *funny, amusing, comical, makes me laugh*. List as many synonyms in each category as possible.

thrilled

_____   _____

_____   _____

_____   _____

_____   _____

_____   _____

small

_____   _____

_____   _____

_____   _____

_____   _____

_____   _____

terrifying

_____   _____

_____   _____

_____   _____

_____   _____

_____   _____

Date: _____ Go to scoring on page 275.

Idea Flow

Homonyms

List as many different meaning of the word in each category as possible. For example, a bat can be a noun such as a *baseball bat* or it can be the *flying nocturnal animal*. It can also be a verb such as *to bat an eyelash*.

line _____ _____

_____ _____

tie _____ _____

_____ _____

set _____ _____

_____ _____

deal _____ _____

_____ _____

state _____ _____

_____ _____

Date: _____ Go to scoring on page 275.

Idea Flow

Concrete

List as many things as possible that you could do with a **brick**.

1. _____

2. _____

3. _____

4. _____

5. _____

6. _____

7. _____

8. _____

9. _____

10. _____

11. _____

12. _____

13. _____

14. _____

15. _____

Date: _____   Go to scoring on page 275.

Idea Flow   *Imaginary*

If people could read minds, what would life be like? List as many things as possible.

1. _____

2. _____

3. _____

4. _____

5. _____

6. _____

7. _____

8. _____

9. _____

10. _____

11. _____

12. _____

13. _____

14. _____

15. _____

Date: _____   Go to scoring on page 275.

Writing Sample

Informative

Write as many interesting things as you can about the state you live in. Use more paper if necessary.

_____

_____

_____

_____

_____

_____

_____

_____

_____

_____

_____

_____

_____

_____

_____

_____

_____

Date: _____   Go to scoring on page 276.

Writing Sample

Write a complete story about the picture. Be sure and tell who, what, where, when, and why. Use more paper if necessary.

_____

_____

_____

_____

_____

_____

_____

_____

_____

_____

_____

_____

Date: _____   Go to scoring on page 276.

Writing Sample

Persuasive

Write your opinion on whether 4th graders should have to do homework or not. Give reasons for your opinion and try to convince the reader to agree with your position. Use more paper if necessary.

_____

_____

_____

_____

_____

_____

_____

_____

_____

_____

_____

_____

_____

_____

_____

Date: _____   Go to scoring on page 276.

Fourth Grade Individual Skills Record

Circle the category that applies to the work on the corresponding page.

3 Exceptional	2 Competent	3 Developing

Cursive page 262

Exceptionally well formed, linked letters; uniform slant and spacing; even with the lines; i's dotted, t's crossed.	Clear, legible letters; slant and spacing generally uniform; occasionally above or below the lines.	Difficult to read; letters irregular and not standard; slanted in random directions; spacing is irregular; lines not conformed to.

Spelling page 263

35–40	17–34	0–16

Punctuation and Capitalization page 264

25–32	14–24	0–13

Grammatical Errors page 265

14-17	8-13	0-7

Grammatical Terms page 266

33–36	26–32	0–25

Idea Flow—Thought Completion page 267

Logical and detailed.	Makes sense.	Doesn't make sense.

Idea Flow—Synonyms page 268

14+	7–13	0–6

Idea Flow—Homonyms page 269

13+	6–12	0–5

Idea Flow—Concrete page 270

12+	7–11	0–6

Idea Flow—Imaginary page 271

12+	7–11	0–6

Fourth Grade Writing Record

Circle the category that applies within each writing sample. Use the chart on the following page for guidelines.

Level	3 Exceptional	2 Competent	1 Developing

Informative Writing page 272

	3	2	1
Cursive	3	2	1
Spelling	3	2	1
Punctuation	3	2	1
Grammar	3	2	1
Vocabulary	3	2	1
Structure	3	2	1
Idea Flow	3	2	1

Descriptive Writing page 273

	3	2	1
Cursive	3	2	1
Spelling	3	2	1
Punctuation	3	2	1
Grammar	3	2	1
Vocabulary	3	2	1
Structure	3	2	1
Idea Flow	3	2	1

Persuasive Writing page 274

	3	2	1
Cursive	3	2	1
Spelling	3	2	1
Punctuation	3	2	1
Grammar	3	2	1
Vocabulary	3	2	1
Structure	3	2	1
Idea Flow	3	2	1

Fourth Grade Scoring Guidelines

3 Exceptional	2 Competent	1 Developing

Cursive

Exceptionally well formed, linked letters; uniform slant and spacing; even with the lines; i's dotted, t's crossed.	Clear, legible letters; slant and spacing generally uniform; occasionally above or below the lines.	Difficult to read; letters irregular and not standard; slanted in random directions; spacing is irregular; lines not conformed to.

Spelling

No spelling errors in an edited final draft.	All phonetic and most sight words are spelled correctly; homonyms (**its, it's**) still may be misused.	All phonetic and most sight words spelled correctly; homonyms frequently used randomly. Silent letters omitted.

Punctuation

Correct use of capitals, periods, commas, quotation marks, colons and parentheses.	Some errors in use of caps, periods & commas, quotation marks, colons and parentheses.	Some errors in use of caps, periods, commas; no use of quote marks, colons or parentheses.

Grammar

Few or no grammar errors; advanced use of conjunctions (**despite, whereas**); no choppiness or few run-on sentences.	A few errors in verb tense, noun/verb agreement; average use of conjunctions (**although**); some choppiness or run-on sentences.	Confusing word order; omitted words; very basic use of conjunctions. (**and, but, so**); sentences either choppy or run-on.

Vocabulary

Extensive variety of vocabulary; specific nouns and vividly descriptive modifiers; alternate words used to avoid repetition.	Good variety of vocabulary—fairly specific nouns; descriptive modifiers; some repetition of words.	Basic, limited vocabulary; scant description or non-specific modifiers; no synonyms; simple repetition of terms.

Structure

Has a developed intro, body, and conclusion; on topic; unity of theme; paragraphs developed; good transitions between paragraphs; variety of sentence structure; very detailed; creative & abstract language.	Short introduction, weak conclusion; on topic; some digressions; uses paragraphs, but some ideas are out of order; some transitions; sufficient detail; at least two types of sentence structure; concrete language.	No intro or ending; little structure or detail; major digressions; few paragraphs; no transitions; limited or fragmented sentence structure; limited use of language. **OR** Off topic.

Idea Flow

Introduces and weaves into the narrative four or more different and interesting concepts and perspectives; imaginative use of abstract words and ideas.	Introduces at least three ideas, and connects them within the narrative; single perspective, day-to-day use of concrete words and ideas.	Introduces one to two ideas, loosely connected to the narrative; single perspective, basic words and ideas.

Fifth Grade
Assessment

Cursive

Write the following in cursive. Pay attention to spacing and punctuation. Write neatly.

About 1,800 workers went on strike at an engine factory in Detroit, forcing Chrysler to immediately close four assembly plants and furlough 12,000 employees who make some of its most popular and profitable vehicles. This will have a strong impact on consumers as the availability of some Chrysler models will be reduced.

_____

_____

_____

_____

_____

_____

_____

_____

Date: _____   Go to scoring on page 291.

Editing

Add the correct punctuation and capitalization to the following sentences. Correct any spelling and grammar errors. Use proofreader's marks (shown below) for corrections.

peter is my best freind last saturday me and peter was gitting a little tired working in his dads busniss we were gonna stay until nine oclock eksept that was to late so insted we desided to closse the store at eihgt (our instructions was-to close at ten we went over to my house and have some choclate ice cream wow it was better then never

Proofreader's marks

^ insert	ɕ insert comma	⊙ insert period
⌿ delete	∩ transpose	≡ capitalize
# insert space	⌒ close up	⌿ lower case

Date: _____ Go to scoring on page 291.

Grammatical Terms

In the box below, write all the appropriate words in each category. Not every word in the paragraph will be used. Don't repeat words that are used more than once.

> In the old days, people almost always left the front door unlocked during the day, and frequently at night. Something has changed in the last fifty years, however, and things everywhere are locked up tight. Hey! Let's unlock everything, throw away the keys, lose the combinations so we can learn to trust again.

Noun	Pronoun	Verb	Adjective	Adverb	Conjunction

See the Answer Key to determine the number of accurate entries. Deduct from that any errors for the total score.

Date: _____ Go to scoring on page 291.

Idea Flow

Thought completion

Write a beginning to each of the following sentences.

1. _____

_____

_____

_____

in spite of the rain.

2. _____

_____

_____

_____

which completely explained why she had left.

3. _____

_____

_____

_____

so this was surprising, as it had never happened that way before.

Date: _____   Go to scoring on page 291.

Idea Flow
Synonyms

Synonyms are words with similar meanings such as *funny*, *amusing*, and *comical*. Write as many as you can for each word.

very

_____   _____

_____   _____

_____   _____

_____   _____

_____

know

_____   _____

_____   _____

_____   _____

_____   _____

_____

get

_____   _____

_____   _____

_____   _____

_____   _____

_____

Date: _____   Go to scoring on page 291.

Idea Flow

A word can have more than one meaning. For example, a bear can be a noun (grizzly bear) or it can be a verb (to carry). List as many different meanings as possible for each word.

block _____   _____

_____   _____

head _____   _____

_____   _____

time _____   _____

_____   _____

letter _____   _____

_____   _____

chip _____   _____

_____   _____

Date: _____   Go to scoring on page 291.

Idea Flow

Concrete

List as many things as possible that you could do with a **mirror**.

1. _____

2. _____

3. _____

4. _____

5. _____

6. _____

7. _____

8. _____

9. _____

10. _____

11. _____

12. _____

13. _____

14. _____

15. _____

Date: _____ Go to scoring on page 291.

Idea Flow   *Imaginary*

If you couldn't see, how would your life change? List as many things as possible.

1. _____

2. _____

3. _____

4. _____

5. _____

6. _____

7. _____

8. _____

9. _____

10. _____

11. _____

12. _____

13. _____

14. _____

15. _____

Date: _____   Go to scoring on page 291.

Writing Sample   *Informative*

Explain what democracy means to you and how it affects your life. Use more paper if necessary.

_____

_____

_____

_____

_____

_____

_____

_____

_____

_____

_____

_____

_____

_____

_____

_____

_____

_____

_____

_____

_____

Date: _____   Go to scoring on page 292.

Writing Sample

Write about what you see in the picture; include who, what, where, when, and why. Discuss the consequences. Use more paper if necessary.

_____

_____

_____

_____

_____

_____

_____

_____

_____

_____

_____

Date: _____ Go to scoring on page 292.

Writing Sample   *Persuasive*

Write your opinion on whether 5th graders should be able to choose the TV programs they watch. Discuss your reasons with supporting facts and arguments. Use more paper if necessary.

_____

Date: _____   Go to scoring on page 292.

Fifth Grade Individual Skills Record

Circle the category that applies to the work on the corresponding page.

3 Exceptional	2 Competent	1 Developing

Cursive page 280

3 Exceptional	2 Competent	1 Developing
Letters are very well formed, evenly spaced. Capitals distinguished from lower case. All letters connected within a word. Ascenders/descenders clearly above and below body letters. Uniform slant. Lines followed.	Letters clear and legible; little variety in spacing. Some capitals printed. Some breaks within words, some printing. Ascenders/descenders not clearly above and below body letters. Generally uniform slant. Lines generally followed.	Letters difficult to read, various sizes; irregular spacing. Capitals not distinguished. Irregular connections or only printing. Ascenders/descenders same height as body letters. Random direction. Lines not followed well.

Editing page 281

33–36	13–32	0–12

Grammatical Terms page 282

28–31	21–27	0-20

Idea Flow—Thought Completion page 283

Logical and detailed.	Makes sense.	Doesn't make sense.

Idea Flow—Synonyms page 284

15+	8–14	0–7

Idea Flow—Homonyms page 285

13+	6–12	0–5

Idea Flow—Concrete page 286

13+	7–12	0–6

Idea Flow—Imaginary page 287

13+	7–12	0–6

Fifth Grade Writing Record

Circle the category that applies within each writing sample. Use the chart on the following page for guidelines.

Level	3 Exceptional	2 Competent	1 Developing

Informative Writing page 288

	3	2	1
Cursive	3	2	1
Spelling	3	2	1
Punctuation	3	2	1
Grammar	3	2	1
Vocabulary	3	2	1
Structure	3	2	1
Idea Flow	3	2	1

Descriptive Writing page 289

	3	2	1
Cursive	3	2	1
Spelling	3	2	1
Punctuation	3	2	1
Grammar	3	2	1
Vocabulary	3	2	1
Structure	3	2	1
Idea Flow	3	2	1

Persuasive Writing page 290

	3	2	1
Cursive	3	2	1
Spelling	3	2	1
Punctuation	3	2	1
Grammar	3	2	1
Vocabulary	3	2	1
Structure	3	2	1
Idea Flow	3	2	1

Fifth Grade Scoring Guidelines

3 Exceptional	2 Competent	1 Developing
Cursive		
Exceptionally well formed individual letters; uniform slant and spacing; even with the lines; i's dotted, t's crossed.	Clear, legible letters; slant and spacing generally uniform; occasionally above or below the lines.	Difficult to read; letters irregular and not standard; slanted in random directions; spacing is irregular; lines no conformed to.
Spelling		
No spelling errors in an edited final draft.	All phonetic and most sight words are spelled correctly.	All phonetic and most sight words spelled correctly; homonyms frequently used randomly. Silent letters may be omitted.
Punctuation		
Correct use of capitals, periods, commas, quotation marks, colons and parentheses.	Some errors in use of caps, periods & commas, quotation marks, colons and parentheses.	Some errors in use of caps, periods, commas; no use of quote marks, colons or parentheses
Grammar		
Few or no grammar errors; advanced use of conjunctions (**nonetheless**); No choppiness or few run-on sentences.	A few errors in verb tense, noun/verb agreement; average use of conjunctions (**although**); some choppiness or run-on sentences.	Confusing word order; omitted words; very basic use of conjunctions (**and, but, so**); most sentences either choppy or run-on.

Vocabulary

Extensive variety of vocabulary; specific nouns and vividly descriptive modifiers; alternate words used to avoid repetition.	Good variety of vocabulary—fairly specific nouns; descriptive modifiers; some repetition of words.	Basic, limited vocabulary; scant description or non-specific modifiers; no synonyms; simple repetition of terms.

Structure

Has a developed introduction, body and conclusion; on topic; unity of theme; paragraphs developed; good transitions between paragraphs; variety of sentence structure; very detailed; creative & abstract language.	Short introduction, weak conclusion; on topic; some digressions; uses paragraphs, but some ideas are out of order; some transitions; sufficient detail; at least two types of sentence structure; concrete language.	No introduction or ending; little structure or detail; major digressions; few paragraphs; no transitions; limited or fragmented sentence structure; limited use of language. **OR** Off topic.

Idea Flow

Introduces and weaves into the narrative four or more different and interesting concepts and perspectives; imaginative use of abstract words and ideas.	Introduces at least three ideas, and connects them within the narrative; single perspective, day-to day use of concrete words and ideas.	Introduces one to two ideas, loosely connected to the narrative; single perspective, basic words and ideas.

Grade Level
Guidelines

Writing
is fun!

The first things a parent with a beginning writer wants to know are: Where do we start? What comes first? What is important?

For children, *outlining, editing,* and *rewriting* make for a big job compared to *telling* a story, which is easier and comes more naturally.

For parents, one of the main difficulties of teaching writing is that they may recognize quality writing when they see it, but it's hard to quantify the elements of quality writing, much less *teach* it.

Fortunately, there is a comfortable sequence for children to learn basic writing skills, which will in turn develop into more complex writing. The steps are:

1. Decide on the **purpose** (*a story, an essay, a report, an article, a poem*, etc.).
2. Decide on the **topic** of the writing, such as *describing the Pueblo Indian culture.*
3. Write an **outline**.
4. Write a **draft** including the following:
   Introduction
   Body
   Conclusion or summary
5. Edit and rewrite.

Developing writing skills

Although writing skills are developed in elementary school classrooms, the foundations are laid at home. As a parent, your attitude and commitment toward communication and expression will shape and direct your child's own attitude. Here's a list of day-to-day suggestions to get your child into the "writing mode."

Guidelines for the parent

1. Encourage oral story telling.
2. Ask your child questions and encourage questions from him.
3. Read a lot yourself to model the reading habit, and have your child read every day. Good writers are good readers.
4. Share reading experiences with your child by discussing the theme and plot. Ask questions that get your child to think about the whole story, such as "Why do you think he did that?" and "What do you think will happen next?"
5. Writing entails thinking—use writing opportunities to create thinking exercises. For example, if you and your child need to make a difficult decision, write a *pro and con list*—all the reasons to do something and all the reasons against it. In the short run, it's putting pencil to paper. In the long run, the child is developing cognitive abilities.
6. Show appreciation, and praise what your child writes.
7. Be non-judgmental about your child's idea flow—even if some of the things seem ridiculous or far-fetched, the point is to encouraging the easy flow of ideas, and afterwards, the pearls can be separated from the rocks.
8. Frequently, for younger children, the act of writing itself is so arduous, that their writing samples alone would indicate limited

narration skills. In order to circumvent this, have your child tell you a story. With no prompting or interrupting, write down or tape record the entire story.

9. Notice the way your child holds the pencil. A proper grip will alleviate the pressure many children put on their fingers, and will enable them to write faster and neater.

Guidelines for the child

1. Write frequently, either helping your parent or on your own—letters, shopping lists, thank you notes, to-do lists.
2. Write daily journal entries about feelings, thoughts, plans, or a narration about what happened during the day.
3. Keep a dream journal by your bed and jot down a few sentences every morning.
4. Keep a scrap book about activities that took place, with comments about your experience.

Types of writing

The three types of writing—informative, persuasive, and descriptive—are developed in the 4th grade. However, the skills needed to write well are learned and practiced in the very early grades as well—starting with the first time a child writes his name. Once a student is able to recognize the three forms, he will be able to write in any of them.

Descriptive

The writer presents a picture with words, telling a story, real or imagined.

It was a dark and stormy night. The thunder raged in the black skies and the lightning sent its jagged bolts to earth. There were three little boys, there in Wisconsin. They were used to playing on the ice, all winter long. They were the best of friends. One day, the oldest boy...

Informative

The writer presents basic information clearly.

The elephant is a large mammal that lives on land. It has a long trunk that it uses to get food, to spray itself, and to scratch its back. Elephants sleep standing up. They can live for more than 50 years.

Persuasive

The writer tries to explain or persuade.

People should not smoke. It is not good for their health. Tobacco causes cancer and emphysema. Half a million Americans a year die from cigarettes. Even though it's very hard, anyone who smokes should try to quit today.

An important function of this book is to show parents the depth and breadth of elementary education. One of the first aptitudes discovered and developed is the fine motor skills. You can see the gradual progression in the following set of typical handwriting samples:

Writing Samples

Kindergarten

R ID⊃

First Grade

riteing

Second Grade

riting

Third Grade

writing

Fourth Grade

Writing

Fifth Grade

Writing

Kindergarten

Basic Skills

At the kindergarten level, there is not much actual writing, which is why drawing is included in the assessment. At this age, drawing is pre-literate expression, and capable of showing a wide range just as written work does. A drawing can be simple, sketchy, static, and monochromatic or a complex, detailed, confident, multicolored story, paralleling a spoken or written narrative.

A kindergartner learns the mechanics of printing, the order of the 26 letters and the idea of putting down letters from left to right.

Kindergarten is the big transition from hearth and home to participation "in the system." Instead of being home with the family or in a small group at pre-school, a child is now one of 20 or 30 students. One of the big, new expectations is that the child listen for directions and follow them. This focusing of attention is initially directed at the alphabet. *"This is the letter A, like in* **apple**. *Copy the A on your paper."* If the child does something completely different from writing an A on a piece of paper, the teacher can redirect the child's attention to the task at hand.

At this level, narrative skills should be highly encouraged, so that when the child is able to write, he will have developed the ability and the willingness to put his thoughts down on paper.

Common Difficulties

1. **Learning the letters of the alphabet**
    This is the first real learning experience for a school child, and there is often confusion about the shapes of the letters, the order in which they are in the alphabet, and the sounds that each letter represents. Children need to first say the alphabet in order, then recognize the individual letters when they see them.

2. **Copying the letters onto paper**
    After a child recognizes the letters, it is time to put them on paper. For some children, it is difficult to look up, see the image, hold that image in their minds, and write it on the paper. For these children, tracing over lightly written letters is an easy solution. There can be little arrows indicating which way the line goes, as this will forestall the problem of starting a **p** at the bottom, for example.

3. **Mirror images**
    It is very common to see backwards letters at this stage. It is helpful to start with one letter, such as **b**, and make sure the child has mastered it before moving on to the next, such as **p**. It is confusing for the child if they are all taught together.

First Grade

Basic Skills

In the 1st grade, children review and master the 26 letters and all the sound combinations (*th, sh, ch,* etc.). By mid-first grade, a child should be able to write a simple sentence, use simple punctuation, and start to spell simple words properly.

First graders should be able to identify these three types of sentences and use the end marks appropriately:

First Grade Term	Formal Term	Mark
Telling statement	Declarative	.
Asking or question	Interrogative	?
Strong feeling statement	Exclamation	!

Both statements and questions are *sentences*. A sentence is a complete thought, and is defined as having a *subject* and a *predicate* (everything after the subject). An example would be, *"The dog sees a cat." The dog* is the subject, and *sees a cat* is the predicate. The predicate can also be short: *"The dog runs."* The shortest sentences of all are commands, *"Run!"*

First graders should recognize and be able to use the most common endings: *s, ed, ing, er.* When writing, children need to pay attention to their grammar. It's easy to skip over little words such as *to, with, by*, but when they are left out, the sentence no longer makes sense. This is why a child should always read back aloud what she has written. Her ear will tell her if it is right or not. If a child puts down actual solecisms such as *"I gots a toy," "They runned away," "She don't know,"* or *"The dog ain't got no food,"* it's best to talk about "standard English," both in writing and speech.

From the beginning, children should practice printing as neatly as their fine motor skills will allow. Penmanship is important. Neatness and correct letter shapes do count because writing must be readable for the writer and the reader. The purpose of writing is to communicate thoughts, ideas, observations, or feelings in a clear, logical, and coherent manner. Good writing habits in the primary grades are a tool to communicate clearly and effectively for a lifetime.

Spelling in the 1st grade is erratic. Children are just becoming acquainted with the letters and the idea of using them to create words, so it is typical to see just the first letter of a word (*g* for *get*), just the consonants (*ppl* for *people*), or completely phonetic spelling (*lidul* for *little*). At this level it is best to stick with phonetic words that completely follow the rules, such as *man* and *take*.

Common Difficulties

1. Complete sentences

In the 1st grade, writing is a very new skill, whereas a child has been speaking for more than half of his entire life. Written language is also more formal, while spoken language is more colloquial. Through writing, a child starts to sort out the difference between a whole sentence and a fragment. In response to a spoken question, *"What did the dog chase?"* the child can quite appropriately respond, *"Fluffy."* But on paper, *"Fluffy"* is not a sentence and a child needs to reengineer her thinking toward *Who did what to whom?* and write, *"The dog chased Fluffy."*

School homework usually includes one syllable spelling words and making sentences out of these words. Use this time to encourage whole sentences. Another exercise is to mix sentences and fragments, and have your child identify which is a sentence, which is a fragment, and why. (See pages 222 and 236.)

2. **End marks**

Since the focus of the 1st grade is the simple sentence, the actual definition of a sentence is "subject with a capital letter, predicate, end mark." Children need to always start with a capital and use one of the three 1st grade end marks, which are period, question mark, and exclamation mark. When your child finishes a piece, have her go over it, sentence by sentence, saying "Is this a sentence? Is there an end mark?" This is the precursor to the writing checklists used later.

3. **Spelling**

Children have a sufficiently large spoken vocabulary in the 1st grade, but they don't know how to spell many words yet. Given that writing is the goal, many teachers across the United States embraced the concept of *inventive spelling* or *temporary spelling*. This allows children to get the words down on paper without losing the idea flow. However, it cannot be emphasized enough that this is only for the first draft in the 1st grade. Proper spelling must be taught, starting with phonics, so the child can learn the basic rules.

4. **Following directions**

Following directions is not the same as being obedient, though there are areas of overlap. In the 1st grade, the directions that are given are much more refined and elaborate than in kindergarten. Because the teacher is talking to 20 or 30 children, there is not as much individual attention as at home. If she says, *"Put your name in the upper right hand corner,"* the child has to pick up her pencil, put the paper right side up, find the upper right hand corner, remember how to spell her name, and print neatly. For some children, this is a difficult and complicated task, as it involves simultaneous processing. If possible, spend a little time in the classroom watching your child's interaction with the teacher. If you notice areas of confusion, you can then work with your child at home.

5. **Legibility**

By the 1st grade, many children are able to reproduce well-formed letters and take pride in this accomplishment. Other children find the skill more difficult and less important.

Very often, children will see how quickly the parent writes and will try to emulate speed while sacrificing legibility. Taking the time to form legible, properly spelled words will form a habit that will benefit the child greatly throughout her education (and career).

6. **Letter formation**

   If left to their own devices, children will form letters in an astonishing variety of ways. They may start at the bottom and go up, or they may start in the middle and go down, and then add a top. This may seem unimportant at first, but the stroke order and direction of the printed word lead directly into the smoothest form of writing: cursive.

   Shape is the first element of printing. The two basic shapes are **o** and **l**. Have your child trace them and copy them. There are two reasons for this. One is that by mastering the basic shape, the child will have an easier time putting together two familiar shapes to form a new letter (**o** and **l** make **a, b, d, p**, and **q**). Second, it is easier to learn the five basic shapes (**o, l, /, **, and **n**) than 26 differently shaped letters. This way, the alphabet is much less daunting.

Second Grade

Basic Skills

If the main skill acquired in kindergarten was the *letter*, and in 1st grade it was the *sentence*, then in 2nd grade it is the *paragraph*. At this level, a paragraph is three to five sentences all on the same topic. As writing skills develop, a paragraph will contain a *topic sentence* for the *central idea* and *supporting details*.

At the 2nd grade level children start learning the contraction rules—the most basic being that the apostrophe replaces the *o* in *not*. Capitalization at the beginning of a sentence is a 1st grade skill, followed by capitalization of proper nouns in 2nd grade. This includes names of people, cities, titles, and so on. A new punctuation skill learned in 2nd grade is the comma in the greeting and closing of letters. Later in the year, the use of a comma to briefly pause in a sentence is introduced.

In 2nd grade, spelling makes the transition from phonetic spelling to standard spelling. Children should know the plurals and the different endings, both regular and irregular: run/runs; fly/flies; child/children; knife/knives. A 7-year-old should recognize and be able to use the prefixes *-er, -est, -ful, -ness, -ous,* and *-y.*

The level of vocabulary should be increasing in a child's writing. Encourage your child to use words that are specific and descriptive. If you see that the child is using the same few words repeatedly, such as *nice, cool, funny, little, cute, really, lots, thing, stuff*, it's a good idea to start asking for synonyms and more specific adjectives. *"Lots of cool stuff is neat, but that funny little thing was really great,"* turns into *"Skateboards and roller-blades are the most fun to play with, but that glow-in-the-dark yo-yo was the most popular."* Go through the process word by word, and the average 2nd grader will come up with at least two synonyms for each generic word.

It is very common for a 2nd grader to start every sentence with *I* or *my*. To help develop his writing skills and broaden his perspective, encourage him to start considering other ways to introduce a topic from a variety of perspectives.

You can help your child develop perspective and complexity in thought and sentence structure by asking questions to elicit further information or feelings. If he writes about his dog Fang you can say, "Tell me what Fang looks like," "How do you feel when you see Fang?" or "Would you feel differently about him if his name were Fluffy?" Ultimately, this type of discussion gives depth, breadth, and sophistication to both a child's writing and his thinking.

Common Difficulties

1. **I can't think of anything to write!**
    Beginning writers may need stimulation and a "jump start" from a parent. If the child is writing about ecology, for example, you can

elicit ideas from him by asking a wide variety of questions, such as, *"What happens to trash after we throw it away?"* or *"What would happen if no one recycled?"* and *"If you were president, what would you do about the environment?"* Make sure that you ask open-ended questions to allow your child plenty of room to explore the topic on his own.

2. **Jumping topic**
   Structure is much more imposed in writing than it is in speaking, so a child who is accustomed to a free ranging conversation will naturally carry this tendency over to writing. While a parent doesn't want to stifle a budding raconteur's narration, it's a good idea to start channeling that creativity into a more structured format. One way of doing this is by having the child do the clustering technique (see page 317). Thus, he can get all the ideas down, then choose one or two on which to focus.

3. **That's all I can write. The end.**
   Even in the 2nd grade, children need to know about wrapping up the subject. Have the child look back over what he has written and come up with one sentence to tie it all together. This is the precursor to the summary or conclusion.

More Second Grade Writing Skills

By now, a child has been exposed to a plethora of rules and conventions. It would be hard for a 7-year-old to remember and apply all of them. Because both under-standing and using the rules are important in these early stages, have your child review a story he wrote, using the following checklist:

Writing Checklist

❑ My name is on my story.

❑ My story has a title.

❑ The first sentence is indented.

❑ I wrote six or more sentences.

❑ Each sentence is complete.

❑ Each sentence begins with a capital letter.

❑ Each sentence ends with correct punctuation.

❑ Each word is spelled correctly.

❑ Each paragraph is indented.

❑ Each paragraph is on one topic.

❑ My margins are straight and wide.

❑ My handwriting is neat.

Parents and teachers can copy and laminate this list so a child can have it handy for each writing assignment.

Letter writing

Letters have their own unique conventions that dis-tinguish them from stories. Have your child write a let-ter to a real person, and prepare the envelope. After the first draft, have him go over the following checklist to ascertain that he hasn't overlooked any important ele-ments of the letter.

Letter Writing Checklist

- ❏ Correct heading
  (name, address, city, state, zip code)—optional in an informal letter
- ❏ Date
- ❏ Comma after the greeting
- ❏ Indented the first sentence of each paragraph
- ❏ Capital letters
- ❏ Correct punctuation
- ❏ Good margins
- ❏ Comma after the closing
- ❏ Neat signature

Parents and teachers can copy and laminate this list so a child can have it handy for each writing assignment.

Letter format

(date) July 20, 1999

Dear Uncle Ben, *(greeting)*
   (body)
   Thank you for taking me to Disneyland for my birthday. I had a really great time.
   I hope that we can do something fun for your birthday, too.
   Let's go to the park this weekend. I have a new baseball bat to show you. I'll see you soon. *(closing)*
                   Your nephew,
                       (signature)
                   Ethan

Third Grade

Basic Skills

A 3rd grader should present information in a logical sequence, and use increasingly complex sentence structure. Stories and reports should have a beginning, middle, and end.

An easy way to help develop these more sophisticated writing skills is to have your child complete a weekly book report. This can be about a book that she has read, or one that was read to her. For variety, she can also do movie reports, changing *author* to *starring*. Be creative in finding ways to make writing fun for your child.

In the 3rd grade, some children still find drawing easier than writing, so encourage illustrations in each report. Both printing and cursive are common at this grade level, but by this time, the writing should be more legible and presentable.

Third grade vocabulary should reflect a child's growing awareness of the world around her and the specific words that can be used to describe it. Because she is reading more than in previous years, she is exposed to a larger and more varied vocabulary. Stories should reflect a stretching of a child's imagination, rather than a recycling of the same words and ideas. In speech and in writing, the parent should encourage more elaborate sentences with introductory clauses, strong supporting adjectives and adverbs, and proper verb tenses. A good familiarity with word roots can help a child dissect words for meaning. A 3rd grader should know the meanings of the most common prefixes: *un, re, pre, ex,* and *dis,* as well as how to use the adverbial ending *-ly* and the noun ending *-tion.*

In terms of punctuation, with these complex sentences a student will have to use more commas than before. A good rule of thumb for commas is that they are used where the writer would naturally pause if she were talking.

Transition words ease the path of a reader from one aspect of a topic to another. If stated baldly, ideas seem merely sequential. When transitioned well, they reveal the underlying logic. For example, here are two facts stated as two separate thoughts:

Bob was sad. He stayed at home.

Here are the same two facts joined by a defining conjunction:

Bob was sad, *so* he stayed at home.
Bob was sad *because* he stayed at home.
Bob was sad, *even though* he stayed at home.
Bob was sad *whenever* he stayed at home.

All in all, at this level a child should start to show a deeper and broader thoughtfulness in the ideas that she expresses and in the language that she uses to convey her thoughts.

Spelling is a big issue in 3rd grade, but, like penmanship, it is not really a part of writing. It is, however, very noticeable in a writing sample, and poor spelling gives the impression of illiteracy. Spelling is a combination of aptitude and knowledge. Children with a strong aptitude for spelling—a natural ability to spell—can glance at a word and retain its correct spelling or even accurately *guess* the spelling of a new word. For children for whom spelling does not come as naturally, a combination of visual (flash cards), auditory (spelling out loud), and kinesthetic (writing the words on paper) learning techniques will aid in learning spelling.

Common Difficulties

1. **Declarative statements only**

   I like to play. I play every day. I play at school.
   Once the subject-predicate rule has been taught, children can adhere to it and never venture further. These children need to be encouraged to be a little more descriptive in their work. Here again, the parent inquiry can help with questions like, "Who *was* that masked man?" or "What did he do?"

2. **And. And. And.**

   The other side of the coin is the child who never met a run-on sentence she couldn't make even longer. Like many a novelist, this child just needs a good editor, and that editor can be herself. If you see an endless thicket of conjunctions, have your child erase every single *and*. Then put in periods and capital letters where they were. It makes an astonishing difference.

3. **Really, really good.**

   There is frequently not much variety in adverbs. Eight-year-olds can think much faster than they write, so all that intensity that they have in their heads comes out as *very* and *really*. Turn those adverbs into more specific adverbs. The main rule for an adverb is that it describes a verb, ends in *-ly,* and answers the question, *How?* So if you ask your child how the game was, and she responds, "Intense!" then she can write, *The soccer game was **intensely** exciting*.

4. **They did it to them.**

   Another characteristic of a 3rd grade writer (not that it is limited to 3rd graders) is to assume that the reader knows everything the writer knows. Children will use general pronouns copiously because inside their heads, they know exactly what happened— while the reader is left wondering, *Who did what to whom?* Until all the facts have been presented, children should be encouraged to write with nouns rather than pronouns. This way, *"He chased him into his castle,"* can become *"The dragon chased the prince into the giant's castle."*

5. **Commas**

   Commas are used to separate words and phrases. Whereas a period is a full stop, a comma is a pause. Until a child learns to hear the cadence of his own speech, it is acceptable for him to use commas only for listing and to pause a sentence before a conjunction.

More Third Grade Writing Skills

A systematic approach to a writing assignment is the well-tested five-step process. The five-step writing process is an organizational tool, a strategy for writing. Specifically, it is the generation and development of an idea, expanded and refined into a finished product. The five steps are as follows:

1. **Pre-writing**

   Before you actually start writing, *brainstorm* the development of your story by clustering: Draw a circle around your central idea or character and then add ideas or description as they come to you. Each one that you write will generate others. This can then be worked into a topic sentence for a first draft:

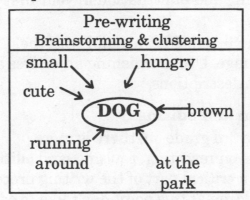

   There was a cute, little dog running around the park last week. He looked hungry, so...

   ♦ Think about what you know. It is easiest to write from your own experience.
   ♦ Think about your audience. How will you tell them your story?

- Make a list or draw pictures of your ideas.
- Choose one idea.
- Think about your idea. What will happen at the beginning? What will happen in the middle? What will happen at the end? This is called an *outline*.

2. **Writing**

- **Experience** Write about what you know, feel or imagine.
- **Setting** Choose the time and place for your story.
- **Characters** Describe who the story is about.
- **Plot** Tell what happens in the story.
- **Rough Draft** Don't worry about perfect spelling and punctuation in your first draft.
- **Experiment** Play around with the language. Use astonishing adjectives and great descriptions.

3. **Revision and editing**

   From the 3rd grade on, there is more emphasis on rewriting, revising, and editing, which is a critical part of the writing process. Most children at this point don't like to edit; they like the idea that they did the work and "it's over," whereas editing means spending more time looking for mistakes and correcting their work.

   Children need to develop editing skills, so a first step is to have them edit work other than their own. Type or handwrite a paragraph with a variety of errors in it and have your child find and correct them. A good strategy is to first have her check the entire paragraph for a single purpose, such as punctuation at the end of a sentence. Go through an entire checklist (see page 311), having your child check for one type of error at a time.

Once your child is fairly proficient at editing your work, she can go on to his own pieces. Here's a summary of what this writing stage entails:

◆ **Story build-up** Read your story. Add words and sentences to tell more.

◆ **Form** Is it a story, a poem, a newspaper article? What changes are necessary so that it seems like the form you have chosen?

◆ Does each paragraph contain one idea?

◆ Read your story to a friend.

◆ Change your story to make it even better.

4. Final proofing

◆ Look at the story one more time.

◆ Fix any mistakes with a colored pencil.

◆ Go through the writing checklist.

◆ Circle any words that you're not sure how to spell. Look them up in the dictionary.

◆ After you edit your story, have your teacher or parent look at it.

5. Publishing

Copy your story neatly and read it to the class or to your family.

9-word outline

To prepare a 9-word outline, think about telling a story to someone in only **9 words**. Think of a beginning part, a middle part and an end part. (Parents may remember this format from the movies: *Boy meets girl, boy loses girl, boy gets girl*.)

Topic: Beauty and the Beast

Prince	becomes	Beast.
Beast	captures	Belle.
Belle	marries	Prince.

Once a child has the basic nine words (approximately), she can use conjunctions and modifiers to make longer, more sophisticated sentences in the pre-outline.

Pre-Outline

Third graders should have enough structure in their writing to be able to start using a simple pre-outline. Before starting to write, they can lay out the basic train of thought. Here's an example based on *Beauty and the Beast*:

Beginning   Spoiled prince is turned into a beast.

Middle   The beast holds Belle captive in the castle.

End   The beast turns into a prince and marries Belle.

Fourth Grade

Basic Skills

By this time, a young writer should be including more detailed information, including chronological references in conjunction with more complex verb tenses (*had done, would have done, will have done*), specific prepositional phrases (*until the dawn, before the mast*), and relative pronouns (*the man who..., the group that..., Einstein's theory, which...*). In terms of the internal structure of a piece, a 4th grader should be using more sophisticated introductory phrases (*initially, first and foremost*), transitional phrases (*meanwhile, on the other hand*), and concluding phrases (*consequently, in summary*).

An introductory clause is a phrase that lets a writer approach a topic less directly—it prepares the reader for what is to follow. Notice how the introductory clause sets the stage: **As had long been suspected**, *the power plant was polluting the groundwater.*

Adjectives can be used to give more information about nouns, and *adverbs* give more information about verbs. Notice how a basic sentence can be shaped:

The boy swam toward shore.
*The **twelve year old** boy swam toward shore.*
*The **suntanned** boy swam **leisurely** toward shore.*

*The **confident** twelve year old boy swam **skillfully** toward the **distant** shore.*

Another benefit of combining phrases in this way is that it will counteract the tendency to chop writing into short sentences à la Joe Friday:

The boy was twelve. He had a suntan. He was swimming. He was a good swimmer. The shore was a long way away.

"What's another word for...?" is an excellent entree into not only vocabulary development and synonyms, but for different styles and levels of writing, as well as for different audiences. Consider how different the following sentences are, although the basic meaning is the same: *Hello, how do you do? Hi, how are you? Hey, what's up?* Each has a particular environment in which it would be appropriate.

In addition to the structures within a writing sample, there are three writing styles that are learned in the 4th grade. These are *informative*, where the writer presents basic information clearly; *descriptive*, where the writer presents a picture with words, telling a real or imaginary story; and *persuasive*, where the writer explains or persuades.

Fourth grade research becomes more fact gathering and report writing than the narration of the previous years. Consequently, rephrasing and paraphrasing become extremely important as children can be tempted to copy whole paragraphs from research sources.

To find a child's "voice" and style, have him read the material and say it back to you in his own words. Then write down what he said, and have him edit it for written English as opposed to spoken English.

Frequently, a young writer, especially on a school deadline for a research project, will sit dejectedly in front of a blank piece of paper, not knowing what to write. Everything seems like a false start.

It may seem to the child like he has nothing to say. Usually, just the opposite is true: He's done the research and there is simply too much to think about and sort out. Have him put the pencil down and start talking. Have him tell you all about the monarch butterfly or the red planet Mars, and he will be amazed at how effortlessly the information flows forth. Stop him gently and say, "Now, start writing some of what you've told me."

If the first draft isn't in the right order—and it probably won't be—that's fine. The point is to get the thoughts from the child's head and onto the paper. Then he can start editing, revising, and rewriting. Don't be afraid to take a pair of scissors and physically cutting up and reorder an essay. It's very hard for a child to visualize that the contents of a paragraph have been moved.

Common Difficulties

1. **Organization**

   Fourth graders have been introduced to the concept of structure though outlines, but it is sometimes difficult for them to apply what they see as abstract (the outline) to what they see as concrete (the actual essay). Young writers tend to feel that because they understand what they are trying to say or because they are aware of the chronology, that it would be redundant to write it all down. They need to go through the journalist's checklist (*who, what, where, when, why,* and *how*) and answer every single question. Then, if something is overstated or redundant, it can always be taken out.

2. Other perspectives

Part of what ails a young writer is that he is doing things that he has probably not had to do before: consider an audience, think objectively rather than subjectively, and put bits and pieces of ideas down on paper as a coherent unit. As has been said before, writing is thinking on paper. Training a person to write is training him to think.

A large part of this has to do with other perspectives. Nine-year-olds generally think of themselves as the center of the web with everything else radiating outward. Getting a 4th grader to place himself on one of the spokes and write from that perspective will help him consider the audience. The new perspective enables him to see how another person could have different but equally valid ideas and helps him think objectively, seeing where a certain idea fits into the whole scheme of things.

A common exercise to work toward this goal is to have the child write an essay as if he were a completely different person (opposite gender, different race, age, size, or personality) and have the writing reflect this person without stating it outright. This is called *showing* the information, not just *telling* it.

3. Serious editing

Young writers feel a great attachment to what they have written down, just the way they wrote it. It seems so permanent, after all. Real editing goes beyond adding commas and a couple of adjectives. Children need to be taught that it is a great technique to "take a pair of scissors to a draft," cutting and pasting, whether they are using paper or a computer. Whole sections can be moved around—frequently the conclusion will have been written first and needs to be shifted to the end, or the introduction will be buried in the body and needs to be highlighted in the beginning.

More Fourth Grade Writing Skills

In the 4th grade, a child needs to display the ability to write more sophisticated essays in any of the three writing styles: descriptive, informative, and persuasive.

Descriptive writing

In descriptive writing, the writer presents a picture with words. One way to practice descriptive writing is for the child to select a favorite place to describe, then close his eyes and visualize that place, adding more and more detail. After he chooses a place, you can elicit the details by prompting him with questions, particularly questions that involved the senses.

For example, if the place is a campground in the woods, you might ask what the weather is like, what kinds of trees there are, what color the leaves are, what season it is, whether there are any mountains or snow visible, if any birds can be heard, if there's a campfire and if so, what it smells like.

Encourage adjectives and the use of metaphors and similes, such as, *"The lake was as smooth as glass."* This is not to be confused with a cliché, as what is old hat to an adult can be new and fresh to a child.

This procedure can be used for indoor or outdoor settings. Instead of a peaceful landscape, there is a lively party scene. The technique can be used for descriptions of people as well as places.

To practice a more narrative type of descriptive writing, the child can think of a story he would like to tell—either a true story, where he would be relating an event or series of events, or a fictitious story, where he would invent a situation and characters. Have the child think of a story, such as when the canoe tipped over and he and his friends lost their belongings.

Have him answer the *who, what, where, when, how,* and *why* questions and then make a brief sequential outline.

Then have him "flesh out" the story by adding thoughts, feelings, and descriptions.

Informative writing

In informative writing, the writer needs to give information to the reader in a clear, comprehensible way, much like an encyclopedia article does.

You can ask your child to pick a topic he likes, such as a type of animal, or airplanes. First have him create a definition of the topic and then write five or six things about the topic that he thinks readers would like to know and that would familiarize readers with the topic.

The opening sentence should be the definition, and it should be accurate and informative. For example, *"A naked mole rat is something like a mouse with no hair."* Prompt the child to tell some facts about his topic by asking him questions.

The closing sentence should be one last fact about the topic—a wrap-up or concluding statement. To clarify informative writing, a young writer should look through an encyclopedia for topical articles.

Another use for informative writing is to explain to the reader how to do something. This type of writing may include recipes, directions to get somewhere, or how-to instructions, such as how to decorate a cake.

The opening sentence(s) should introduce the topic. For example, *"Chocolate chip cookies are a delicious snack. Here's how to make them."* Then the child can list the steps in the process, finishing with a concluding sentence, such as, *"Now the cookies are ready to eat."*

Persuasive

The purpose of persuasive writing is to get the reader to accept the author's point of view. In other words, the writer is moving the reader from point A to point B, or in the vernacular, talking someone into something. This is accomplished by using powerful, emotional, or logical reasons why his position should be accepted.

To get an initial understanding of persuasive writing, the child can look at a commercial. The purpose of a commercial or an advertisement is to get people to buy things. The child can observe the words and arguments that are used to that end: *Easy! Fun! Cheap! Get one today! Limited time only!*

The ad writers thought about what would motivate people and used words that would connect the buyer with the product.

For a 4th grade writer, a good persuasive writing project would be to take one side of an issue and lay out his argument either for or against it.

Once children have grasped the concept of identifying the goal and laying out the path toward the reader's arriving at it, they can practice persuasive speaking in real life. For example, if a child wants his parents to take him and his sister camping, but they don't want to go because they are too tired, the child can make a list of ideas that will persuade the parents to go. For instance, the child knows that Mom would like a little tranquillity, she would prefer not to be stuck with a ton of dishes, and she doesn't want to sit in the car for hours. Dad likes nature, but he is tired of driving and he needs some time off. So, using this information, the child comes up with the following persuasive arguments for both parents:

1. The woods are beautiful and peaceful.
2. There is a lovely spot not far from home.
3. The kids will put up the tent and pack the food.
4. They promise not to argue.
5. They will do the cooking and cleaning up.

An exercise of this type will be a good start in the art of persuasive writing.

Simple Outline

Fourth graders can expand on the pre-outline form used in 3rd grade. Following is an outline of the story

Beauty and the Beast, with a more developed framework than in the previous grade.

I. **Introduction**	About the prince and Belle before they met
II. **Body**	
A. *Main Point #1*	Belle's father goes to the castle
B. *Main Point # 2*	Belle gets trapped in the castle
C. *Main Point #3*	Belle gets to know the beast
III. **Conclusion**	The spell is broken and the prince marries Belle

Fifth Grade

Basic Skills

By the 5th grade, a student should be able to use an outline; develop themes; write comfortably using different writing styles, such as descriptive, informative, and persuasive; and clearly distinguish between formal and colloquial language. In addition, knowing what the eight parts of speech are (see page 203), and what they do in a sentence will help a child when the teacher refers to a part by its name in class.

As there is more editing in this level than before, it is important for every 5th grade writer to be fully conversant with the proofreader's marks. This will enable a young writer to understand the teacher's corrections as well as edit her own work more effectively.

Proofreader's marks

^ insert	⸰ insert comma	⊙ insert period
ϒ delete	∬ transpose	≡ capitalize
# insert space	◠ close up	⸓ lower case

Also at this level, outlines become more important and more detailed. Third graders used a pre-outline format with a beginning, middle, and ending. Fourth graders expanded on the introduction and conclusion, and learned to break the middle, or body, into at least three major points. By the 5th grade, students are ready for even more sophisticated techniques to clarify and organize their thinking.

The 5th grade is where a child really starts to develop her "voice" in writing. She can write or type quickly and organize her thoughts well enough to develop and express more complicated or philosophical ideas. She can also analyze her own writing and recognize flaws in logic, contradictions, and weaknesses in positions. She is ready to start letting her writing become a reflection of herself.

Common Difficulties

1. **Erratic or nonsequential chronology**
   Chronology weakness is when the writer has difficulty explaining the order of events in a logical sequence. There are several chronology techniques that can be used:

   A. A straight chronology: *The order in which events happened.*

   B. Present time: *With reference to the past or future in dialogue or flashbacks*

   C. Order revealed: *Presentation of the information in the order it was received.* (This places the author or character center stage, as all time relates to him and his perception of it.)

2. **Unrelated cause and effect**

When something happens out of the blue, with nothing leading up to it, the reader will feel that a logical conclusion has not been reached. A young writer is often unable to understand the consequences of actions, or see to the patterns of cause and effect in either a sequential linear direction or a multi-directional ripple effect. The cause-and-effect maps on page 155 can be used to practice perception and reasoning.

3. **Details and "the big picture"**

This aspect of writing is actually a reflection of an individual's aptitude—there are "detail oriented" people and "big picture" people. It only becomes a problem, however, when a piece is unbalanced—either too detailed or too general. If neither the writer nor the reader can "see the forest for the trees," the writer has over-emphasized the details, while missing the main point. Outlining for major topics will help the writer hold his focus on the main point without drifting off into minutia.

Conversely, some pieces read more like an overview, with highlights and main points, but no supporting details. This writer needs to go back to the outline, and under each main point, list at least three supporting facts.

More Fifth Grade Writing Skills

In the 5th grade a student should be able to use a variety of techniques to develop a well written essay.

Developing a theme

After a writer gets an idea of something she wants to write about, she needs to develop that idea. The student might want to write about dolls, but have no thoughts on what she would like to say about dolls.

The parent can elicit the development of the idea by asking questions. For example, "What aspect of dolls would you like to tell about? The history of dolls? How different types of dolls are made? The many ways to play with dolls? Doll costuming around the world? Or perhaps a combination of these topics?" This open ended type of questioning will spark a response in the child.

Suppose the child picks the history of dolls around the world as her topic. She must research it to get information on primitive dolls and dolls in different eras. She must pick out what she considers the most important or interesting facts about dolls through the ages. Then she can write the outline and develop the theme.

The writer must expand her thoughts from a bare bones outline to a fully "fleshed out" piece. Adjectives and adverbs must be added to make the writing more interesting and accurate. Sentence structure should be varied and synonyms used to avoid becoming repetitive.

After the first draft, the parent can ask some more *why, how,* and *what* kind of questions to develop more details. For example, a sentence such as *"Ballet is a form of theatrical entertainment,"* can be developed to be *"Ballet is one of the most thrilling and vivid forms of theatrical entertainment."*

In a fictional piece, more dialog might be written to replace prose, to enliven the story. For example, the sentence, *"Benny was angry at his sister because she was playing with his computer and had deleted his home work by mistake,"* could be changed to *"Benny yelled at his sister, 'Sally! You are in such big trouble! You ruined my homework! Don't touch my computer again!'"*

The writer should add color by adding supporting details and expanding thoughts. The following story maps can be used to organize the chronological, logistical, or consequential aspects of the work.

Story mapping

Story mapping is a form of pre-outlining. It is an interesting technique for organizing thoughts for chronology, similar and/or different characteristics, and cause and effect. Story maps are akin to the clustering that was introduced in the 3rd grade. They provide a visual format showing temporal, spatial, or consequential relationships that might not otherwise have been apparent to the writer. The information derived from the story mapping can then immediately be put to good use in the outline. Here's what a story map might look like.

Chronological
A. Before they met
B. The first day
C. The rest of their lives

Cause and effect
A. They meet
B. They both like to swim
C. They become friends

Similarities and differences
A. Bob
B. Mary
C. Bob and Mary
    1. Similarities
    2. Differences

Once the writer's thoughts are clear, the act of writing itself is just a question of putting pen to paper, or fingers to the keyboard—the student need only begin writing about each item on the outline, using transition sentences where appropriate, to create a smooth flow from paragraph to paragraph.

A good outline will ensure that each paragraph contains a single idea, and has good transitions that carry the reader along from idea to idea, with no gaps or unnecessary overlaps. For example, the last sentence of a paragraph might be, *"He swept the floor and put the papers away."* The opening sentence of the next paragraph might be, *"Now that the room was cleaned up, Jim set up the table and chairs for the meeting."*

When starting to write, it is best to get something down on paper, even if it is not perfect. Later, the writing can be edited and revised. As George Bernard Shaw said, "Good writing is not written. It is rewritten."

Story map—Chronology

Clearly establishing a chronology enables a writer to develop a logical sequence for his story. There are groups of phrases that help establish time, such as:

- ◆ Before, during, after.
- ◆ First, in the beginning, next, then, after that, later on, in the end, finally, at last.
- ◆ 1 a.m., 2 a.m., 8 p.m., noon, midnight.
- ◆ In the morning, that afternoon, all night.

On Monday, they planned the bank robbery.	➡	On Friday, they broke into the vault.	➡	By Sunday, they had been arrested and put in jail.

Have your child write a sequential outline for his story, like the one illustrated on page 335. No matter what the time span, divide the story or informational piece at major breaking points. For example, 1) *a boy lost his dog;* 2) *first he looked all over his house;* 3) *the next day he put up a notice at school;* 4) *a week later he put an ad in the newspaper offering a reward;* 5) *a few days after that a girl found the dog.* Writers at this level need to make sure extraneous information does not stray in, such as 3.5) *he ate lunch.*

Story map—Venn diagram

A Venn diagram is prepared by making overlapping circles—grouped by characters, places, or events. This will enable a beginning writer to show differences and similarities. In making a Venn diagram for the characters in her story, for example, your child will have one circle per character, all overlapping in the center. In the part of each circle that does not overlap any other circle, your child should write traits that are unique to that character. In parts that overlap, she can write traits that the overlapping characters have in common.

Have your child make one or more Venn diagrams about the characters, locations, or events in her story. Even if she doesn't use all the information, it will help clarify the ideas in her own mind. Elicit the information for the diagrams by asking, *"What things are the same about Bob and Mary?"* and *"What things are different about them?"* The information gathered through the Venn diagram can then be used to develop a good outline.

Story map—Cause and effect

Determining cause and effect allows a beginning writer to answer the questions, *Why did this happen?*

How did this come about? and *What are the consequences of this action?* The words *because, so, since, therefore, as a result, thus,* and *caused by* are words that are used to indicate a cause and effect relation.

Have your child use the main event of the story as a starting point and then list the consequences of each event. The writer can go from cause to effect or from effect back to cause. For example, *a fire broke out in an office building.* What was the cause? A reporter who is interviewing people who worked there finds out that: 1) the wiring of electric heater was defective; 2) someone was smoking in the building; and 3) there had been a storm earlier. One of these facts is probably the cause of the fire.

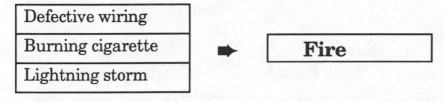

Conversely, the writer can also tell what the effect of the fire (which in this case becomes the cause) was, in terms of 1) how much damage was done to the building; 2) how many people were displaced; or 3) how much money it cost.

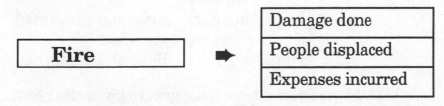

Once a writer become conversant with cause/effect, similarities/distinctions, and chronology, his writing is on its way to being well developed.

Basic outline

From the 3rd through the 5th grade and beyond, there are appropriate levels of writing structure—the 3rd grade *pre-outline*; the 4th grade *simple outline*; the 5th grade *basic outline* with more supporting facts; and ultimately, the detailed *standard outline* as shown in the following example.

I. **Introduction**

    A. Main Point #1   About the spoiled prince

    B. Main Point #2   Belle and her father's life

    C. Main Point #3   setting (town and towns people)

II. **Body**

    A. Main Point #1   Belle's father goes to the castle

        1. Supporting Fact   Belle and the towns people

        2. Supporting Fact   Belle and the beast

    B. Main Point # 2   Belle gets trapped in the castle

        1. Supporting Fact   Belle and enchanted servants

        2. Supporting Fact   Belle and her father

    C. Main Point #3   Belle gets to know the beast

        1. Supporting Fact   Beast shows kindness

        2. Supporting Fact   Belle rethinks her situation

III. Conclusion

A. *Main Point #1*		Beast defends Belle
B. *Main Point #2*		Belle falls in love with Beast, which breaks the spell
C. *Main Point #3*		Prince and Belle get married

Of course, you may have more than three or more supporting points under certain main points, but two is the minimum and one is insufficient.

Vocabulary development

Vocabulary is a tool with which the writer builds his story. Just as a builder builds a house with bricks, so a writer builds a story or essay with words. The vocabulary of a written piece determines its ease of readability and its approximate grade level.

One of the best ways to develop one's vocabulary is to read (and look up new words in the dictionary when they aren't clear by the context alone). Encourage your child to keep a list of new words and their meanings in a notebook. Encourage your child to borrow books at her reading level from the library. If she is not motivated, she can be helped to find books along the lines of her interests. If the homework load leaves too little time for extra book reading, a magazine subscription is a good idea.

Learning the roots of words is another way to build vocabulary. For example, think of as many words as you can that begin with the same prefix, for example, *tele* (meaning far): *television, telephone, telegram, telepathy*.

When a student writes an essay or story, he should be encouraged to read it over and see if he can change any of the words to more interesting or descriptive words. If he finds that this is difficult, a handy tool is a thesaurus, which lists synonyms for words.

As a challenge, play a game where your child has to change at least five words to more colorful words. For example, the sentence, *"On the hike, we saw some flowers along the trail,"* could be changed to *"On the hike, we spotted some pretty yellow daisies, beautiful little violets, and wild red roses along the trail."*

Another way to expand vocabulary is to play Scrabble® and other word games frequently. This will stimulate thought about words.

Over time, the child's vocabulary will increase, and her facility with words will improve to the point where writing will become more of a joy and less of a chore.

Reassessments

Kindergarten

Printing: Have your child print the alphabet.

Drawing: Have your child draw a self-portrait.

Idea Flow—Thought Completion: Have your child dictate an ending to each of the following sentences.

    1. The kids were laughing because…

    2. My friend told me that…

    3. There was a loud noise, so…

Idea Flow—Categories: Have your child dictate as many in each category as possible.

    1. clothes   2. scary things

Idea Flow—Concrete: Have your child dictate as many things as possible that she could do with a **box**.

Writing Sample—Informative: Have your child print her **name** and **age**.

Writing Sample—Descriptive: Have your child write about a pet she would like to have.

Verbal Narrative: Have your child tell a story about the picture.

First Grade

Printing: On a separate piece of paper, print the following.

The car was going very fast.

Spelling: Cross out the words that are spelled wrong, and then write the correct spelling below.

bote	plane	beby	booke	care
had	apple	nos	bal	mouse
cake	upe	fish	bear	pencil

Grammar—Sentence or Fragment: Read the following groups of words and decide if each group forms a complete sentence or not. Put **Y** for **yes** and **N** for **no**.

1. The bikes are behind the house. _____
2. They want. _____
3. The bunnies ate the food. _____
4. Ran away. _____
5. Sandy to school. _____
6. Tell me your name. _____
7. Our teacher is nice. _____
8. What doing? _____
9. Where is the puppy? _____
10. Not now. _____

Idea Flow—Sentence Construction: Use the words to write or dictate as many complete sentences as you can. Endings, such as *-s, -ed, -ing, -er,* may be used.

the	fly	bird	will
pretty	is	a	in
are	sky	house	not

Idea Flow—Thought Completion: Dictate an ending to each of the following sentences.

1. The dog jumped over the fence and...
2. The trees had fallen down because of...
3. Larry saw the door fly open and then...

Idea Flow—Categories: Dictate as many in each category as possible.

1. family members (not names)   2. green things

Idea Flow—Concrete: Dictate as many things as possible that you could do with a **penny**.

Writing Sample—Informative: On a separate piece of paper, print your **name**, **age**, **telephone number**, and **address**.

Writing Sample—Descriptive: On a separate piece of paper, write a story about the picture, using as much detail and description as possible.

Second Grade

Printing: On a separate piece of paper, print the following:

It was very hot yesterday. All of the kids wanted to play in the water.

Spelling: Underline and correct any spelling errors.

1. Pam has blak hair.
2. Were did you go?
3. Please thinck hard.
4. That was very funy.
5. The shert is so nise.
6. His freind turned on the lite.
7. Wat is in yor hand?

Contractions: Write the contractions for the following:

do not _____	can not _____
I am _____	have not _____
I will _____	she is _____
you are _____	would not _____
I have _____	are not _____

Punctuation and Capitalization: Add the correct punctuation and capitalization to the following phrases.

1. carla smith
2. he is asleep
3. are you coming
4. I told mike about my new toy
5. didnt you take a nap
6. jill cant jump rope
7. help

Grammar—Sentence or Fragment: Read the following groups of words and decide if each group forms a complete sentence or not. Put **Y** for **yes** and **N** for **no**.

1.　　We lost the race.　　　　　_____
2.　　Getting a new toy.　　　　_____
3.　　Bobby laughed because.　　_____
4.　　Trees in the park.　　　　　_____
5.　　We forgot Calvin's birthday.　_____
6.　　It's very sunny today.　　　_____
7.　　Manny said that he wanted.　_____
8.　　Lou was late for school today.　_____
9.　　Summer is fun.　　　　　　_____
10.　　Put on the table.　　　　　_____

Idea Flow—Thought Completion: Write an ending to each of the following sentences.

1. It wasn't true, so…
2. We couldn't stop laughing because whenever…
3. No one could figure out what…

Idea Flow—Synonyms: Write as many synonyms as possible for each of the following words.

1. small　　　2. funny　　　3. quick

Idea Flow—Concrete: Write as many things as possible that you could do with a **piece of tape**.

Writing Sample—Informative:
On a separate piece of paper, write as much as you can about **friends**.

Writing Sample—Descriptive:
Write a story about the picture using as much detail and description as possible.

Third Grade

Cursive: Write the following in cursive.

Isn't it true that it feels like there's never enough time to do something right the first time, but we always seem to find time to do it over?

Spelling: Underline and correct any misspelled words in the following paragraph.

My favrit uncle is fameus. He worked for a newspapper for meny yers. He was in charje of writting all of the most importent storys. He sez that if the facts are not writen down, peopel won't no what is going on. He also tolld me that I need to pay closs atention to what I read, becuse I shoudn't beleive everything. He is quiet smart.

Punctuation and Capitalization: Add the correct punctuation and capitalization to the following sentences.

1. is your uncle from houston texas
2. charlies father is named mr wong
3. jack can dance but he cant sing
4. ouch
5. lily plays the piano violin flute and harmonica

Grammatical Errors: Correct the grammatical errors in this paragraph, including nouns, pronouns, verb tenses, run-on sentences, and sentence fragments.

It was the most warmest day of the year. Me and my sister wanted to go to the beach but. We asked our mom if could we go and they said that we would have to cleaned the yard first and we didn't think that was fair, but we very wanted to go to the beach, so we started to raking right away. Couldn't finish very quickly. My friend holded the trash bag while I raked the leaf. When Mom saw what we had did. She was so glad that she said that she would drive us there.

Grammatical Terms: Circle each noun. Underline each verb. Put a square around each adjective.

Why does the ice cream man go so fast? When he comes down the street, he drives about fifty miles an hour. How are little kids supposed to catch him if he goes that fast?

Idea Flow—Thought Completion: Write an ending to each of the following sentences.

1. Nick took one look inside the box and ...
2. Patty kept running until ...
3. This is not what I expected, thought Vincent as he

Idea Flow—Synonyms: Write as many synonyms as possible for each of the following words.

1. happily   2. look   3. say

Idea Flow—Concrete: List as many things as possible that you could do with a **pin**.

Idea Flow—Imaginary: If you had all the wishes you wanted, what would they be? List as many as you can.

Writing Sample—Informative: Write as much as you can about the 3rd grade.

Writing Sample—Descriptive: Write a complete story about the picture, using as much detail and description as possible.

Fourth Grade

Cursive: On a separate piece of paper, write the following.

A <u>noun</u> is a person, place or thing. It usually functions as the subject or object of a sentence. A <u>verb</u> is an action word or a state of being word, such as the verb "to be." The various forms of a verb are called tenses—including the present, the past, and the future. An <u>adjective</u> is a word that describes a noun. It is called a modifier, because it modifies or changes the noun—for example, from a "duo" to a "dynamic duo."

Spelling: Underline and correct any misspelled words in the following list.

receive	participate	suddenly	should
takeing	finaly	latly	beginning
totally	exellent	views	hevey

Punctuation and Capitalization: Add the correct punctuation and capitalization to the following paragraph.

Michael matthew and shawn went to new york for the day while they were there they visited the metropolitan museum of art. they saw works of many famous artists there, such as paintings by henri matisse mary cassat and even boticelli They also saw many sculptures by auguste rodin wow it must have taken a long time to create such masterpieces wouldnt you like to visit the museum so you could see this art, too

Grammatical Errors: Correct the grammatical errors in the paragraph, including nouns, pronouns, verb tenses, run-on sentences and sentence fragments.

When I'm growed up I wants to be a author of famous books. I'll travel to all over the world and will be writing stories about the place I visit. I will go to Istanbul, Bombay, Prague, and other faraway place and I will climb Mt. Everest and swim in the Indian Ocean, maybe I can even go to the North Pole. So someday when you'll see my name on a book just you remember that I tell you I was going to be real famous someday.

Idea Flow—Thought Completion: Write a beginning to each of the following sentences.

1. . . .and then they all just stared at each other.
2. . . .because it had all been a huge joke.
3. . . .from then on, she cried whenever she heard that song.

Idea Flow—Synonyms: On a separate piece of paper, write as many synonyms as possible for each word.

1. friend   2. lose   3. wet

Idea Flow—Homonyms: On a separate piece of paper, write as many homonyms as possible for each word.

1. bore   2. tire   3. groom
4. file   5. dream

Idea Flow—Concrete: On a separate piece of paper, write as many things as possible that you could do with a **paper clip.**

Idea Flow—Imaginary: If everyone in the whole world spoke the same language, how would things be different from the way they are now? On a separate piece of paper, list as many things as you can.

Writing Sample—Informative: On a separate piece of paper, write as much as you can about a foreign country of your choice.

Writing Sample—Descriptive: On a separate piece of paper, write a description of one of your friends.

Writing Sample—Persuasive: On a separate piece of paper, write your opinion on whether 4th graders should have free choice about the kinds of food they eat. Give reasons for your opinion and try to convince the reader to agree with your position.

Fifth Grade

Cursive: On a separate piece of paper, write the following in cursive.

A <u>noun</u> is a person, place, or thing. It usually functions as the subject or object of a sentence. A <u>verb</u> is an action word or a state of being word, such as the verb "to be." The various forms of a verb are called tenses—including the present, the past, and the future. An <u>adjective</u> is a word that describes a noun. It is called a modifier, because it modifies or changes the noun.

Editing: Add the correct punctuation, capitalization, and paragraphs to the following text. Correct any spelling or grammar errors. Use proofreader's marks for correction.

when you live to a country, it is importent to feel like you are a part of that sociaty you cando this by voteing _ choseing where you live _ starts a bussiness or diciding to partisipate in local goverment. _ is a powerfull country_ but unfortunatly _ meny people dont now what its means to be a responsable citizen _ for example _ if a adult want to complane about politics_ but he didnt vote_ then he should of went to the polling booth on election day.

Grammatical Terms: List all the nouns, verbs, adjectives, adverbs, and conjunctions you can find in the following paragraph. Not all of the words in the paragraph will be used.

Soon it will be summer. I really look forward to this time of year because life is so carefree. I spend my time reading, getting together with friends, or just lazing by the pool. After ten months of challenging school work, summer vacation is a welcome change of pace. Usually, though, I am glad when school starts again because learning is fun and exciting.

Idea Flow—Thought Completion: On a separate piece of paper, write a beginning to each of the following sentences.

    1. . . . and that's why my dog's name is Homer.

    2. .   so won't you go there and offer to help?

    3. . . . and I don't think you should worry about it.

Idea Flow—Synonyms: On a separate piece of paper, write as many synonyms as possible.

    1. flee   2. recall   3. glue

Idea Flow—Homonyms: On a separate piece of paper, write as many homonyms as possible.

    1. place   2. trip   3. gum
    4. paste   5. tire

Idea Flow—Concrete: List as many things as possible that you could do with a **fork**.

Idea Flow—Imaginary: List as many things as possible that would be different if you were **president**.

Writing Sample—Informative: On a separate piece of paper, write as much as you can about **ecology**.

Writing Sample—Descriptive: On a separate piece of paper, write a complete story about a place you visited recently. Use as much detail and description as possible.

Writing Sample—Persuasive: On a separate piece of paper, write about why you think people should recycle. Discuss your reasons with supporting facts and arguments.

Answer Key

First Grade

Assessment
Spelling
1. dog   2. ball   3. cat   4. rose   5. bell
6. frog   7. duck   8. tree   9. star   10. egg
11. mitt 12. baby   13. man   14. truck 15. hand

Grammar
1. Y   2. N   3. N   4. Y   5. N
6. N   7. Y   8. Y   9. Y   10. N

Reassessment
Spelling
1. boot   2. plane   3. baby   4. book   5. car
6. hand   7. apple   8. nose   9. ball   10. mouse
11. cake 12. up   13. fish 14. bear 15. pencil

Grammar
1. Y   2. N   3. Y   4. N   5. N
6. Y   7. Y   8. N   9. Y   10. N

Second Grade

Assessment

Spelling

1. truck   2. laughed   3. walked   4. are 5. house
6. said   7. happy   8. fine   9. you 10. who

Punctuation and Capitalization

1. <u>B</u>ob <u>G</u>omez
2. <u>I</u> am hungry<u>.</u>
3. <u>W</u>here are you<u>?</u>
4. <u>H</u>e saw <u>T</u>im in the yard<u>.</u>

5. <u>D</u>on<u>'</u>t you like to play ball<u>?</u>
6. <u>J</u>ump<u>!</u>
7. <u>S</u>am can<u>'</u>t tell time<u>.</u>

Contractions

1. I'm   2. don't   3. you're   4. he's   5. we're
6. isn't   7. they're   8. haven't   9. can't   10. wouldn't

Grammar

1. Y   2. N   3. N   4. Y   5. N
6. Y   7. N   8. N   9. Y   10. N

Reassessment

Spelling

1. black   2. Where   3. think   4. funny 5. shirt
6. nice   7. friend   8. light   9. What 10. your

Punctuation and Capitalization

1. <u>C</u>arla <u>S</u>mith
2. <u>H</u>e is asleep<u>.</u>
3. <u>A</u>re you coming<u>?</u>
4. <u>I</u> told <u>M</u>ike about my new toy<u>.</u>

5. <u>D</u>idn<u>'</u>t you take a nap<u>?</u>
6. <u>J</u>ill can<u>'</u>t jump rope<u>.</u>
7. <u>H</u>elp<u>!</u>

Grammar

1. Y	2. N	3. N	4. N	5. Y
6. Y	7. N	8. Y	9. Y	10. N

Third Grade

Assessment

Spelling

have, two, has, green, lives, away, four, children, twins, babies, very, tall, named, they, nice, to, many, and, you, have

Punctuation and Capitalization

1. <u>I</u> live in <u>P</u>ortland<u>,</u> <u>O</u>regon<u>.</u>
2. <u>A</u>re you going with <u>M</u>r<u>.</u> <u>S</u>mith<u>?</u>
3. <u>W</u>e like cars<u>,</u> trains<u>,</u> boats and bikes<u>.</u>
4. <u>G</u>o away!

Grammatical Errors

Zelda and her cat <u>was</u> playing. <u>They</u> like to play. Oops! The kitty <u>bit</u> her on the finger and it <u>really hurt.</u> Zelda <u>ran</u> and told her mother what the <u>cat</u> had <u>done.</u> <u>Her</u> mother put a bandage on <u>her</u> (Zelda's) finger and <u>put</u> the cat outside. The cat sat down and ... (<u>finish sentence</u> or <u>remove *and*</u>).

Grammatical Terms

<u>Nouns</u>: Jordan, Jaime, home, school, distance, boys, test, children, test, mother, ice cream

<u>Verbs</u>: walked, was, were, took, did, was going, buy

<u>Adjectives:</u> short, happy, difficult, glad, delicious

Reassessment

Spelling

favorite, famous, newspaper, many, years, charge, writing, important, stories, says, written, people, know, told, close, attention, because, shouldn't believe, quite

Punctuation and Capitalization

1. Is your uncle from Houston, Texas?
2. Charlie's father is named Mr. Wong.
3. Jack can dance, but he can't sing.
4. Ouch!
5. Lily plays the piano, violin, flute and harmonica.

Grammatical Errors

It was a warm, sunny day. It was the ~~most~~ warmest day of the year. ~~Me and my sister~~ My sister and I wanted to go to the beach. ~~but.~~ We asked our mom if ~~could we~~ we could go and she said that we would have to cleaned the yard first. ~~and~~ We didn't think that was fair, but we ~~very~~ really wanted to go to the beach, so we started to ~~raking~~ clean right away. We couldn't finish very quickly. My friend ~~holded~~ held the trash bag while I raked the ~~leaf~~ leaves. When Mom saw what we had ~~did~~ done she was so happy that she said that she would drive us there.

Grammatical Terms

Nouns: man, street, miles, hour, kids
Verbs: does, go, comes, drives, are, supposed to catch, goes
Adjectives: ice cream, fifty, little

Fourth Grade

Assessment

Spelling

believe, people, friend's, would, coming, Christmas, didn't, thought, forgotten, called, cancelled, gotten, message, beginning, then, your, there, tomorrow, delighted, too

Punctuation and Capitalization

<u>B</u>obby is a little boy<u>.</u> <u>H</u>e has a brother named <u>I</u>rwin and a dog called <u>H</u>arry<u>.</u> <u>O</u>ne day<u>,</u> <u>B</u>obby<u>,</u> <u>I</u>rwin and <u>H</u>arry fell in a well<u>.</u> <u>T</u>hey yelled<u>,</u> "<u>H</u>elp!" They couldn<u>'</u>t get out on their own<u>.</u> <u>D</u>o you think anyone will find them? <u>L</u>et<u>'</u>s hope so<u>.</u>

Grammatical Errors

In order to build a bicycl<u>e</u>, it is importan<u>t</u> to follow the instructions <u>that</u> <u>are</u> included with every <u>kit</u>. <u>The</u> difficulty of buildi<u>ng</u> bikes has increase<u>d</u> <u>over</u> <u>(in)</u> the past ten years. <u>A well built bicycle</u>, <u>(A bicycle that is built well)</u>, <u>is</u> guaranteed to work. If you start early in the morning, you will finish it in a day if you <u>work very carefully.</u> Before you put the bike together<u>,</u> <u>m</u>ake sure <u>that</u> you have all the pieces. No matter how long it takes, do a good job <u>b</u>ecause it is worth it.

Grammatical Terms

Noun: Ellie, Zack, room, key, door, gate, sign, town
Pronoun: it, she, everyone, they

Verb: ran, looking, wanted, to find, could unlock, could escape, had...started, had known, weren't supposed, to go, was

Adjective: dark, dusty, silver, rusty, No Trespassing, different, drab, little

Conjunction: and, so, but, because

Reassessment

Spelling

participate   taking   finally
lately   excellent heavy

Punctuation and Capitalization

Michael, matthew, and Shawn went to New York for the day. While they were there they visited the Metropolitan Museum of Art. They saw works of many famous artists there, such as paintings by Henri Matisse, Mary Cassat and even Boticelli. They also saw many sculptures by Auguste Rodin. Wow! It must have taken a long time to create such masterpieces. Wouldn't you like to visit the museum so you could see this art, too?

Grammatical Errors

When ~~I'm growed~~ grow up I wants to be an author of famous books. I'll travel ~~to~~ all over the world and ~~will be writing~~ write stories about the places I visit. I will go to Istanbul, Bombay, Prague, and other faraway places. ~~and~~ I will climb Mt. Everest and swim in the Indian Ocean. Maybe I can even go to the North Pole. So,

someday when you~~'ll~~ see my name on a book, just
~~you~~ remember that I ~~tell~~ <u>told</u> you I was going to
~~be~~ become real<u>ly</u> famous someday.

Fifth Grade

Assessment
Editing

peter is my best freind, last saturday, me and peter
was gitting a little tired working in his dads
busniss, we were gonna stay until nine oclock
eksept that was to late, so insted we decided to
closse the store at eihgt (our instructions was to
close at ten, we went over to my house and have some
choclate ice cream, wow, it was better then never.

Grammatical Terms

Noun: people, door, day, night, year, things, keys,
    combinations, trust

Pronoun: something, we

Verb: left, unlocked, has changed, locked up, unlock,
    throw away, lose, learn to trust

Adjectives: old, front, fifty

Adverb: almost always, frequently, last, tight

Conjunctions: and, however, so

Reassessment
Editing

when you live to a country, it is important to feel like you are a part of that society you cando this by voteing, choseing where you live, starts a bussiness, or diciding to partisipate in local goverment. is a powerfull country, but unfortunatly, many people dont now what its means to be a responsable citizen. for example, if a adult want to complane about politics, but he didnt vote, then he should of went to the polling booth on election day.

Grammatical Terms

Noun: summer, time of year, life, time, friends, pool, months, school work, summer vacation, pace, school

Verb: will be, look forward, is carefree, spend, reading, getting together, lazing, is welcome, glad, starts, learning is

Adjective: soon, carefree, ten, challenging, welcome, glad, fun, exciting

Adverb: really, so, usually

Conjunction: or, after, though, because

Index

361

How Well Does Your Child Do Math?

A Step-by-Step Assessment of Your Child's Math Skills and Techniques to Develop Them

For Nate

Special thanks to Susan Greenberg.

Contents

Introduction

You've probably noticed that times have changed since you were in school. The math work your son or daughter brings home seems quite different from what *you* were learning at that age. Children today are expected to be more familiar with the underlying concepts than with the rote memorization of math facts. You're left to wonder: "What is normal for a child in my daughter's grade?" or "What are the national standards in arithmetic?"

You also begin to worry that report cards and scores on standardized tests aren't telling you enough about how your son or daughter is *really* performing academically. After all, news reports are assaulting you with discouraging statistics about American education. In 1996, the National Assessment of Educational Progress (NAEP), an arm of the U.S. Department of Education that monitors academic achievement through periodic testing of 4th, 8th, and 12th graders, found that, of the nation's 4th graders, 36 percent were not mastering basic math skills, such as measuring something longer than a ruler, and 38 percent cannot solve a problem involving money or identify the fraction that represents the shaded portion of a rectangle. By the 4th grade, 100 percent of students should be testing at or above basic-skill level, but the latest NAEP math test results showed that the state with the highest percentage (Maine) had only 75 percent of 4th grade students at or above that level. The 1996 assessment also showed that almost 40 percent of 8th graders still lack even basic number skills.

It's no longer safe to assume that everything must be okay if your child continues to be promoted, as there is often an unpublicized "no-fail" policy in schools, where children are routinely advanced to the next grade when they have not achieved even a remedial level in the previous grade. The thinking was that "flunking" stigmatized a child and separated him from his peer group, and that the child would continue to do poorly and possibly end up not graduating. It was deemed preferable to put a child into the next grade and give additional academic support. Unfortunately, this support was not always available, but the policy was in place and the child would be passed along nonetheless. So how do you make sure that your child is on the right track—that he doesn't become a part of these bleak statistics?

You *can* identify specific learning problems by checking the results of whatever standardized test your child is required to take in school every year. But these tests vary from state to state, and not all teachers support the findings. Part of the problem is that America, unlike most advanced nations, does not have a national curriculum. The states' constitutional right to establish their own educational systems means that some schools have a wonderful school curriculum, but others leave much to be desired. It also means that students' annual standardized test scores might only reflect their performance on a regional level.

Furthermore, school report cards indicate only your child's *overall* performance. If you see a low grade in math on your 4th grader's report card, you know only that there's a problem—not what the problem is. You can, of course, schedule a conference with the teacher, but if the teacher is simply not strong in math, it will be difficult to isolate the problem.

But what if you could figure out that your 4th grader can add, subtract, multiply, and divide with 80 percent accuracy, but is struggling with fractions? This is what *How Well Does Your Child Do Math?* can help you do. Then, you can work with your child with workbooks, discussions, games, and exercises.

Why I wrote this book

As a parent, I had the same concerns you do. When my son was in the 2nd grade, I noticed that he and his classmates were picking up the concepts of arithmetic with the classroom manipulative exercises, but there was little or no emphasis on memorizing sums and differences.

Current educational theory has often caused math books to be eliminated from the curriculum, replacing them with manipulative blocks and beads. The consequence of this is that many children, in spite of being able to explain the underlying concepts, can't do addition and subtraction quickly and accurately. This carried over into 3rd grade, where the children understood that if seven children each have eight toys, they could line up seven rows of eight blocks and count them up to find the sum or to determine that it was a multiplication problem. However, to answer the question, "What is seven times eight?" it is common practice for American 3rd graders to be encouraged to use a times table chart to look up the answer. This handicaps children because they will be forced to rely on these charts permanently, whereas when they memorize the information, they own it for life.

Because of my concerns about my son's performance in math, I had my son tested at a local math tutoring center and found that his arithmetic skills were at least a year below grade level. Because this particular center focuses on mastery of each level, there is a great deal of repetition. In the current vernacular of "guess and check" math proponents, this is called "drill and kill."

At that point, I had already put together *How Well Does Your Child Read?*, so I realized that something like it could also be used to monitor a child's math skills on an ongoing basis. As a linguist and the director of American Accent Training, a nationwide program to teach foreign-born students to speak standard American English, I had experience creating diagnostic analyses and other kinds of tests. I used what I knew about testing to create a math "inventory" to test my own son, as well as with the children in the ACE (After Class Enrichment) Program I had founded at the local elementary school.

This became the foundation for *How Well Does Your Child Do Math?*, which led me to write another book featuring tests to help you assess your child's writing performance, *How Well Does Your Child Write?*

The material for my diagnostic tests has been garnered from a number of reliable sources. I studied the NAEP's assessments of American students' abilities in reading, mathematics, and writing. It has been conducting such tests since 1969, ranking the results of the tests by state and providing appropriate achievement goals for each age and grade. I also relied on the Third International Math and Science Study (TIMSS), which is an assessment of the math and science achievement of students in the United States and 40 other nations; books on test research; advice from the director of a Kumon Math Center, and online information. (See page 545 for online resources.)

Finally, my diagnostic tests went through a series of trial runs with children, in addition to being evaluated by experienced elementary school teachers and reviewed by an educational therapist.

How to use this book

How Well Does Your Child Do Math? contains a mathematics diagnostic/placement test for children in kindergarten through grade 5. It will help you determine the grade level at which your child has mastered the concepts and computation of elementary arithmetic. You can use this assessment to target areas that may need additional work. Or, if you discover that your child is performing at or above his grade level, this book can allay your doubts about your child's ability and help you guide him to the next level.

The book contains the following sections:

- ◆ Definitions of the terms used in kindergarten through 5th grade math, such as *lowest common denominator*, *integer*, and *fraction* (pages 387-389).

- ◆ A learning style pre-test to determine whether your child's learning style is primarily auditory (does your child acquire and retain information by what he hears?) or visual (does your child acquire and retain information by what he sees)? (pages 381-382).

♦ Test-taking tips and tricks (pages 383-836).

♦ A shapes, numbers, and counting assessment for kindergartners, testing the ability to recognize and write numbers (pages 392-395).

♦ Arithmetic assessments for children in grades 1 through 5, testing knowledge of numbers, time and money, patterning, addition, subtraction, fractions, word problems, charting, division, estimation, and averaging (pages 396-426).

♦ A chart to help you track your child's progress (pages 427-428).

♦ A chapter on grade level guidelines to familiarize you with math skills that are or should be covered at each grade level, along with difficulties your child may have and ways to overcome them (pages 429-496).

♦ Reassessments (pages 467-532).

♦ An answer key for some of the more advanced test questions (pages 432-433).

♦ An explanation of the NAEP's latest math assessment, with a chart showing children's performance in individual states (pages 535-539).

♦ Listings of educational services and online resources (pages 545-555).

The mathematics assessment

For many years, educators had students memorize sums, equations, and times tables without relating their understanding of math facts to practical application, such as figuring out a baseball player's batting average or the tax on a long list of grocery items.

More recently, teachers were trained to teach concepts to children that would do away with laborious rote memorization. The TIMSS, however, found that American children may be *introduced* to more concepts than students in much higher-scoring nations, but they do not *master* these concepts. The highest students in America ranked lower than the lowest students in Asia, according to the study.

Studies show that American students are weak in computation, concepts, and application. Educators have been divided on the best way to teach students these skills—"guess and check" or "drill and kill." Guess and check, another term for estimation, gives students the skills necessary to make a ballpark judgment about "how much" or "how many" of something. The proponents of guess and check feel that if children have an understanding of the principles, pure memorization of facts is not necessary, especially with the availability of calculators. Drill and kill is straight memorization of math facts. Its proponents say that arithmetic has no exceptions, so knowing the rules makes learning the concepts easier and faster because the child is focusing on ideas, with the underlying foundation having already been laid.

Educators are now coming to the conclusion that the guess and check/drill and kill debate is not an "either/ or" situation. Memorizing the fundamental rules of addition, subtraction, multiplication, and division is the first logical step, followed by applying the basic concepts to higher math. This, then, is how the diagnostic test in this book is organized.

Scoring the assessment

In these tests, the goal is for your child to succeed at a minimum of 80 percent accuracy. As you give each test, check the bottom of the page for the allowable number of errors, which will depend on the number of items in the section.

Using the chart on page 427, put a check mark next to the category each time your child passes a particular level. If your child misses more than the allowable number, leave the chart blank and stop the testing at that point. Work with your child on that concept until he masters it. Then reassess him at a later date—two to three months (see page 497 for reassessments).

For example, check marks up to single digit addition indicate that your child has learned his numbers up to 100 and can add up to 9 + 9, but doesn't fully understand carrying in addition, or single digit subtraction. This is an indicator of his grade level and of the particular functions that he needs to practice.

Because it is frustrating to be tested on unknown or half-understood material, its is not recommended that you go beyond the specific point where your child is unable to succeed. But it must be noted that many children are able to succeed at levels higher than at which they are having difficulty. For example, some children are able to do single digit multiplication (a 3rd grade skill) while still struggling with borrowing in double digit subtraction (a 2nd grade skill). Therefore parents should use their own discretion in deciding how much further in the testing they wish to proceed, based on the abilities of their child.

Math skills consist of sequential building blocks. Arithmetic skills are taught in a particular order because more advanced skills require knowledge of the basic skills for mastery. Although a national arithmetic curriculum has not been established in America, and standards may vary from school to school, the assessments in this book will be a good general indicator of your child's math level.

Is this an intelligence test?

No. It is extremely important to remember that early or late arithmetic skills are not an indicator of intelligence. Through practice, any child can learn the four functions using the nine integers and zero. Late bloomers can be given the tools to develop quick and accurate skills. Children need to be helped through the transition from arithmetic and basic comprehension of it, to enjoying and relating to the numbers in their daily lives.

Before you begin

Before you plunge into the rest of this book, are you sure that no physical or learning impediments are hampering your child's ability to do math? For example, has your child's eyesight been checked recently? If he or she has been displaying learning problems, have you ruled out the possibility of Attention Deficit Disorder (ADD) or dyslexia? Only after you've determined that your child is ready, willing, and *able* to learn should you give the diagnostic test to determine what your child's math level is and what you may do to improve it.

How to give the test

Set aside 20 minutes alone with your child in a quiet room. Make sure there are no distractions—turn off the TV, and never try to give the test just before a big soccer match or gymnastics practice.

Tell your child that this will only take a few minutes and that the results will help make math more enjoyable. Stress that there's no pressure, no punishment, no failing.

Depending on the age of your child, the two of you can sit side by side while you score and he answers the questions. Direct your child's attention to the numbers on the page, not the marks you're making. Some children can become anxious if they pay too much attention to your scoring.

Students in kindergarten through 2nd grade should be monitored closely because they cannot always read the instructions, and they will have a greater tendency to get sidetracked. Independent study starts in the 3rd grade, so children at the 3rd grade level or higher can have greater autonomy during the test. (Of course, the behavior of individual children can vary greatly, so there will be exceptions to this.)

For younger children (kindergartners to 2nd graders), the test will take from one minute, because they don't know numbers well, to 20 minutes. I recommend a 20-minute limit to combat the "fatigue factor"; boredom or exasperation can lower children's scores even in subjects they know better than the characters on the latest Saturday morning TV cartoons. Older children (grades 3 to 5) can take the test within 20 minutes to an hour, depending on their motivation, cooperation, and stamina.

What if your child takes longer? Well, computational skills need to be quick and accurate. If your child takes too much time, he doesn't know the material. At that point, the test should be stopped and the previous lessons drilled. If your child is spending a lot of time on one math problem, remember a good rule of math test-taking: Never let the clock run out on 20 questions because you're stuck on one. If your child is spending an inordinate amount of time on one problem, this could mean the child hasn't grasped that "type" of problem just yet. Encourage him to move on to other problems and come back to that one later.

What to do after the test

Once your child reaches the point in the test where the questions are beyond his grade level, you can end the test. The answer key is at the back of the book. Turn to the scoring section and determine the grade level that corresponds to your child's score. Once that has been determined, consult the chapter on standards for each grade level—kindergarten through 5th. Here you will find suggestions on helping your child with any areas of difficulty that have been identified in the assessment. These standards and guidelines can help you with remediation if your child scores below grade level. This chapter also introduces you to the next level or levels if your child is at or above grade level.

One of the primary functions of the test is to familiarize you with the materials that should be taught at each level. Once that familiarization has taken place, you can seek out appropriate materials for your child.

You can obtain flash cards or worksheets that are appropriate to your child's level by calling Matrix at 800-457-4255. Keep in mind that when practicing by themselves, children need materials that are interesting and challenging, not overwhelming. Also, it's okay if your child wants to do the same easy problems over and over. That's an excellent way to reinforce the basics and build math confidence and fluency.

Retesting

If you feel your child has made progress after the work you've done together, you can test him again. Or even if he performed at the appropriate level the first time around, you still may want to give the test periodically to monitor his skills. In the first case, your child needs to be tested on the same material as before, but he may have memorized the answers. So you should use the reevaluations in the back of the book. In the second scenario, you can just pick up at the point in the test where your child left off.

Each time you give the test, record the date so you can chart your child's progress. Continue giving the test until your child is at or above grade level.

How often should you retest your child? This depends upon the age of the child. A 5-year-old who is just learning his numbers could be tested every four to six months, while a 7-year-old, who needs to master the concepts for school, could be tested every two to four months. Children who are on track could be tested at the beginning and end of each school year.

Now, if you're ready (and your child is ready), let's find out how well your child can do math!

Learning Style Pre-test

It is helpful for parents to understand their child's learning style. Some children's learning strength is *auditory*—they acquire and retain information by what they hear; others learn *visually*—by what they see; and some children learn the best in a *tactile* or *kinesthetic* way—by physically touching or manipulating the objects that they are counting.

This quick test will help determine if your child's learning style is markedly auditory or visual.

Auditory Sequential Memory

Say the groups of digits at a rate of one digit every two seconds. Then ask your child to repeat the digits back. Keep adding a new set until she makes a mistake.

1. 5-2-1
2. 6-3-5-8
3. 2-5-4-8-7
4. 4-9-1-6-2-8
5. 3-8-9-1-6-2-4

Visual Sequential Memory

Show the digits to your child, allowing two seconds for each digit. Then remove or cover the paper and ask her to repeat the digits back. Keep adding a new set until she makes a mistake.

1. 6-8-2
2. 4-1-5-9
3. 6-5-1-8-4
4. 8-1-3-6-7-0
5. 7-8-2-1-0-6-9

Interpretation

Most people use a combination of learning styles, but usually one is dominant. If your child shows a marked preference for *visual memory*, she would benefit by practicing math with flash cards, pictures and graphs.

If your child shows a marked preference for *auditory memory*, she would benefit by practicing math out loud—chanting the times tables, reciting the problem and answer, or listening to a tape.

A child with a marked preference for *kinesthetic memory* would benefit by practicing math with manipulatives—blocks, pieces of paper, coins, and beads.

The main point is that not all approaches work for all people. Experiment with different approaches and see what works best for your child.

Test-taking Techniques

There are two elements to taking a test successfully. Most important, of course, is knowing the information. The other is knowing the test.

Tests are written according to basic standards and practices. This is why school tests are called *standardized*. It is very helpful for your child to be familiar with test standards and formats before starting a test, so that he can focus on the content, rather than on the test itself. Here are some basic guidelines:

First, look the whole test over. This includes noting how much time you have for the test, how long the test is, and what kind of test it is—multiple choice or fill-in-the-blank. In the 4th and 5th grades, word problems get longer and more difficult, and often you have to "show your work." Many a 10-year-old has gotten to the end of a math test with 10 minutes left to go, only to be dismayed to find two pages of complicated word problems!

Next, put your pencil down and read the instructions. Then read them again.

Following this, prioritize to determine if questions are equally weighted. If some questions are worth only 1 point and others are worth 10 points, spend more time and energy on the more heavily weighted problems.

Next, know *what you need to solve for* in the problem. If it is a word problem, write a number equation to help you solve it. Circle each number in the word problem and underline what function should be used. Make sure that the number equation matches exactly and every element is accounted for. An example would be:

Bobby had <u>*three*</u> *apples; he ate [minus]* <u>*one*</u> *and gave [minus]* <u>*two*</u> *to Cindy. How many were left?*

3 − 1 = 2 and 2 − 2 = 0

One of the easiest techniques for a multiple choice test is the process of elimination. If there are four possibilities, chances are that one of them will be way off base, so first, eliminate the ridiculous. Another one will probably be fairly unlikely. Cross that one out, too. Of the two remaining, both will be possibilities, but since you've eliminated the clearly wrong answers, you can concentrate on finding the correct one of two, instead of the correct one of four. For example, these are questions from a typical 3rd grade standardized math test:

The chart below shows the results of a survey when 20 students were asked to choose their favorite ice cream. Which flavor was the favorite?

vanilla	cherry	peach	mint

❑ cherry ❑ peach
❑ mint ❑ vanilla

This is reading and interpreting a graph, which is well within the 3rd grade skill range. The first step is to *eliminate the ridiculous*. Because the question asks for the favorite ice cream, you can immediately eliminate the visibly smaller segments of *peach* and *vanilla*. This leaves you with two fairly similar segments for *mint* and *cherry*. This is where you look for additional information. Because *cherry* has 8 grids shaded and *mint* has only 7, then this would indicate that *cherry* was the favorite flavor.

Another excellent technique is to convert numbers into pictures. This will help you visualize the problem.

Mark buys 24 bags of potato chips. The chips come 8 bags to a box. How many boxes of chips does Mark buy?

❑ 32   ❑ 3
❑ 192   ❑ 4

You know that Mark bought 24 bags. You also know that there are groups of 8 (8 bags to a box). Make 32 little marks for the total number of *bags* and group them by 8 for the number of *boxes*:

You can see that there are 3 groups. Whenever the process involves counting smaller groups within a whole, it will probably be a division problem: **24 ÷ 8 = 3.**

You can also eliminate the ridiculous. You can immediately eliminate 192 and 32, because if the bags are *within* the boxes, you will obviously end up with fewer boxes than there are bags. The two reasonable answers are 3 and 4, which are easily checked by doing division, and double checked by doing the reverse operation, multiplication (**3 x 8 = 24**).

Once you have figured out how to do a certain problem, look for more problems of that type and use the same technique to solve it.

Test-taking tips

1. Look the whole test over.
2. Prioritize.
3. Read the instructions.
4. Read the instructions again.
5. Make sure that you have scratch paper for working out problems.
6. After you read each problem, look for key words that tell you what kind of computation is needed, such as *more than, less than, greatest, least, closes, between,* etc.
7. Make sure that you know *what you need to solve for* in the problem, for example, how much is left, how much the total is, and so on.
8. In multiple choice questions, eliminate the obviously wrong answers and then be sure to check all possible correct answers. Don't choose the first one that looks likely.

Terms You Should Know

Four functions

Addition The process of uniting two or more numbers into one sum, represented by the symbol +.

Subtraction To take away (withdraw) one number or quantity from another, represented by the symbol −.

Multiplication Adding a number (the *multiplicand*) to itself a certain number of times in order to find the *product*, represented by the symbol **x**.

Division How many times one quantity is contained in another—the inverse of multiplication, represented by the symbol ÷.

Fractions

Numerator The top number in a fraction.

Denominator The bottom number in a fraction.

LCD *Lowest Common Denominator* The least common multiple of the denominators of a set of fractions.

Common Fraction A fraction having an integer as a numerator and an integer as a denominator. Also called a vulgar fraction.

Proper Fraction A numerical fraction in which the numerator is less than the denominator (2/3).

Improper Fraction A fraction in which the numerator is larger than or equal to the denominator (3/2).

Mixed Number A whole number and a fraction (1 ½).

Decimal Fraction A linear array of integers that represents a fraction, every decimal place indicating a multiple of a negative power of 10. For example, the decimal 0.1 = 1/10; 0.12 = 12/100; 0.003 = 3/1000.

Decimal Point A dot written in a decimal number to indicate where the place values change from whole numbers to tenths, hundredths, thousandths, etc. of a number.

Reciprocal A number related to another in such a way that when multiplied together their product is 1. For example, the reciprocal of 2/3 is 3/2.

Numbers

Digit One of the ten Arabic number symbols, 0 through 9.

Number Any quantity, including positive numbers (1), negative numbers (-1), zero (0), fractions (½), percentages (10%), and decimals (.5). A number is made up of digits.

Whole Number Any of the set of numbers including zero and all negative and positive multiples of 1.

Integer Any positive whole numbers (1, 2, 3...), negative whole numbers (-1, -2, -3...), and zero (0). This excludes fractions, percentages and decimals.

Natural Number Any positive whole number, excluding zero.

Factor One of two or more quantities that divides a given quantity without a remainder. For example, number 2 has two factors, 2 and 1, because 2 ÷ 1 = 2 and 2 ÷ 2 = 1. Number 6 has four factors, 1 and 6, 2 and 3.

Prime Number A number having only two factors—itself and 1. Example: the number 7, which can only be divided by itself and one to end up with no remainder.

Composite Number A number having more than two factors.

Geometry

Point A dimensionless geometric object having no properties except location.

Line The shortest distance between two points.

Ray A straight line extending from a point. Also called half-line.

Right Angle An angle formed by the perpendicular intersection of two straight lines. An angle of 90°.

Acute angle An angle less than 90°.

Obtuse Angle An angle greater than 90° and less than 180°.

Vertex The point at which the sides of an angle intersect.

Diameter A straight line segment passing through the center of a figure, especially of a circle or sphere, and terminating at the periphery.

Circumference The boundary line of a circle.

Cube An object having six equal square faces.

Octagon A closed plane figure bounded by eight line segments and eight angles.

Polygon A closed plane figure bounded by three or more line segments.

Congruent Coinciding exactly when superimposed. The same size and shape.

Horizontal Parallel to the horizon

Vertical At right angles to the horizon; upright.

Parallel Two or more straight lines that do not intersect.

Perpendicular A line at right angles to a given line.

Assessments

Kindergarten
through
Fifth Grade

Shapes & Sizes

Kindergarten

1. Color the mailbox that is the biggest.

2. Color the telephone that is in the middle.

3. Color the A that is above the line.

   A A —A—

4. Write the number of white triangles. _____

   △ ▲ ▲ △ △ ▲ △

5. How many stars do you see? _____

   ★ ○ ★ ○ ○ ○ ★ ★

---

0 to 1 ✗, put a check in the chart on page 427 and go to the next page. 2 or more ✗s, stop here and review skills; retest at a later date.

Patterns & Counting

Kindergarten

1. Draw a line from the number to the group that it matches.

   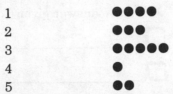

   1
   2
   3
   4
   5

2. How many balloons do you see? _____

3. Color the circle red, the square blue, and the triangle yellow.

4. Color the matching shape.

   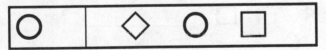

5. Circle the group that has the most in it.

---

0 to 1 ✗, put a check in the chart on page 427 and go to the next page. 2 or more ✗s, stop here and review skills; retest at a later date.

Recognizing Numbers 1-10 *Kindergarten*

Have your child say each number.

	✓	✗	answer given
4	☐	☐	_____
6	☐	☐	_____
1	☐	☐	_____
3	☐	☐	_____
9	☐	☐	_____
2	☐	☐	_____
7	☐	☐	_____
10	☐	☐	_____
5	☐	☐	_____
8	☐	☐	_____

✓ = immediate response   ✗ = slow or incorrect response
0 to 2 ✗s, put a check in the chart on page 427 and go to the next page. 3 or more ✗s, stop here and review skills; retest at a later date.

Writing Numbers 1-10   *Kindergarten*

Have your child write each number on his own, in order. Start with 0 and work up to 10.

_____

_____

_____

_____

_____

_____

_____

_____

_____

_____

0 to 2 ✖s, put a check in the chart on page 427 and go to the next page. 3 or more ✖s, stop here and review skills; retest at a later date.

Recognizing Numbers 1-100   *First Grade*

Have your child say each number.

	✓	✗	answer given
42	☐	☐	_____
61	☐	☐	_____
57	☐	☐	_____
38	☐	☐	_____
94	☐	☐	_____
12	☐	☐	_____
45	☐	☐	_____
24	☐	☐	_____
78	☐	☐	_____
83	☐	☐	_____

✓ = immediate response   ✗ = slow or incorrect response
0 to 2 ✗ s, put a check in the chart on page 427 and go to
the next page. 3 or more ✗ s, stop here and review skills;
retest at a later date.

Writing Numbers 1-100 *First Grade*

Dictate the following numbers to your child and have him write them on the line.

fifty five _____

twenty six _____

sixty seven _____

twenty one _____

thirty nine _____

forty eight _____

seventeen _____

seventy _____

one hundred and six _____

eighty three _____

0 to 2 ✖s, put a check in the chart on page 427 and go to the next page. 3 or more ✖s, stop here and review skills; retest at a later date.

Signs & Skip Counting _First Grade_

Fill in the blanks by skip counting by 2s.

1. 5   7   _____   11   13

2. 12   _____   _____   _____   20

Fill in the blanks by counting by 3s.

3. 2   _____   8   _____   14   _____

4. 3   _____   _____   12   _____

Put the correct sign on the line (>, <, =).

5. 8 _____ 6

6. 0 _____ 3

7. 15 _____ 14

8. 4 _____ 2+2

9. 11 _____ 15

10. 36 _____ 36

0 to 2 ✗s, put a check in the chart on page 427 and go to the next page. 3 or more ✗s, stop here and review skills; retest at a later date.

Sequencing & Ordering   *First Grade*

Answer the following questions.

1. What is one more than 69? _____
2. What is one less than 30? _____
3. What is ten more than 23? _____
4. What is ten less than 58? _____
5. What is five more than 45? _____

Fill in the numbers that would come next.

6. 2 4 6 _____ _____
7. 25 35 45 _____ _____
8. 300 400 500 _____ _____
9. 296 297 298 _____ _____

Circle the larger number in each set.

10. 4   8   12. 21   12
11. 1   11   13. 11   2

Rewrite these numbers in order from the largest to the smallest.

14.   8   5   11   4   6

_____ _____ _____ _____ _____

15.   125   100   90   45   62

_____ _____ _____ _____ _____

---

0 to 3 ✖ s, put a check in the chart on page 427 and go to the next page. 4 or more ✖ s, stop here and review skills; retest at a later date.

Single & Double Digit Addition   *First Grade*

Solve the following problems.

1. $\begin{array}{r} 9 \\ +\ 1 \\ \hline \end{array}$

2. $\begin{array}{r} 3 \\ +\ 6 \\ \hline \end{array}$

3. $\begin{array}{r} 6 \\ +\ 2 \\ \hline \end{array}$

4. $\begin{array}{r} 3 \\ +\ 4 \\ \hline \end{array}$

5. $\begin{array}{r} 4 \\ +\ 4 \\ \hline \end{array}$

6. $\begin{array}{r} 72 \\ +\ 19 \\ \hline \end{array}$

7. $\begin{array}{r} 42 \\ +\ 37 \\ \hline \end{array}$

8. $\begin{array}{r} 54 \\ +\ 35 \\ \hline \end{array}$

9. $\begin{array}{r} 36 \\ +\ 43 \\ \hline \end{array}$

10. $\begin{array}{r} 72 \\ +\ 17 \\ \hline \end{array}$

> 0 to 2 ✗s, put a check in the chart on page 427 and go to the next page. 3 or more ✗s, stop here and review skills; retest at a later date.

Single & Double Digit Subtraction   *First Grade*

Solve the following problems.

1.   6
    − 3

6.   87
    − 11

2.   9
    − 5

7.   39
    − 28

3.   29
    − 14

8.   73
    − 51

4.   8
    − 3

9.   98
    − 55

5.   7
    − 4

10.   25
    − 12

> 0 to 2 ✗s, put a check in the chart on page 427 and go to the next page. 3 or more ✗s, stop here and review skills; retest at a later date.

Time & Money
First Grade

Answer the following questions.

1. What time is it? _____

2. Draw hands on the clock
   to show 7:00.

3. About how long would it take to eat dinner?

   ❑ 3 minutes   ❑ 30 minutes

4. About how long would it take to comb your hair?

   ❑ 1 minute   ❑ 1 hour

5. How many cents is each coin? Write the amount below
   the coin.

_____   _____   _____   _____

> 0 to 1 ✗, put a check in the chart on page 427 and go to the
> next page. 2 or more ✗s, stop here and review skills; retest
> at a later date.

Patterns
First Grade

Copy the pattern.

1. ◇　□　△　◇　_____

2. ✖　◯　◯　✖　_____

What would come next?

3. ⊡　△　⊡　△　⊡　_____

4. ●　□　□　●　□　_____

5. **1　A　2　B　3　_____**

> 0 to 1 ✖, put a check in the chart on page 427 and go to the next page. 2 or more ✖s, stop here and review skills; retest at a later date.

Time & Money

Second Grade

1. About how long would it take you to have dinner?
   ❑ 1 minute   ❑ 20 minutes   ❑ 4 hours

2. Draw hands on the
   clock to show 3:35.

3. Which one is more?

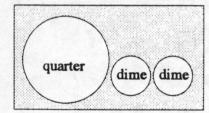 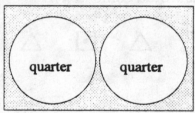

4. How many dimes do you need to equal one dollar?
   ❑ 10   ❑ 20   ❑ 4

5. What is the total?

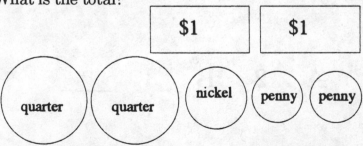

0 to 1 ✗, put a check in the chart on page 427 and go to the
next page. 2 or more ✗s, stop here and review skills; retest
at a later date.

Computation with Regrouping   *Second Grade*

Solve the following problems.

1.   29
   + 32

6.   75
   − 56

2.   81
   + 25

7.   65
   − 48

3.   76
   + 28

8.   27
   − 19

4.   55
   + 37

9.   43
   − 38

5.   43
   + 27

10.   44
    − 16

---

0 to 2 ✗ s, put a check in the chart on page 427 and go to the next page. 3 or more ✗ s, stop here and review skills; retest at a later date.

Simple Fractions

Second Grade

Look at each picture and write the fraction, with the numerator represented by the white space. A sample is given.

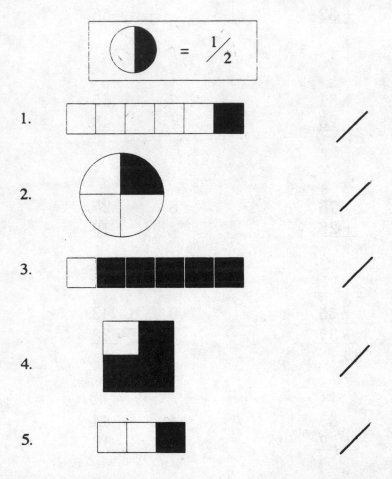

0 to 1 ✖, put a check in the chart on page 427 and go to the next page. 2 or more ✖s, stop here and review skills; retest at a later date.

3 Digit Mixed Computation   *Second Grade*

Solve the following problems.

1.   446
     + 575

6.   748
     − 669

2.   723
     − 408

7.   512
     + 389

3.   687
     + 245

8.   300
     − 129

4.   425
     + 398

9.   801
     − 799

5.   916
     − 787

10.   122
     + 188

0 to 2 ✖s, put a check in the chart on page 427 and go to the next page. 3 or more ✖s, stop here and review skills; retest at a later date.

Word Problems

Second Grade

Read the following questions and mark the correct answer.

1. If a train travels 10 miles east and then 22 miles
    north, how many miles has it gone in all?

    _____

2. If a farmer has 17 eggs for sale, and someone
    buys 9, how many eggs are left?

    _____

3. 7 children go to a party and play in the back
    yard. 3 children go into the kitchen for some
    juice. 2 children go into the house to rest.
    How many children are left in the back yard?

    _____

4. Write the following words in number form:
    one hundred forty two _____

5. Write the following words in number form:
    four hundred eighty three _____

> 0 to 1 ✗, put a check in the chart on page 427 and go to the
> next page. 2 or more ✗ s, stop here and review skills; retest
> at a later date.

Single Digit Multiplication/Division *Third Grade*

Solve the following problems.

1.   7
       x 2

6.   9 x 5 =

2. $2\overline{)8}$

7.   4 ÷ 2 =

3.   7
       x 3

8.   9 x 7 =

4. $3\overline{)6}$

9.   8 ÷ 2 =

5.   3
       x 6

10.   5 x 0 =

---

0 to 2 ✖ s, put a check in the chart on page 427 and go to the next page. 3 or more ✖ s, stop here and review skills; retest at a later date.

Double Digit Multiplication/Division *Third Grade*

Solve the following problems.

1.   12
    x 2

6.   3 / 27

2.   8 / 32

7.   9 / 45

3.   48
    x 3

8.   69
    x 4

4.   6 / 36

9.   8 / 56

5.   37
    x 6

10.   98
    x 6

0 to 2 ✕s, put a check in the chart on page 427 and go to the next page. 3 or more ✕s, stop here and review skills; retest at a later date.

Time & Money

Solve the following word problems.

1. If it is 8:05 a.m. now, what time will it be in four hours?

_____

2. Chizuko went to sleep at 9 p.m. and woke up at 7 a.m. How long did she sleep?

_____

3. If a loaf of bread costs $1.25 and milk costs $2.50, how much do they cost together?

_____

4. Pierre has a dollar. He buys a toy that costs 69 cents. How much change does he get?

_____

5. Sonya earns $5.25 per hour. If she works for six hours, how much does she earn?

_____

---

0 to 1 ✗, put a check in the chart on page 427 and go to the next page. 2 or more ✗s, stop here and review skills; retest at a later date.

Graphs   *Third Grade*

Based on the graph, answer the following questions.

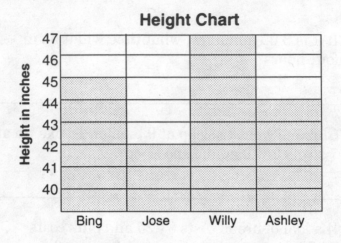

1. Which child is the tallest?

    _____

2. Which child is the shortest?

    _____

3. How much taller is Bing than Ashley?

    _____

4. How tall is Bing?

    _____

5. If all the children stood on top of each other, how tall would
    they be?

    _____

> 0 to 1 ✘, put a check in the chart on page 427 and go to the
> next page. 2 or more ✘s, stop here and review skills; retest
> at a later date.

Division with Remainders   *Third Grade*

Solve the following division problems.

1. $3\overline{)11}$ 6. $2\overline{)21}$

2. $5\overline{)36}$ 7. $9\overline{)40}$

3. $7\overline{)48}$ 8. $5\overline{)68}$

4. $8\overline{)100}$ 9. $6\overline{)50}$

5. $4\overline{)51}$ 10. $9\overline{)12}$

0 to 2 ✗s, put a check in the chart on page 427 and go to the next page. 3 or more ✗s, stop here and review skills; retest at a later date.

Mixed Word Problems   *Third Grade*

Read the following questions and check the correct answer.

1. If 8 children each have 4 toys each, how many toys do they have in all?

   _____

2. If a cake is cut into 9 pieces, and there are 3 children, how many pieces does each child get?

   _____

3. If Mario had four bags of marbles and each bag held sixteen marbles, how many marbles did he have in all?

   _____

4. If there are 32 children in a class and there are 8 rows, how many children were in each row?

   _____

5. Write the following words in number form:
   Five hundred sixty five thousand two hundred seventy four

   _____

> 0 to 1 ✗, put a check in the chart on page 427 and go to the next page. 2 or more ✗ s, stop here and review skills; retest at a later date.

Rounding Off & Estimating   *Fourth Grade*

Round off each number to the nearest 10:

1. 42 _____   2. 26 _____

Round off each number to the nearest 100:

3. 119 _____   4. 462 _____

Estimate

5. 10 feet is approximately how many yards?

_____

6. 23 inches is approximately how many feet?

_____

7. 125 days is approximately how many months?

_____

Average

8. Hector is 3 feet tall. Jamaal is 4 feet tall. Yuzi is 5 feet tall. What is the average height?

_____

9. The soccer team took the following days off: 6 in January; 3 in February; 4 in March; 7 in April. What is the monthly average?

_____

10. Luis has $10 to spend per day on a four-day trip. His trip took five days instead of four. How much is his daily allowance for the five days?

_____

---

0 to 2 ✗s, put a check in the chart on page 427 and go to the next page. 3 or more ✗s, stop here and review skills; retest at a later date.

Multiple Digit Computing　　　*Fourth Grade*

Solve the following problems.

1.　　13
　　x 32

6.　75 ⟌ 425

2.　　43
　　x 61

7.　53 ⟌ $6.89

3.　　27
　　x 39

8.　71 ⟌ $4.97

4.　　56
　　x 65

9.　58 ⟌ 291

5.　　35
　　x 65

10.　90 ⟌ 400

> 0 to 2 ✖ s, put a check in the chart on page 427 and go to the next page. 3 or more ✖ s, stop here and review skills; retest at a later date.

Computing with Fractions   *Fourth Grade*

Reduce each fraction to its lowest terms.

1. $\dfrac{2}{4}$ 2. $\dfrac{8}{24}$ 3. $\dfrac{75}{100}$

Compare using >, <, = .

4. $\dfrac{2}{4}$ $\dfrac{1}{4}$ 5. $\dfrac{5}{6}$ $\dfrac{1}{2}$ 6. $\dfrac{1}{3}$ $\dfrac{3}{9}$

Reduce and write a mixed number or a whole number.

7. $\dfrac{4}{4}$ 8. $\dfrac{20}{5}$

9. $\dfrac{9}{2}$ 10. $\dfrac{11}{6}$

Add or subtract these fractions and reduce to lowest terms.

11. 3/4 + 3/4 =   12. 4 1/4 + 2 3/4 =

13. 7/8 − 5/8 =   14. 1 3/6 + 3 4/12 =

---

0 to 3 ✘s, put a check in the chart on page 427 and go to the next page. 4 or more ✘s, stop here and review skills; retest at a later date.

Measurements

Fourth Grade

Read the following questions and mark the correct answer.

1. If there are 10 kids playing and they need drinks, about how much juice would be needed for them altogether?

    ❑ a pint   ❑ a quart   ❑ a gallon

2. If there are 10 millimeters in a centimeter and 100 centimeters in a meter, how many millimeters are in a meter? _____

3. To measure the distance between your eyes, which unit of measurement should be used?

    ❑ mm   ❑ cm   ❑ m   ❑ km

4. To measure how far a person can walk in 1 hour, which unit of measurement should be used?

    ❑ mm   ❑ cm   ❑ m   ❑ km

5. Compare using > or <.

    16 feet _____ 6 yards

---

0 to 1 ✖, put a check in the chart on page 427 and go to the next page. 2 or more ✖s, stop here and review skills; retest at a later date.

Mixed Word Problems   *Fourth Grade*

Read the following questions and check the correct answer.

1. What is the chance of drawing a red marble from a bowl
    that has one red, one blue and one green marble?
    ❑ even   ❑ 1 in 2   ❑ 1 in 3

2. An oak tree is 50 feet tall. If it can grow three times that
    height, how tall can it grow?
    ❑ 50 feet   ❑ 150 feet   ❑ 300 feet

3. 37 children are going in vans to Disneyland. Each van
    seats 8 children. How many vans are needed?
    ❑ 4 vans   ❑ 5 vans   ❑ 6 vans

4. Ali spent one third of his money for lunch, and he gave
    one sixth of it to his brother. How much did he have left?
    ❑ 1/6   ❑ 1/3   ❑ 1/2

5. Twelve children are at a party. Half of the children are
    drinking punch and half of those children are also eating
    popcorn. How many children are having both popcorn
    and punch?
    ❑ four   ❑ six   ❑ three

---

0 to 1 ✖, put a check in the chart on page 427 and go to the
next page. 2 or more ✖s, stop here and review skills; retest
at a later date.

Multiplying & Dividing Fractions   *Fifth Grade*

Multiply or divide these fractions. Reduce if necessary.

1. 3/4   x   4/3   =

2. 2/5   x   3/5   =

3. 3/9   x   3/9   =

4. 2/2   x   4/12   =

5. 1/4   x   3   =

6. 1/3   ÷   1/4   =

7. 2/3   ÷   4/5   =

8. 5/8   ÷   3/4   =

9. 7/10   ÷   1/10   =

10. 2/5   ÷   1/3   =

---

0 to 2 ✗s, put a check in the chart on page 427 and go to the next page. 3 or more ✗s, stop here and review skills; retest at a later date.

Graphs

Fifth Grade

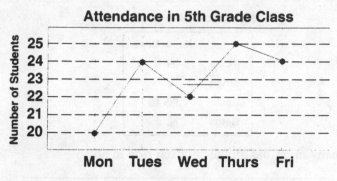

Attendance in 5th Grade Class

1. How many students were at school on Tuesday?

   _____

2. How many more students were in school on Thursday than on Monday?

   _____

3. What is the average attendance for the week?

   _____

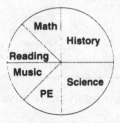

4. What fraction of the day is used by Math and PE?
   ❑ 1/8   ❑ 1/4   ❑ 1/2   ❑ 1   ❑ 2   ❑ 4

5. How much more of the day is used by Science than PE?
   ❑ 1/8   ❑ 1/4   ❑ 1/2   ❑ 1   ❑ 2   ❑ 4

---

0 to 1 ✖, put a check in the chart on page 427 and go to the next page. 2 or more ✖s, stop here and review skills; retest at a later date.

Tables

Fifth Grade

5th Grade Bike-a-thon

	No. of Miles
Lina	||||| ||
Brian	||||
Miguel	||||| |||||
Helga	|||||	

1. How many miles did all the children ride in all?

    _____

2. If Lina received 50 cents for every mile she rode, how much money did she bring in?

    _____

3. What is the average number of miles ridden?

    _____

	# of Days		# of Days
January	31	July	31
February	28	August	31
March	31	September	30
April	30	October	31
May	31	November	30
June	30	December	31

4. If today is August 1, how many more days until Christmas (December 25)?

    _____

5. What is the average number of days in a month?

    _____

0 to 1 ✗, put a check in the chart on page 427 and go to the next page. 2 or more ✗s, stop here and review skills; retest at a later date.

Measurements

Use the centimeter side of your ruler to make the following measurements to the *nearest centimeter*.

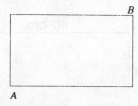

1. What is the length in centimeters of one of the longer sides of the rectangle?_____

2. What is the length in centimeters of the diagonal from A to B?_____

3. On the grid below, draw a rectangle with an area of 12 square units.

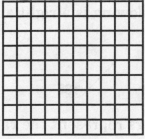

4. How many pints equal one gallon?
    ❑ 4   ❑ 8   ❑ 12

5. How many quarts of water are in a 5 gallon jug?
    ❑ 16   ❑ 20   ❑ 40

---

0 to 1 ✖, put a check in the chart on page 427 and go to the next page. 2 or more ✖s, stop here and review skills; retest at a later date.

Geometry

1. What is the perimeter of this polygon?

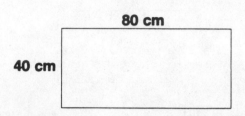

2. What is the perimeter of an octagon where each side measures two inches?

3. How many faces does a cube have?

4. Which of the following is a right angle? Circle your answer.

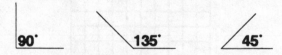

5. Which two letters represent the radius of the circle?

❑ B C

❑ B D

❑ A C

> 0 to 1 ✖, put a check in the chart on page 427 and go to the next page. 2 or more ✖ s, stop here and review skills; retest at a later date.

Fractions & Decimals   *Fifth Grade*

Write the decimal or fraction for each problem.

1. $\dfrac{3}{5}$ _____

2. .40 _____

3. $\dfrac{1}{4}$ _____

Solve the following decimal problems.

4. .5 + .25 = _____

5. .75 − .25 = _____

Write the following as percentages.

6. 7/10 _____

7. 4/5 _____

8. 2/8 _____

9. 11/20 _____

10. .78 _____

---

0 to 2 **✗** s, put a check in the chart on page 427 and go to the next page. 3 or more **✗** s, stop here and review skills; retest at a later date.

Word Problems

Fifth Grade

Read the following questions and check the correct answer.

1. It took Chelsea 2 hours and 15 minutes to fill out 45 forms. What was the average time spent on each form?

    _____

2. 16 children collected rocks along the beach, finding a total of 48 rocks. What was the average number of rocks found per child?

    _____

3. Quincey bought four lobsters for $3 a pound. They weighed 13 oz., 14 oz., 17 oz., and 20 oz. How much did she spend?

    _____

4. If it is now 11:45 a.m., what time will it be in 20 minutes?

    _____

5. Twenty people are swimming in a pool. Another 16 join them, but the pool becomes crowded and 9 people have to leave. What fraction of the people had to leave?

    _____

> 0 to 1 ✗, put a check in the chart on page 427 and go to the next page. 2 or more ✗s, stop here and review skills; retest at a later date.

Progress Chart

In these tests, the goal is for your child to succeed at a minimum of 80 percent accuracy. As you give each test, check the bottom of the page for the allowable number of errors, which will depend on the number of items in the section. If your child completes a test at 80 percent accuracy or better, enter the date the test was passed on this chart.

Level	Topic	Passed
Kindergarten	Shapes & sizes	
	Patterns & counting	
	Recognizing numbers 1-10	
	Writing numbers 1-10	
1st Grade	Recognizing numbers 1-100	
	Writing numbers 1-100	
	Signs & skip counting	
	Sequencing & ordering	
	Single & double digit addition	
	Single & double digit subtraction	
	Time & money	
	Patterns	

Level	Topic	Passed
2nd Grade	Time & money	
	Computation with regrouping	
	Simple fractions	
	3 digit mixed computation	
	Word problems	
3rd Grade	Single digit multiplication/division	
	Double digit multiplication/division	
	Time & money	
	Graphs	
	Division with remainders	
	Mixed word problems	
4th Grade	Rounding off & estimating	
	Multiple digit computing	
	Computing with fractions	
	Measurements	
	Mixed Word problems	
5th Grade	Multiplying & dividing fractions	
	Graphs	
	Tables	
	Measurements	
	Geometry	
	Fractions & decimals	
	Mixed word problems	

Grade Level Guidelines

I love math!

Starting point

The first things a parent of a child just beginning to learn math wants to know are: Where do we start? What comes first? What is important?!

The main problem with parents teaching math is that they don't realize how much time and repetition is involved in cementing the basics of arithmetic in a child's mind.

For children, math (learning the numbers, putting them in the right order, printing them neatly and correctly, knowing the function and understanding the computation) is like trying to see the forest for the trees. Each element may be clear, but putting them all together for the big picture is extremely difficult. Months of flash cards, pages of sums, and hours of practicing are necessary to make those facts and relationships clear in a child's memory and fully at hand to be recalled instantly.

Fortunately, math is a step-by-step, cumulative system. There is a comfortable sequence for children to follow in learning arithmetic, leading naturally into higher math.

In terms of working with your own child, however, it is crucial to remember that there are stages of learning, types of memory, ways of learning, and internal time frames in which children learn. In general, children learn by doing. They are more successful with hands-on, colorful, concrete exercises, instead of more abstract, black-and-white, pencil-and-paper exercises. For example, having a child rearrange number cards to manipulate sums will make a stronger, more lasting impression than if she just sits and looks at numbers on a page. Children will easily learn the pre-basics of math from manipulation—the handling and moving around of blocks, coins, or pieces of fruit. In time, with gentle encouragement, they will start to make the connection between numbers printed on the page, the physical realities, and the abstract concepts.

There are two general techniques that work well in finding out what is going on with a child's math skills. First, check what *type* of error was made. For instance, if a child carries the wrong number, this would require different practice from a child who lined up the numbers wrong.

The other technique is to ask the child to say what she is thinking and doing *while* she is doing the problem. When the words stop making sense, then the parent can step in to assist. Some children have a more purely intuitive sense of math, though, and would have great difficulty articulating the thought process, so like everything, this is a process of trial and error.

Each grade level in this section lays out the typical types of mistakes for that particular range. Of course, there will be some overlap from grade to grade, because the skills are cumulative.

Math should be fun, not work

There will be a wide range in ability, interest, and performance among children. It may extend from an engaged interest to complete detachment and disinterest in numbers and counting. Some children make the connection between the objects or pictures (🔔🔔🔔), the spoken number *(three bells)*, and the printed numeral (**3**) at an earlier age than others. To a small child, there is not much difference between drawing six bells and counting six bells, so incorporate objects as well as pictures and numbers into your play time.

Math *is* serious, but 5-year-olds need to be taught playfully. Play counting games and sing counting songs. Have the child count the place settings as he sets the table, or count the number of knobs in the kitchen. This will help lay the foundation for understanding sequencing and order.

Stay calm

Parents are well aware of the importance of arithmetic and the enormous effect it will have on a child's future. All parents want their children to understand math, and to use it well and often. These days especially, with television such an omnipresent attraction, the official window of opportunity—the 2nd and 3rd grades—for children to start becoming numerate can be a worrisome period for parents.

Hovering anxiously over children while they pick through their numbers, stumble over "easy" sums, and write large, messy numbers, a parent may become frustrated. Sometimes kids like to tease their parents. They may pretend to forget large amounts of information (*Dad! What's six plus two again?*). If you feel yourself getting upset (*But you know the answer to this!* or *We've been over this!* or *We're going to sit here until you finish!*), it's time to back off and make a fresh start later.

There are not many guarantees in life, but if you sit patiently night after night, playing with flash cards, explaining the rules of math to your child, reinforcing this understanding with her own experiences, and finally, pointing out where you use math everyday, you will have a child who is good at arithmetic. If you go through these steps, you will achieve 100 percent numeracy in your home.

Arithmetic is an enjoyable activity, not a punishment, and it should be taught playfully and lovingly. It is extremely important to keep it positive so that your child won't be permanently put off by math. One day, it will all make sense to her. Your job, as a parent, is to keep practicing the fundamentals until that day comes.

So, stay calm, and turn off the TV.

Kindergarten

Basic skills

Most kindergartners should know how to count up to 15 or 20 objects and recognize numbers up to 20. Some may know how to print 0 to 9, but this depends on their fine motor skills. Importantly, children need to know that there are *numbers* and an association between each number and its amount (three = **3** = △△△).

In texts appropriate for kindergartners, there should be a picture for every number so that they can *see* the idea.

A 5- or 6-year-old should recognize the basic shapes: circle, square, triangle. Children should know the names and be able to point each one out from a group of shapes.

Circle   Square   Triangle

They should know the positions—right, left, top, and bottom—so they can put their names on their papers in the proper position, they can count numbers from right to left and top to bottom, and can open the math book at the front, rather than the back.

Once a child is comfortable with counting, he needs to be able to start putting amounts together: adding. Adults tend to take addition for granted. Children need to have it reinforced. Start with concrete information. Ask your child, *"If you and Bobby were playing ball, how many kids would that be? Then if Billy and Sue came, how many would there be?"* She will naturally know the answer. But having to stop, think about it, and explain it will help develop simple addition. As a parent and adult, you have to recognize that concepts that you take for granted need to be pointed out to children with concrete examples.

Kindergartners are now ready for more games and songs. Songs that work well are some of the old standards such as "One Potato, Two Potato"; "There Were 10 in the Bed" (this teaches counting backwards which is helpful for subtraction). Counting games, such as dominoes, help a child count "for a reason."

A further support for your child's arithmetic skill building is the use of flash cards. Flash cards are helpful for visual learners.

Start with counting cards that have pictures on them and work up to recognizing the numbers and then simple addition.

Common difficulties

1. **Number discrimination**
   Children have to learn to recognize the visual configurations of a given number. When they are learning the ABCs and 0 to 9, kindergartners who are having trouble may either not know how to write a number or may confuse it with a letter, such as **9** and **p** or **9** and **q**. When practicing with the child, it is helpful to keep numbers and letters separate until the distinction is made. Have the child find and circle the same numbers from a list of similar ones.

2	6	8	2	9

This helps a child recognize the visual shape of the number and compare it with the others.

2. **Sequencing**

   Adults know that there is sequential order in counting, but in the beginning, children are perfectly happy to say 1–2–3–7–5–9–6–10! Proper sequencing is simply a matter of engraining the order in a child's mind with number songs, counting stories and number games. Fill-in-the-blank exercises give a child practice in sequencing and writing. He *says* the numbers, *thinks about* the number that comes next, and *writes* the missing number in the box.

1	2	3	4	___
6	___	8	9	10

   When you are helping a kindergartner with this type of exercise, cover up everything except the row you are working on. The whole exercise may look too "busy" to a child's eye.

3. **Math concepts**

   Objects are concrete and real, numbers are abstract and intangible. An association between a *number* and an *amount* of things must be formed. For example, put four apples on a table and talk to your child about the number **4**. Sesame Street videos are excellent for counting and numbers.

4. **Fine motor coordination**
   Fine motor skills for writing numbers are
   generally lacking in 5-year-old fingers. Have
   your child trace numbers to develop an
   understanding of the shapes involved and the
   order of the stroke (top to bottom). Practicing
   drawing little circles and sticks is easy and
   fun for a child. Combining the circles and
   sticks for numbers allows the child to see the
   basic shapes and combinations, while
   memorizing the nine digits.

5. **Math vocabulary**
   In this first year of school, a child's
   vocabulary increases to include specific
   "school words." Part of this is the language of
   math and the vocabulary of spatial concepts.
   Children need to understand verbal
   meanings of words such as *under, over, more,
   less,* and *between* in order to follow directions
   in the math lessons.

More kindergarten skills

♦ **Counting**
  Counting starts in kindergarten and
  kindergartners need to know how to count
  from 0 to 9. Counting simple groups of objects
  and writing the answers in number form
  allows a child to understand the correlation
  between a number of objects and the written
  number.

A good way to practice is by having your child put dots in boxes. They are neat and easy to keep track of. Have your child practice writing the correct number:

What number is shown in each box?

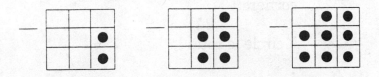

...as well as putting the correct number of dots in the boxes:

Draw the correct number of dots in each box.

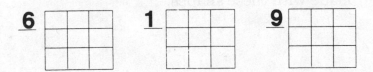

♦ **Shape recognition**
The three shapes that are introduced first are the circle, the square, and the triangle. Have your child find and color the same shape from a list of similar ones.

This exercise helps a child recognize visual shapes and compare them with the others.

Parents can help a child identify these three shapes by pointing out the characteristics:

☐ A square has 4 equal sides and 4 corners;

○ A circle is round;

△ A triangle has 3 sides and 3 corners.

In order to familiarize a child with these shapes, call the shapes by their names and use them in drawing, so a child can see, for example, that a house or a person can be made with these shapes.

First Grade

Basic skills

Simple addition and subtraction should be mastered in the 1st grade. First graders should be able to count up to 100, and be completely familiar with basic addition and subtraction facts up to **9 + 9 = 18** and **9 − 9 = 0**. They should be able to figure out simple addition word problems. They should know the coins and denominations and be able to add up to a dollar.

By the end of 1st grade, students should be familiar with the *mechanics* of arithmetic—the rules of addition, such as the commutative rule. For example, **1 + 2 = 3** and **2 + 1 = 3** have the same answer, even though the digits being added are in a different order. When explaining this number concept to a child, it's essential for him to visualize the problem:

● + ●● = ●●● and ●● + ● = ●●●

First graders should be able to count by 2s, 5s, and 10s and should know the easy way to add 9s (see pages page 457-458).

It is not unusual to see a child still counting on his fingers at this stage, but memorization is the preferred way to learn math facts. While finger counting is not a cause for worry, it should be used only if a child has a specific memory recall deficit. For a child who has trouble memorizing things, it is better to have finger counting as a backup than to simply start randomly guessing answers. If you suspect that there is a specific difficulty—whether it is a behavioral problem or a learning disability—do not hesitate to discuss this with the school principal, teacher, or school psychologist. Hearing and vision should also be checked.

A 1st grader should know that when you put two numbers together, they make certain bigger numbers but not others (**2 + 4 = 6** and not **2 + 4 = 24**).

Being able to find the small sum within a bigger problem is a great advantage in early math. For example, **23 + 23** is a *big* number to a 1st grader, but **2 + 2** and **3 + 3** can be easily figured out. So by learning the basic skills, a child will be ready to grasp more advanced skills that follow.

A child can have fairly good addition skills, but have great difficulty with subtraction. Therefore, subtraction should not be started until addition is second nature.

Familiarity with the **number families** will help a child understand the relationship between addition and subtraction. Subtraction is the *reverse* of addition. It is important for children to see and understand this relationship. Manipulatives (blocks, coins, etc.) help a child see that *subtracting 3* is just the opposite of *adding 3*. If a child can count backwards, it will help him understand subtraction.

The math vocabulary of addition and subtraction needs to be explained. You can correlate familiar words with the new terms your child is learning. **Addition** means **putting together** and can also be called **adding** or **plus**. Other addition words are **more than, increased,** and so on. **Subtraction** means **taking away** and can also be called **minus, subtract,** and **take away**. Other subtraction words are **less than** and **fewer than**.

When a child doesn't understand the relationship between *-teen* and *ten*, it can impede simple addition. "Teen" and "ten" are the same thing. Six*teen* is really *six-ten*, or six plus ten, so when a child is adding a number between 3 and 9 to *ten*, he just needs to think *-teen*.

Trouble with addition can also be caused by a sequencing difficulty. Before a young child memorizes a math fact, such as **8 plus 5 equals 13**, he starts counting—or sequencing—from 8 and adds on another 5. If he has trouble sequencing, this will show up in his having trouble with days of the week, putting things in order, prioritizing, and even in social situations where appropriate behavior follows certain sequential patterns. If you notice that your child has trouble sequencing, focus him on tasks that help him prioritize.

In addition to numbers and patterns, 1st graders refine some distinctions among shapes. Kindergartners learn the three basic shapes: *circle, square,* and *triangle*; 1st graders add on variations of those with *oval, rectangle,* and *pentagon*. If these are not making sense spatially, it helps to use words to clarify, such as *round* for a circle and *egg-shaped* for oval. The difference between a *square* and a *rectangle* is not immediately obvious, so the parent can point out that a rectangle has two opposite sides that are longer, while a square has four *equal* sides. *Pentagons* are five-sided and stop signs are *octagons* (eight-sided).

Another form of numbers, patterns, shapes, and counting is money. First graders need to understand the relationship of coins to value. If a parent has ever traveled to another country where different coins are used, he will empathize with how difficult it is to associate an actual amount with a little round piece of metal—and then to quickly add them together in order to buy something! Children need to learn which number is represented by which coin and, conversely, how much each coin is worth (a nickel is 5 cents, a dime is 10 cents, etc., but there is no "7 cent coin").

Common difficulties

1. **Math signs**

   Confusion between **addition** and **subtraction** is common. While a 1st grader should know both functions, he may forget to look for the sign. You might see either a total disregard for the sign—adding when it's easier and subtracting when it's easier—or perhaps adding no matter what the sign. Before starting each problem, have the child circle the sign and say *plus* or *minus*.

2. **Illegible numbers**

   Boys generally have good large motor skills, but often have trouble with their fine motor skills. The consequence of this is messy writing of numbers and math problems, which can either cause a wrong answer or be read as a wrong answer. If this is the case with your child, get out the graph paper and have him write one number per grid box. This will confine his numbers as well as align his sums.

3. **Faulty memory**

   When a child forgets sums he knows well, there could be a variety of factors at play. Perhaps it has been a long time since he used the skill and he is rusty. Perhaps he is in the process of acquiring a new skill such as multiplication, which in the short run, can cause lapses in addition, or perhaps he has poor memory recall. It could also be that as he sees math getting progressively more difficult, he chooses to rest at a comfortable spot for a while as he gears up for the more difficult problems ahead. In this situation, go back to the basics. Review, starting from a level where he has 100 percent mastery and gradually add higher level work.

More 1st grade skills

♦ **Vertical sums vs. horizontal sums**
One of the fascinating aspects of math is that it is a language—a *symbol language*. This will become apparent at two early stages. The first place the symbols come into play is when you switch from vertical sums to horizontal sums:

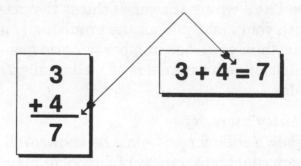

These are two different symbols representing **equals**. Children need to practice both vertical and horizontal sums until they are equally easy.

♦ **Counting and adding**
First graders need to solidify their
understanding of amounts and the numbers
that represent those amounts. Exercises in
which the child counts objects and writes the
numbers help make the connections for him.
For 6-year-olds, make sure that the pictures
are large and easy to count.

How many planes, cats, and ducks are there?

Practice making groups of dots
to be added together. Allow
your child to use colored
markers so that the groups of
dots can be distinguished. This
is a good way to explain how to
add two amounts.

♦ **Writing numbers**
A 1st grader should be able to write each
number in order from 1 to 100. Use lined
paper to form a grid and have your child
practice writing the numbers if he is not yet
proficient in doing so.

♦ **Number families**
First graders should know that for each
equation and its inverse equation (for
example, addition and its inverse,
subtraction), there are number families.

These are made of three numbers that will be used in four different equations. Use the following steps to teach this concept to your child.

Step 1: Introduce the three numbers you will be using (in this case 1, 2, 3).

Step 2: Have your child use the three numbers to make four different equations. This exercise is first written and then read aloud. Have your child focus not only on the *order* of the numbers, but on the *signs*.

$$1, 2, 3$$
$$\boxed{1} + \boxed{2} = \boxed{3}$$
$$\boxed{2} + \boxed{1} = \boxed{3}$$
$$\boxed{3} - \boxed{1} = \boxed{2}$$
$$\boxed{3} - \boxed{2} = \boxed{1}$$

◆ **Groups of five**
A 1st grader should learn the concept of a group of five, so he doesn't have to start from 1 each time he adds. He can start with 5, and then say "6, 7...". This concept of counting groups rather than individual units will hold a child in good stead for more advanced addition and multiplication. Use a group of objects, such as raisins, to practice the concept of a group of five with your child. For example, group five raisins together and work

with your child to show him how one more makes six, two more make seven, and so on.

♦ **More than (>), less than (<), equal to (=)**
A 1st grader should have enough of a grasp of the relationship between numbers to understand the quantity a number represents. This can then be applied to comparing numbers to determine *more* and *less*. In math symbols, *more* is represented by > and *less* is represented by <. A helpful hint is that the bigger side of the shape is next to the bigger number, and the smaller side is by the smaller number. Therefore, you would write **24 > 7** or **7 < 24**. If the numbers being compared are equal, the symbol is =.

♦ **Using flash cards**
Flash cards aid in memory recall and discourage finger counting. At the 1st grade level, 10 minutes of review per day is sufficient to drill the sums from **1 + 1** to **10 + 10**. Repetition is the soul of learning, and the more reinforcement of the basics that a child has, the better he will do at every subsequent level in math.

In the beginning, have your child write the problem *and the answer* on the card. Participation will encourage a child to use the cards, the actual writing will be a memory aid, and the visual reinforcement of saying and *seeing* the sum is important. After your child demonstrates a facility for reading the sums and answers, move on to sumless cards.

Second Grade

Basic skills

Second graders should have the basic addition and subtraction skills down cold. Simple sums should be second nature and the child should start adding longer and longer problems, rather than just one digit to one digit.

Consistency is important. Every child should sit and do computation for 15 minutes a day. She can be with the parent or on her own, doing flash cards with a parent or a sibling or silently to herself. Choosing the function herself (addition or subtraction) will give a child greater incentive to practice. Although the level may seem too easy to you, or it may seem that she has gone through the cards so many times, let her choose the function for the 15-minute drills. As the parent, your job is to make certain that your child sits still and practices. This means checking to make sure that her answers are correct. Encourage her to ask for help and discourage her from counting on her fingers.

After adding and subtracting, a child starts working with more difficult word problems. This is where her math vocabulary will start expanding to include real-life situations in word problems, with people joining and leaving groups, eating portions of pizza, and sharing toys.

Second graders can run into difficulty with sequencing because they are using both larger numbers and larger increments of skip counting.

By the end of the 2nd grade, a child should understand the concepts of "parts" and "a whole." This is the basis of fractions. A fraction is part of a whole. The most simple and common is 1/2, which is 1 part of 2 parts of a whole.

One half can be illustrated with any variety of regular and irregular shapes:

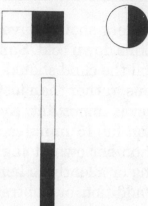

For computational purposes, 1st graders generally become familiar with the front of coins, because there are clearly different heads and faces there. Second graders need to start recognizing the backs of coins, as well as be able to identify them by size and color.

Second graders should be able to count by 5s very well, so this leads naturally into using a clock, which is in increments of five. As a child tells time, she is automatically practicing counting by 5s, which in turn leads into multiplication. For example, if the little hand is on the **12** and the big hand is on the **4**, she skip counts up to 20, for 12:20, or multiplies **4 x 5** for the same result.

Common difficulties

1. **Math signs**
   Confusion between addition and subtraction is still common at the 2nd-grade level.

Although these are 1st grade skills, 2nd graders can get caught up in the harder numbers or regrouping, and forget to look for the sign. If this is a consistent problem, have your child resume the habit of circling the sign and saying the words *plus* or *minus* to refocus attention.

2. Misalignment and errors in place values

A 2nd grader needs to understand that each *column* has a place value. This will ease her understanding of adding numbers (as well as the other functions). Often poor alignment will cause the wrong numbers to be computed. For children who consistently misalign, graph paper is an excellent way to line up columns of numbers.

3. Confusion in regrouping

Particularly with problems involving regrouping, children can get confused about what stays and what gets carried. Often, a child will have a sum such as 13, but write down the 1 and carry the 3. If you see this problem occurring, it means the child does not understand place notation. Ask her which number is in the ones column and which is in the tens. If she responds correctly, work with her concentration and attention to detail. If she responds incorrectly, work on place notation. Do exercises like these:

Circle the number

in the tens column: **452**
in the ones column: **429**
in the hundreds column: **672**

4. Random guesses

Sometimes a child may just make a wild guess and put down random numbers. This would indicate that she needed more work at the previous level. In this case, spend time reviewing skills previously learned.

5. Illegible numbers

If a child has poor motor coordination or tries to write too fast, the resulting numbers will be difficult or impossible to read. Children usually write sentences before they do sums, and it is possible to figure out one poorly shaped letter from context. Children need to know that this is *not* true of math. The parent should spend time with the child practicing writing the numbers 0 through 9.

More 2nd grade skills

♦ **Math vocabulary**
Math vocabulary is a major factor in converting word problems to number problems.

*It took **15** minutes to get dressed <u>and</u> **5** minutes to eat breakfast. How long did it take to get ready <u>all together</u>?*

The key to word problems is to take them step by step. After the child reads the problem, first have her pick out the numbers: **15** and **5**. With addition, there is no "right order," as there is with subtraction, but in order to get ready for subtraction, have her put the larger number on top.

15 minutes to get dressed

5 minutes to eat
_____

The next step is deciding on the sign. Go over the problem again, and find the word that would indicate addition or subtraction—*and, plus, with, more, all together* are addition words; *took out, lost, left behind, forgot* are subtraction words.

15 minutes

+ 5 minutes
_____

20 minutes all together

◆ **Tens complements**
Each number has a set of combinations that when added together equal that number. These are called *complements*.

0	+	10	=	10
1	+	9	=	10
2	+	8	=	10
3	+	7	=	10
4	+	6	=	10
5	+	5	=	10
6	+	4	=	10
7	+	3	=	10
8	+	2	=	10
9	+	1	=	10
10	+	0	=	10

The *tens complements* indicate when it's time to carry, because whenever the total from a column is more than 10, anything over 10 stays in that column and the whole 10 is carried over to the next column. For example, if in a column you are adding 7 and 6, the tens complement would be 7 and 3, leaving an extra 3. So the 3 would stay in that column, and the whole 10 (written as 1) would be carried to the next column.

◆ **Adding 10 to a number**
Adding 10 to a number is very easy. Drop off the **zero** from the **10**, and replace it with the number you are adding.

10 +	0	=	10	"teen"
10 +	1	=	11	"oneteen"
10 +	2	=	12	"twoteen"
10 +	3	=	13	thirteen
10 +	4	=	14	fourteen
10 +	5	=	15	fifteen
10 +	6	=	16	sixteen
10 +	7	=	17	seventeen
10 +	8	=	18	eighteen
10 +	9	=	19	nineteen
10+	10	=	20	twenty

For children, the distinction between a *number* and a *digit* helps clarify place notation. They can think of the whole number as being made up of digits in the ones column, tens column, and so on. **10** is a number, made up of two digits (**1** in the tens column and **0** in the ones column).When adding a number from 1 to 9 to a ten, the number being added goes in the ones column, in place of the zero.

♦ **Adding 9 to a number**
Adding with 9 is just like adding with 10, but one number smaller—that is, add 10 and subtract 1. You can think of it as:

9	=	10 − 1
9 + 9	=	10 + 10 − 2
9 + 9 + 9	=	10 + 10 + 10 − 3

♦ **Number families**

As was introduced in the 1st grade, for every group of three numbers, there are four problems—two addition and two subtraction. Here we will use **7, 8,** and **15**.

$$7 + 8 = 15$$

$$8 + 7 = 15$$

$$15 - 8 = 7$$

$$15 - 7 = 8$$

A child should be able to quickly recognize and recall these number families along with the individual computations. Fill-in-the-blank exercises use skills that are effective for both addition and subtraction:

$$7 + \underline{\quad} = 15$$

$$15 - \underline{\quad} = 7$$

Here are some of the common but difficult combinations that need to be practiced a lot. Make cards and put them up around the house. Choose one group per day and work on it. Don't mix groups until each one is mastered.

5. 6. 11
11 = 5 + 6
11 = 6 + 5
11 − 6 = 5
11 − 5 = 6

5. 7. 12
12 = 5 + 7
12 = 7 + 5
12 − 7 = 5
12 − 5 = 7

5. 8. 13
5 + 8 = 13
8 + 5 = 13
13 − 8 = 5
13 − 5 = 8

6. 7. 13
6 + 7 = 13
7 + 6 = 13
13 − 7 = 6
13 − 6 = 7

6. 8. 14
6 + 8 = 14
8 + 6 = 14
14 − 8 = 6
14 − 6 = 8

7. 8. 15
7 + 8 = 15
8 + 7 = 15
15 − 8 = 7
15 − 7 = 8

◆ Addition and carrying

In addition, when the ones column is full, we need to start filling up the tens column. To many children, it seems that, in carrying, the number has to *jump* over to another column.

$$9$$
$$\underline{+\ 1}$$
$$10$$

The question is, how do you add these two groups together, and how do the numbers in the *ones column* jump over to the *tens column?* Using the grids below, imagine that the dots are pennies, as **10 pennies = 1 dime** is an easy concept for 2nd graders. As the child can see, there's just no room in the box for that 10th penny.

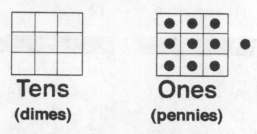

Tens
(dimes)

Ones
(pennies)

So, what happens? All **10** penny dots need to *move over* to the left and turn into one shiny new dime, with no leftover pennies.

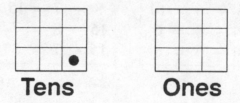

Tens

Ones

What happens if you want to add other numbers? It's the same process—let's try **6 + 6**.

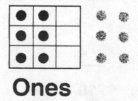

Ones

Of course, all six of the new dots won't fit into the ones box with the six that are already there, so 10 of those dots form one ten, and the remaining dots (2) are the ones.

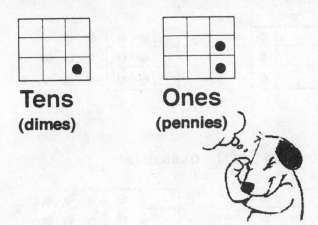

Tens
(dimes)

Ones
(pennies)

◆ **Borrowing**
Subtraction is just the inverse of addition. With addition, the question is, "Where do we carry to?" With subtraction, the question is, "Where do we borrow from?" And both times in double digit addition, the answer is the *tens column*. (As children get into three-or-more digit addition and subtraction, they can apply this rule to carrying to or borrowing from the hundreds column, the thousands column, and so on.) Let's start with **46:**

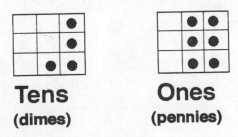

Tens
(dimes)

Ones
(pennies)

Then we are going to subtract **9**. One **10** decompresses itself back into 10 temporary **ones**:

 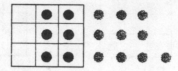

Remove 9 of the **ones** dots:

 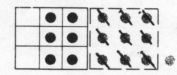

And you are left with 37:

Third Grade

Basic skills

Math starts to accelerate in the 3rd grade. Children do larger and more complicated addition and subtraction problems, with regrouping (carrying and borrowing).

$$
\begin{array}{r} 4396 \\ + 2844 \\ \hline \end{array}
\qquad
\begin{array}{r} 7891 \\ - 2908 \\ \hline \end{array}
$$

Strong basics are extremely important at this level. Arithmetic is strictly sequential, with addition being a fundamental component of multiplication, and subtraction being the inverse of addition. Addition and subtraction skills must be stimulus/response—with no hesitation whatsoever. The multiplication facts also need to be similarly memorized.

Third graders are expected to be accurate in the use of greater than (>) and less than (<) signs. They should be able to identify fractions of a whole number, such as **1/2 of 10 is 5**. They are becoming familiar with the concepts of decimal values such as tenths and hundredths—using money to represent these values.

Children learn that multiplication is a shortcut for addition.

$$7 + 7 + 7 + 7 + 7 + 7 = 42$$
and
$$7 \times 6 = 42$$

Counting by 1s, 2s, 5s, and 10s was learned in 1st grade and reviewed in 2nd. Multiplication by 3s, 4s, 6s, 7s, 8s, and 9s should be mastered in the first half of the 3rd grade in order to lay the foundation for division in the second half.

Reviewing and learning multiplication and division facts up to **10 x 10** and **100 ÷ 10** can take up through the end of 3rd grade to memorize. Children also start to learn multiplication and division of two- and three-digit numbers by a single-digit number.

$$
\begin{array}{ccc}
39 & 135 & \\
\underline{\times 3} & \underline{\times 6} & 7\overline{)28}
\end{array}
$$

A good check for children just learning to multiply is to remember that when both numbers multiplied are even, the answer will be even. When one number is even and the other odd, the answer will still be even. The answer is only odd when both numbers multiplied are odd.

Once a child has arrived at an answer (any of the four operations), it can be easily checked by the reverse operation. For example, when multiplying **8 x 4 = 32**, the answer can be checked by doing the problem in reverse—division: **32 ÷ 4 = 8**.

Third grade probabilities are encountered in tally exercises where children predict the probability of an event, such as heads and tails in a coin toss. The coins are then tossed and the actual results are noted.

Statistics are used when reading simple graphs in order to obtain the data and convert it to usable information. In order to convert data from chart form to sentence form, children need to practice gathering information and creating their own charts first. This way, they are familiar with the types of underlying facts that go into a chart. Spatial visualization is necessary to understand graphs (correlating two sets of information) and fractions (parts of a whole).

Common difficulties

1. **Multi-step problems**
   With double-digit multiplication, long division, and longer series of sums, children need to hold more information in their heads for a longer period of time while doing these multi-step computations. There are two things that support a child's memory. One is a good command of the basic arithmetic facts, because that lessens the time needed to finish the problem. The other is a good understanding of the whole problem, which has to do with place holders and columns for carrying and borrowing.

2. **Complex word problems**
   When children first learned word problems, there was generally one operation that needed to be completed. In the 3rd grade, there are frequently many steps and a variety of functions. For example, the following typical problem contains two functions, division and addition:

   A sailboat traveling 50 miles per hour took a 250 mile trip. If the sailors left at 9 a.m., what time did they return?

   First you have to divide (**250 ÷ 50**) to find out how long the trip took. Then you have to add the hours to 9 a.m. for the answer of 2 p.m.

More 3rd grade skills

♦ **Times tables**

In the 3rd grade, children are expected to know the times table up to 10 x 10. Work with your child until each set of numbers is mastered.

1	2	3	4	5	6	7	8	9	10
2	4	6	8	10	12	14	16	18	20
3	6	9	12	15	18	21	24	27	30
4	8	12	16	20	24	28	32	36	40
5	10	15	20	25	30	35	40	45	50
6	12	18	24	30	36	42	48	54	60
7	14	21	28	35	42	49	56	63	70
8	16	24	32	40	48	56	64	72	80
9	18	27	36	45	54	63	72	81	90
10	20	30	40	50	60	70	80	90	100

♦ **Times tables—9s**

Nines are magical, of course. One of the easiest tricks you can do with 9s is a quick multiplication technique.

When 9 is multiplied by a number (3, for example), the number in the tens column of the answer (27) will be one less than the number you are multiplying by (**9 x 3 = 27**) and the two numbers of the answer will always add up to 9 (**2 + 7 = 9**)!

Here's a chart to illustrate this technique:

0	9
1	8
2	7
3	6
4	5
5	4
6	3
7	2
8	1
9	0

♦ **Squares**

Squares are important in the practical world in terms of measuring floor space or other shapes. They also lead into roots and powers, which can be written in exponential notation. (**2 x 2 = 4 or 2²**)

5^2

1	2	3	4	5	6	7	8	9	10
2	4	6	8	10	12	14	16	18	20
3	6	9	12	15	18	21	24	27	30
4	8	12	16	20	24	28	32	36	40
5	10	15	20	25	30	35	40	45	50
6	12	18	24	30	36	42	48	54	60
7	14	21	28	35	42	49	56	63	70
8	16	24	32	40	48	56	64	72	80
9	18	27	36	45	54	63	72	81	90
10	20	30	40	50	60	70	80	90	100

♦ **Decimals**

In the 3rd grade, children should become familiar with the concept of decimals and percentages. An easy way for a 3rd grader to grasp this is in terms of 100 cents being equal to *one whole* dollar. Then any amount less than the whole, 67 cents, for example, can be .67 of a dollar (a whole) which is the same as 67%.

♦ **Standard measurements**
In the 3rd grade, measurements are also learned, generally consisting of *lengths, volume, weights,* and *temperature.*

Standard Ruler Facts	Abbreviations	
12 inches in a foot	inch	in.
36 inches in a yard	foot	ft.
3 feet in a yard	yard	yd.

Standard Volume Facts	Abbreviations	
8 ounces in a cup	ounce	oz.
2 cups in a pint	pint	pt.
2 pints in a quart	quart	qt.
4 quarts in a gallon	gallon	gal.

Fluid Weight

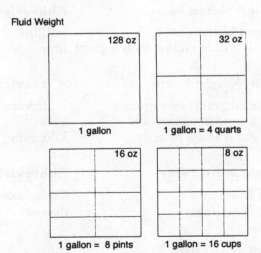

Standard Weight Facts	Abbreviations	
8 ounces in a cup	ounce	oz.
16 ounces in a pound	pound	lb.

Temperature Facts	Abbreviations	
32°F is freezing	Fahrenheit	F
212°F is boiling	degree	deg.

♦ Metric measurements

Metric refers to *meter*, which is the basis for this system. It is based on divisions of 1, 10, 100, and 1,000. It is used exclusively in most countries outside the United States. In recent years, the metric system has come to be used in many aspects of American life.

Metric Ruler Facts	Abbreviations	
10 millimeters in a centimeter	millimeter	mm
100 centimeters in a meter	centimeter	cm
1,000 millimeters in a meter	meter	m
1,000 meters in a kilometer	kilometer	km

Metric Volume Facts	Abbreviations	
1,000 milliliters in a liter	milliliter	ml
A liter is a little smaller than a quart	liter	l

Metric Weight Facts	Abbreviations	
1,000 milligrams in a gram	milligram	mg
1,000 grams in a kilogram	gram	g
A kilogram is 2.2 pounds	kilogram	kg

Temperature Facts	Abbreviations	
0°C is freezing	Centigrade	C
100°C is boiling	degree	deg.

♦ Short division

The first big step in the early part of 3rd grade was multiplication. The next big step toward the end of 3rd grade is the introduction of division. Just as addition and subtraction started off with no regrouping, so does division. This is called short division.

quotient **5**

divisor **5** / **25** dividend   **25 ÷ 5 = 5**

These problems can be expressed as *25 divided by 5,* or *5 goes into 25.* Because 5 goes into 25 an even number of times, there is no remainder.

With division, a student can always check his work by multiplying the quotient (**5**) by the divisor (**5**). **5 x 5 = 25**, which is the original dividend.

♦ **Simple fractions**
The third big step in the 3rd grade is fractions. It's important to realize that fractions and division are the same thing.

What are fractions?
Fractions are *parts* of a *whole*. The most simple and common fraction is **1/2**, which is **1 ÷ 2**, or one part out of a whole divided into two equal parts.

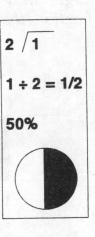

2 / **1**

1 ÷ 2 = 1/2

50%

In terms of what has been presented so far, the connections have been addition and its opposite, subtraction; addition and its short form; and multiplication and its opposite, division. Now we come to division and its short form, fractions. In a nutshell, fractions are division. 4/5 is simply

$$5\overline{)4}$$

5 can't go into **4**, so a **0** preceded by a decimal point needs to be added after the **4**.

$$5\overline{)4.0}^{.8}$$

The answer is **.8**, which is the same as **80%**. So **4/5 = 80%**.

Another key fact to remember about fractions is that when the numerator is the same, the *larger the denominator*, the *smaller the fraction (the piece of the whole)*.

numerator $\dfrac{1}{2}$ denominator $> \dfrac{1}{3}$

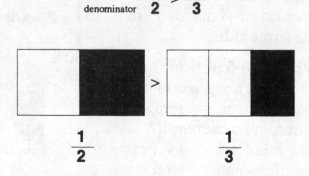

$$\frac{1}{2} \qquad\qquad \frac{1}{3}$$

Fourth Grade

Basic skills

By the 4th grade, a student should be able to add, subtract, multiply, and divide single and multiple whole numbers with multiple steps, quickly and accurately, as well as add and subtract simple decimal numbers and percentages such as 10%, 50%, and 100%.

Basic geometry comes into play in the 4th grade, including such concepts as right, acute, and obtuse angles.

Children in 4th grade should also be able to estimate measurements, and use standard units to measure length, area, weight, volume, and temperature.

Both digital and analog clocks should be used to tell time for purposes such as calculating a duration or determining a time in the past or future, including crossing the meridian from a.m. to p.m.

Probability and statistics at this level include sampling techniques in order to collect information or to conduct a survey, then collating the data into a graph (*pie, bar,* or *line*), and averaging the results.

Common difficulties

1. **Alignment in division**

   One of the most difficult skills at this level is lining up long division problems. Children don't always realize why they are moving over— they just memorize the process of indenting and bringing down the next number in the dividend. The key to understanding is in place holders, which show that we are moving from ones to

tens to hundreds and so on. Either writing in
the zeros or using grid paper makes short work
of long division. Look at the difference in
these two examples:

```
       192696              192696
  5 / 963480          5 / 963480
     -5                   500000
  ───────              ─────────
     46                   460000
    -45                   450000
  ───────              ─────────
     13                    13000
    -10                    10000
  ───────              ─────────
     34                     3400
    -30                     3000
  ───────              ─────────
     48                      480
    -45                      450
  ───────              ─────────
     30                       30
    -30                       30
  ───────              ─────────
      0                        0
```

2. **Mechanics of long division**
   It's easy to lose track in long division, so it's
   helpful to remember that it's a pattern:

   division → multiplication → subtraction;
   division → multiplication → subtraction,

   over and over until the end.

3. **Place holders and commas**
   Children often forget to put the commas in
   numbers larger than 100. The rule is one
   comma for every three digits, starting from
   the ones place:

   1,000; **10,000**; **100,000**; **1,000,000**.

4. **Aligning the decimal point**
   The decimal point marks the boundary

between a whole number and the decimal fraction. The point always lines up, no matter how many numbers there are. For example:

$$3.75 \qquad 3.000$$
$$+ \ \underline{0.50} \qquad + \ \underline{0.003}$$
$$4.25 \qquad 3.003$$

5. **Understanding the concept of fractions**
Children should be able to understand that fractions are parts of a whole and that the same amount—half, for example—can be written in many ways. At first, it is difficult to grasp what fractions and their equivalencies are, that **1/2** and **2/4** are the same as **4/8** and **5/10** of a whole, and that **.5 = 50/100 = 5/10 = 1/2**. Explain fractions to your child by using tangible examples, such as pieces of a pie.

6. **Converting charts to words**
Charts are visual representations of numbers (amounts, duration, etc.), and children must be able to change what they see in a chart into clear sentences and accurate computations.

More 4th grade skills

♦ **Long division**
When the dividend cannot be evenly divided by the divisor, there will be an amount left over. If the amount is smaller than the divisor, it will be a remainder.

$$\begin{array}{r} 5 \text{ R } 1 \\ 5\overline{)26} \end{array}$$

If the amount is larger, it will be divided by the divisor and the problem becomes long division. Depending on the dividend, there may still be a remainder.

$$\begin{array}{r} 33 \\ 5\overline{)165} \\ -150 \\ \hline 15 \\ -15 \\ \hline 0 \end{array} \qquad \begin{array}{r} 33 \text{ R } 1 \\ 5\overline{)166} \\ -150 \\ \hline 16 \\ -15 \\ \hline 1 \end{array}$$

Here are the steps:

1. The divisor, **5**, can't go into the first number of the dividend, **1**.

2. Calculate how many times the divisor **5** goes into **16** (three times), with **1** left over.

3. Write the **3** above the line, directly over the **6**.

4. Write the **15** below the **16** and add a place holder **0**.

5. Subtract **150** from **165**.

6. Write the difference, **15**.

7. Calculate how many times the divisor **5** will go into **15** (three times).

8. Write **3** above the line, to the right of the other **3**. This gives the answer **33**.

♦ **Double digit multiplication**

When a child gets to the double digits, you should get out the graph paper. There is a lot of aligning, and one misalignment will result in an incorrect answer. As with the other functions, it is important to align the numbers in the correct columns—ones, tens and so on.

$$
\begin{array}{r}
\overset{1}{2}5 \\
\times\ 31 \\
\hline
25 \\
+750 \\
\hline
775
\end{array}
$$

1. Multiply **1** times **5**. Write **5** below the **1**.

2. Multiply **1** times **2**. Write **2** below the **3**.

3. Add a place holder **0** below the **5**.

4. Multiply **3** times **5**. Write **5** below the **2**.

5. Carry the **1** (over the **2** in **25**).

6. Multiply **3** times **2**. Add the carried **1**.

7. Write **7** to the left of the **5**.

8. Add **25** and **750**.

9. The total is **775**.

♦ **Multiple digit division**

Multiple digit division is not much different from single digit division.

$$\begin{array}{r} 91 \text{ R } 12 \\ 14\overline{\smash{\big)}\,1286} \\ -1260 \\ \hline 26 \\ -14 \\ \hline 12 \end{array}$$

1. Estimate the result to compare against the final total. This will eliminate large errors. **14 x 10** is **140**, so **10** is too high. Try **14 x 9**. **126** does go into **128**. This tells you that your answer will be approximately **90**.

2. **14** goes into **128 9** times (with **2** left over).

3. Write the **9** above the line, directly over the **8**.

4. Multiply **9** by **14**. **9 x 14 = 126**.

5. Write the **126** below the **128** and add a place holder **0**.

6. Subtract **1,260** from **1,286**.

7. Write the difference, **26**.

8. **14** goes into **26 1** time (with **12** left over).

9. Write the **1** over the **6**.

10. Multiply the **1** by **14**. **1 x 14 = 14**.

11. Subtract **14** from **26**. **26 - 14 = 12**.

12. **14** does not go into **12**. So **12** is the remainder.

13. The answer is **91** remainder **12**. The answer can also be written **91 12/14**, which reduces to **91 6/7**.

♦ **Rounding and estimating**

Accuracy is very important in arithmetic, but not always necessary. Two skills to be mastered in the 4th grade are *estimating* and *rounding off*.

Estimating is making an educated guess. For example, if you need to find out how large a room is, but you don't need the exact inches, you can estimate by "pacing off" to find the general number.

Rounding off is a way of removing the insignificant digits from the equation so that you can work with the significant digits. For example, if you are talking about $1,000, it doesn't matter about a few dollars one way or the other. Tens of dollars may not be highly significant either. The first decision is what digit is significant for your estimation—and that will probably be 100s, and definitely 1,000s. So if something costs $985 dollars, that number can be rounded up to the next 100, which brings it to $1,000.

However, rounding off needs to be balanced in order not to skew high or low. If you always round up, then the total will be high and always rounding down will pull down the total.

In order to counter this skewing, round up half the time and round down the other half. Here are some general rules to follow:

Number ends in	Process
0	Leave it as it is
1, 2, 3, 4	Round down
6, 7, 8, 9	Round up
5	Look at the preceding number; if it is odd (3̲5), round up; if it is even (4̲5), round down. If there is no preceding number, round down.

◆ **Geometry**

Fourth grade geometry is limited to lines and angles. Children need to know the two main line relationships. They also need to know the three basic angles and the rules for them.

Lines

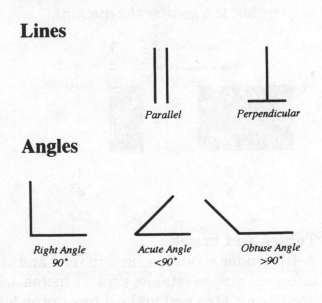

Parallel   *Perpendicular*

Angles

Right Angle   *Acute Angle*   *Obtuse Angle*
90°   *<90°*   *>90°*

- **Comparing fractions**
  In the 3rd grade, it was introduced that with fractions, when the numerator is the same, the *larger the denominator*, the *smaller the fraction*. This is the case when comparing **unlike fractions**. (An unlike fraction is when the denominators are different.)

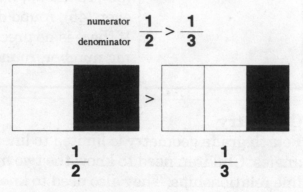

When comparing like fractions, the *larger the numerator*, the *greater the amount*.

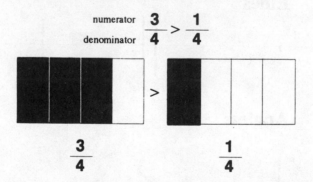

- **Tables and graphs**
  A 4th grader should be able to read and interpret graphs (stable, erratic, increasing, decreasing, etc.) and make a line graph for

each set of data, with a title and labeling for the vertical scale and the horizontal scale. The first step is to find the *range of the data*, choose an interval that best represents it, and mark off equal spaces on the vertical scale. Then round off the data to the nearest 10. The scale should begin with zero. The vertical scale notes time (years, in this case).

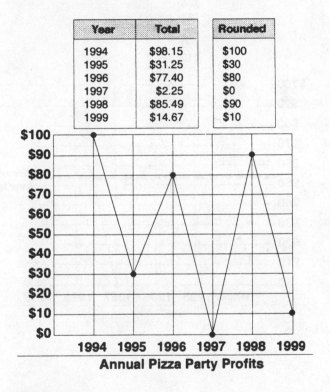

Year	Total	Rounded
1994	$98.15	$100
1995	$31.25	$30
1996	$77.40	$80
1997	$2.25	$0
1998	$85.49	$90
1999	$14.67	$10

Annual Pizza Party Profits

◆ **Averaging**
Averaging is a simple yet useful math skill. It is particularly convenient with graphs. Once a chart has been plotted, it's helpful to eliminate the highs and the lows and find out what the middle is.

Averaging is adding and dividing. In the previous graph, there were six dollar amounts. The rounded numbers totaled **$310**. Divide **$310** by **6** and the average amount for 1994–1999 was **$52**.

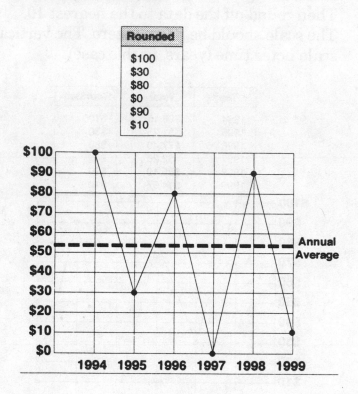

Fifth Grade

Basic skills

In the 5th grade, children review, consolidate, and build upon the principles acquired in the previous years.

They hone their skills in the four functions (addition, subtraction, multiplication, and division) with whole numbers, as well as with fractions, decimals, numeral problems, word problems, and graphs. They learn how to compute percentages and relate percentages to fractions and decimals. They need to understand fraction relationships: *comparisons* (3/5 > 1/2), *equivalence* (2/3 = 4/6), *reducing* (3/9 = 1/3), and *mixed numbers* (1 1/3) vs. *improper fractions* (4/3).

By this time, because they have mastered the basics, they can go on to using a calculator for computation as they work alone or in cooperative groups. Concentration, comprehension, and focus should be at the point where the child does not lose track in a multiple-step problem.

Commonalties are used in the 5th grade, with *common divisors* and *common multiples*.

Fifth grade geometry deals with *circle* relationships, including *diameter, circumference,* and *radius*, along with recognizing, measuring, and drawing angles of various kinds.

Fifth graders should have no trouble converting or reducing fractions and are in a position to compute fractions with the four functions.

Arithmetic is intuitive—if you divide a number, it gets smaller. When you divide by a fraction, the number gets bigger, because rather than dividing something into parts, you are counting parts of a whole. For example, if you are dividing the number **4** into **1/10**, you are dividing 4 *wholes* into 10 parts each. So you end up with 40 parts.

Division of
a Fraction
4 ÷ 1/10 = 40

Common difficulties

1. **Borrowing in subtracting fractions**
   When the problem involves regrouping, it is a difficult concept to think of breaking up the whole number and carrying it over to the fraction *as a fraction*. If you have the problem

   2 ¼ – 1 ¾ =

   you have to convert the numbers to fractions with a common denominator (which they already have in this case). This is done as follows: For each mixed number (**2 1/4**, for example), multiply the whole number (**2**) by the denominator (**4** or a *fourth*). This will tell you how many *fourths* are in the whole number **2** (**8**). To that add the fourth you already had (**1/4**). You now have **9/4**. Hence, **2 1/4** is equal to **9/4**.

   4 x 2 + 1 = 9 → 9/4

   4 x 1 + 3 = 7 → 7/4

   Then subtract.

   9/4 – 7/4 = 2/4 (or 1/2)

2. **Decimal place values**
   Remember that the number *left* of the decimal is the whole number, and the number *right* of the decimal is the fraction.

   $$3.4 = 3\ 4/10$$

   .4 and **.40** are the same because in both the **4** is in the tenths place. However, **.04** would be **4/100**, because the **4** is in the hundredths place, hence **.04** is 4 hundredths.

3. **Converting mixed fractions**
   Converting an improper fraction such as **7/5** to a mixed fraction is simple division. An easy way to convert it is by dividing the numerator by the denominator (**7 ÷ 5**) and then writing the remainder as a fraction with the whole number equaling **1 (1 2/5)**. The remainder is the numerator and the denominator stays the same.

4. **Crossing from a.m. to p.m.**
   The problem with clocks is that most things are on a base 10 system, but time is base 12. This makes it difficult to go from 8 p.m. to 2 a.m., as the meridian must be crossed. Have your child count from 8 to 12 (4 hours) and then from 12 to 2 (2 hours), and add them together (6 hours).

5. **Common factors**
   A factor is one of two or more quantities that divides a given quantity without a remainder. For example, 2 has two factors, **2** and **1**. The number 6 has four factors, **1**, **6**, **2**, and **3**

488

because all can be divided into 6 without a remainder.

$$6 \div 6 = 1$$
$$6 \div 1 = 6$$
$$6 \div 3 = 2$$
$$6 \div 2 = 3$$

Factors are used in reducing fractions and finding common denominators.

More 5th grade skills

◆ **Geometry**
Fifth grade geometry expands upon angles and includes circles. Children should understand circle relationships, including the diameter, circumference, and radius. They should be able to recognize congruent shapes (the same size or shape) when they are in different positions.

Circles

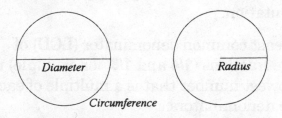

Diameter

Circumference

Radius

Congruent shapes

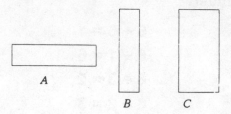

A and B are congruent shapes because they both measure ¼ by 1. B and C are not congruent (although they are both rectangles) because C is wider.

♦ **Adding and subtracting fractions**
When you are adding or subtracting **like fractions** (common denominator), you just add or subtract the numerators, and the denominator stays the same.

$$\frac{1}{4} + \frac{1}{4} = \boxed{\frac{2}{4}} = \boxed{\frac{1}{2}}$$

When you are adding or subtracting **unlike fractions**, you need to find a common denominator before completing the computation.

The least common denominator (LCD) of unlike fractions (**1/4** and **1/6**, for example) is the lowest number that is a multiple of each of the denominators:

The multiples of 4: **4, 8, 12, 16, 20, 24** ...

The multiples of 6: **6, 12, 18, 24, 30, 36** ...

The least common multiple is **12**. Use the LCD to write like fractions for **1/4** and **1/6**.

---

1. Calculate how many times each of the uncommon denominators (**4** and **6**) can go into the common denominator (**12**). **4** goes into **12, 3** times. **6** goes into **12, 2** times.

2. Multiply the **1/4** by **3/3** and the **1/6** by **2/2**.

$$\frac{1}{4} \times \frac{3}{3} = \frac{3}{12}$$

$$\frac{1}{6} \times \frac{2}{2} = \frac{2}{12}$$

3. Now you have like fractions to work with.

$$\frac{3}{12} + \frac{2}{12} = \frac{5}{12}$$

♦ **Reducing fractions**
When reducing a fraction, the first thing is to see if the denominator can be divided by the numerator, as in the following example:

$$\frac{6}{12} \div \frac{6}{6} = \frac{1}{2}$$

If the denominator can't be divided by the numerator, try to find a number that goes into both the top and the bottom numbers. For example:

$$\frac{9}{12} \div \frac{3}{3} = \frac{3}{4}$$

In a word problem or in a practical situation, the fraction or remainder must be treated as a whole. If you have a car that holds 4 people, and 10 people are going somewhere, you want to find out how many cars you need. If you do the math, it will come out to be 2 1/2 cars. In real life, of course, this is impractical, so you need 3 cars.

♦ **Multiplying and dividing fractions**
With whole numbers, addition and subtraction is easier than multiplication and division. With fractions, however, multiplication and division are actually easier than addition and subtraction, because you don't have to find a common denominator.

Multiplication: Simply multiply the numerator by the numerator and the denominator by the denominator.

$$\frac{3}{4} \times \frac{2}{3} = \boxed{\frac{6}{12}}$$

To reduce this answer, divide the numerator and the denominator by **6**.

$$\boxed{\frac{6}{12}} \div \frac{6}{6} = \boxed{\frac{1}{3}}$$

Division: The first fraction stays as it is and the second (the divisor) gets inverted. So,

$$\frac{3}{4} \div \frac{2}{3} = \boxed{}$$

becomes:

$$\frac{3}{4} \times \frac{3}{2} = \frac{9}{8} = \boxed{1\frac{1}{8}}$$

- ◆ **Converting fractions to decimals**
  Because fractions and decimals are the same thing (division), this is an extremely simple process. Simply divide the numerator by the denominator.

$$\boxed{\frac{1}{2}} = 2\overline{)1} = 2\overline{)1.0}^{.5} = \boxed{.5}$$

- ◆ **Converting decimals to fractions**
  This is even easier, because the decimal point tells you that it's a fraction.

$$\boxed{.5} = \frac{5}{10} = \boxed{\frac{1}{2}}$$

The number to the right of the point is the numerator. The denominator is always 1 followed by as many 0s as there are number places after the point. For example:

.1 = 1/10   .01 = 1/100   .001 = 1/1000

.5 = 5/10   .15 = 15/100   .625 = 625/1000

Again, this is easily understood by knowing place values. Whereas in whole numbers we work with ones, tens, hundreds, and so on, in decimals, we work with—from left to right—tenths, hundredths, thousandths, and so on. Percentage is just *per 100*. **15% = 15/100**.

The decimal equivalents of these common fractions should be memorized:

Aliquot Parts		
1.00	=	1
.50	=	1/2
.25	=	1/4
.125	=	1/8
.0625	=	1/16

Reciprocals				
1	x	1.00	=	1
2	x	.50	=	1
4	x	.25	=	1
8	x	.125	=	1
16	x	.0625	=	1

◆ **Graphs and tables**
Fifth graders are in the position to present information in a variety of forms. In a survey, for example, a student will first collect the basic information. This can be presented in paragraph form.

> *Raw data: There are 25 students, 12 boys and 13 girls. They are majoring in math, English, history, biology, and PE.*

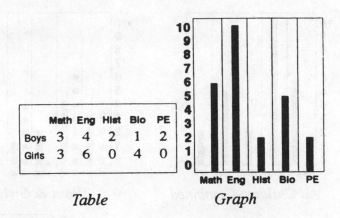

	Math	Eng	Hist	Bio	PE
Boys	3	4	2	1	2
Girls	3	6	0	4	0

Table   *Graph*

Numbers can be presented in a table, which is an arrangement of data in columns and rows.

Comparisons can be presented in a graph, which is a picture to illustrate quantitative relationships.

Fifth graders should be able to gather the data, compile it into a table, and present the findings in a graph. They should also be able to read a table or a graph and extrapolate the basic information.

Students should be able to select what they feel is the pertinent comparison and present it in graph form, with a corresponding legend to explain what is being compared within a category.

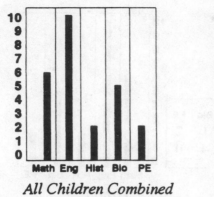

All Children Combined

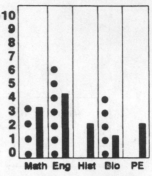

Boys & Girls

A 5th grader should be confident and accurate converting data among the three main graph formats: *bar, line,* and *pie.*

Types of Graphs or Charts

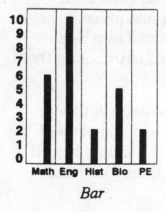

Bar

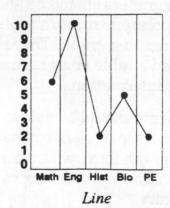

Line

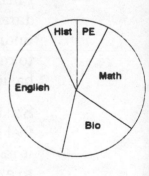

Pie

Reassessments

Kindergarten
through
Fifth Grade

Shapes & Sizes   *Kindergarten*

1. Circle the biggest bell.

2. Circle the clock that is on the right.

3. Color the **Z** that is below the line.

    ___Z___   _____   ___Z___
                     Z

4. Write the number of white squares. _____

    ☐ ☐ ◆ ☐ ☐ ■ ☐ ☐

5. How many stars do you see? _____

    ★ ☽ ★ ★ ☽ ★ ★ ★

---

0 to 1 ✖, put a check in the chart on page 427 and go to the next page. 2 or more ✖s, stop here and review skills; retest at a later date.

Patterns & Counting   *Kindergarten*

1. Draw a line from the number to the group that it matches.

   1
   2
   3
   4
   5

   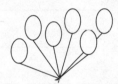

2. How many baloons do you see? _____

3. Color the circle blue, the square yellow, and the triangle red.

   △   ○   □

4. Color the matching shape.

5. Circle the group that has the most in it.

---

0 to 1 ✗, put a check in the chart on page 427 and go to the next page. 2 or more ✗s, stop here and review skills; retest at a later date.

Recognizing Numbers 1-10 *Kindergarten*

Have your child say each number.

	✔	✗	answer given
6	☐	☐	_____
7	☐	☐	_____
0	☐	☐	_____
4	☐	☐	_____
8	☐	☐	_____
5	☐	☐	_____
3	☐	☐	_____
1	☐	☐	_____
9	☐	☐	_____
2	☐	☐	_____

> ✔ = immediate response   ✗ = slow or incorrect response
> 0 to 2 ✗s, put a check in the chart on page 427 and go to the next page. 3 or more ✗s, stop here and review skills; retest at a later date.

Writing Numbers 1-10 *Kindergarten*

Have your child write each number on his own, in order.
Start with 0 and work up to 10.

_____

_____

_____

_____

_____

_____

_____

_____

_____

_____

> 0 to 2 ✖ s, put a check in the chart on page 427 and go to the
> next page. 3 or more ✖ s, stop here and review skills; retest
> at a later date.

Recognizing Numbers 1-100 *First Grade*

Have your child say each number.

	✓	✗	answer given
18	☐	☐	_____
31	☐	☐	_____
75	☐	☐	_____
28	☐	☐	_____
88	☐	☐	_____
63	☐	☐	_____
42	☐	☐	_____
94	☐	☐	_____
58	☐	☐	_____
89	☐	☐	_____

✓ = immediate response   ✗ = slow or incorrect response
0 to 2 ✗s, put a check in the chart on page 427 and go to the next page. 3 or more ✗s, stop here and review skills; retest at a later date.

Writing Numbers 1-100 *First Grade*

Dictate the following numbers to your child and have him write them on the line.

fifty seven   _____

twenty six   _____

nineteen   _____

seventy nine   _____

thirty four   _____

forty five   _____

sixty two   _____

eighty   _____

one hundred and four   _____

ninety three   _____

> 0 to 2 ✖ s, put a check in the chart on page 427 and go to the next page. 3 or more ✖ s, stop here and review skills; retest at a later date.

Signs & Skip Counting *First Grade*

Fill in the blanks by counting by 2s.

1. 4 6 ____ 10 12

2. 8 ____ ____ ____ 16

Fill in the blanks by counting by 3s.

3. 5 ____ 11 14 ____

4. 1 ____ ____ 10 ____

Put the correct sign on the line (>, <, =).

5. 4 ____ 7

6. 2 ____ 0

7. 19 ____ 18

8. 2 ____ 1+1

9. 13 ____ 17

10. 50 ____ 50

0 to 2 ✗s, put a check in the chart on page 427 and go to the next page. 3 or more ✗s, stop here and review skills; retest at a later date.

Sequencing & Ordering   *First Grade*

Answer the following questions.

1. What is one more than 29? _____
2. What is one less than 50? _____
3. What is ten more than 44? _____
4. What is ten less than 62? _____
5. What is five less than 25? _____

Fill in the missing numbers.

6. 5   10   15   _____   _____
7. 22   24   26   _____   _____
8. 400   500   600   _____   _____
9. 197   198   199   _____   _____

Circle the larger number in each set.

10. 7   2   12. 2   18
11. 5   13   13. 24   42

Rewrite each set from the smallest to the largest.

14.   8   15   12   6   2

_____   _____   _____   _____   _____

15.   115   136   3   25   16

_____   _____   _____   _____   _____

0 to 3 ✘s, put a check in the chart on page 427 and go to the
next page. 4 or more ✘s, stop here and review skills; retest
at a later date.

Single & Double Digit Addition   *First Grade*

Solve the following problems.

1.   7
    + 3

6.   81
    + 15

2.   8
    + 5

7.   53
    + 37

3.   2
    + 6

8.   48
    + 35

4.   4
    + 5

9.   19
    + 67

5.   5
    + 3

10.   35
    + 61

---

0 to 2 ✗s, put a check in the chart on page 427 and go to the next page. 3 or more ✗s, stop here and review skills; retest at a later date.

Single & Double Digit Subtraction   *First Grade*

Solve the following problems.

1.   8
    − 5

6.   64
    − 11

2.   5
    − 4

7.   49
    − 38

3.   54
    − 14

8.   46
    − 22

4.   7
    − 3

9.   87
    − 44

5.   6
    − 3

10.   68
    − 25

---

0 to 2 ✗s, put a check in the chart on page 427 and go to the next page. 3 or more ✗s, stop here and review skills; retest at a later date.

Time & Money
First Grade

Answer the following questions.

1. What time is it? _____

2. Draw hands on the
   clock to show 9:00.

3. About how long would it take to brush your teeth?

☐ 2 minutes   ☐ 2 hours

4. About how long is lunch recess at school?

☐ 1 minute   ☐ 1 hour

5. How much is each coin? Write the amount below
   the coin.

_____   _____   _____

---

0 to 1 ✗, put a check in the chart on page 427 and go to the
next page. 2 or more ✗s, stop here and review skills; retest
at a later date.

Patterns

Copy the pattern.

1. ◇ △ ☐ ◇ _____

2. O ✗ O ✗ _____

What would come next?

3. ◇ ☐ ◇ ☐ ◇ ☐ _____

4. △ △ ▽ △ △ ▽ _____

5. **A 1 B 2 C 3 D** _____

> 0 to 1 ✗, put a check in the chart on page 427 and go to the next page. 2 or more ✗s, stop here and review skills; retest at a later date.

Time & Money

Second Grade

1. What time is it? _____

2. Draw hands on the
   clock to show 6:55.

3. Circle the set that is more.

4. How many quarters do you need to make one dollar?

   ❑ 10   ❑ 20   ❑ 4   ❑ 100

5. What is the total? _____

0 to 1 ✖, put a check in the chart on page 427 and go to the
next page. 2 or more ✖s, stop here and review skills; retest
at a later date.

Computation with Regrouping   *Second Grade*

Solve the following problems.

1.   57
    + 24

6.   44
    − 25

2.   72
    + 57

7.   71
    − 44

3.   35
    + 65

8.   26
    − 18

4.   25
    + 56

9.   88
    − 79

5.   99
    + 11

10.   65
    − 48

> 0 to 2 ✘s, put a check in the chart on page 427 and go to the next page. 3 or more ✘s, stop here and review skills; retest at a later date.

Simple Fractions   *Second Grade*

Look at each picture and write the fraction, with the numerator represented by the white space, and the denominator by the dark space. A sample is given.

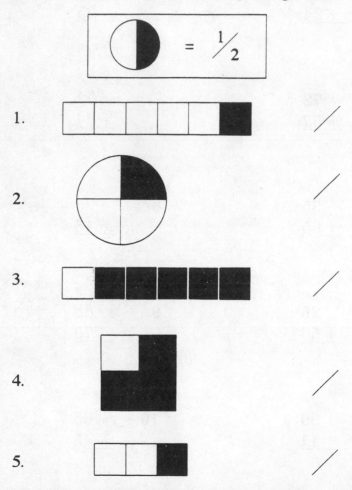

0 to 1 ✗, put a check in the chart on page 427 and go to the next page. 2 or more ✗s, stop here and review skills; retest at a later date.

3 Digit Mixed Computation   *Second Grade*

Solve the following problems.

1.   358
    + 645

6.   448
    − 219

2.   845
    − 517

7.   203
    + 707

3.   842
    + 178

8.   500
    − 219

4.   555
    + 555

9.   901
    − 299

5.   816
    − 807

10.   344
    + 499

> 0 to 2 ✖ s, put a check in the chart on page 427 and go to the next page. 3 or more ✖ s, stop here and review skills; retest at a later date.

Word Problems

Second Grade

Read the following questions and mark the correct answer.

1. If a snail crawls 15 inches to the left and then 20 inches down, how many inches has it gone in all?

   _____

2. If there are 19 birds on a wire, and 11 fly away, how many birds are left?

   _____

3. 20 kids go out to recess on the playground. 5 kids go to the soccer field. 6 kids go to the monkey bars to play. The rest are in the sandbox. How many kids are in the sandbox?

   _____

4. Write the following words in number form: nine hundred fifty two

   _____

5. Write the following words in number form: three hundred eighty

   _____

---

0 to 1 ✘, put a check in the chart on page 427 and go to the next page. 2 or more ✘s, stop here and review skills; retest at a later date.

Single Digit Multiplication/Division *Third Grade*

Solve the following problems.

1.   8
     x 2

6. $4 \times 4 =$

2. $2\overline{)6}$

7. $10 \div 2 =$

3.   3
     x 7

8. $9 \times 5 =$

9. $10 \div 5 =$

4. $4\overline{)8}$

5.   7
     x 8

10. $6 \times 8 =$

> 0 to 2 ✗s, put a check in the chart on page 427 and go to the
> next page. 3 or more ✗s, stop here and review skills; retest
> at a later date.

Double Digit Multiplication/Division *Third Grade*

Solve the following problems.

1.   23
      x 3

6.   3 ⟌ 36

2.   8 ⟌ 24

7.   9 ⟌ 72

3.   36
      x 3

8.   54
      x 4

4.   6 ⟌ 24

9.   7 ⟌ 56

5.   56
      x 7

10.   79
       x 8

> 0 to 2 ✗s, put a check in the chart on page 427 and go to the next page. 3 or more ✗s, stop here and review skills; retest at a later date.

Time & Money

Third Grade

Solve the following word problems.

1. If it is 9:55 a.m. now, what time will it be in five hours?

_____

2. Carla went to sleep at 8:30 p.m. and woke up at 6:30 a.m. How long did she sleep?

_____

3. If a pair of shoes costs $22.75 and a shirt costs $24.25, how much do they cost together?

_____

4. Tina has two dollars. She buys some candy that costs $1.59. How much change does she get?

_____

5. Sam earns $15.50 per day. If he works for four days, how much does he earn?

_____

0 to 1 ✗, put a check in the chart on page 427 and go to the next page. 2 or more ✗ s, stop here and review skills; retest at a later date.

Graphs

Third Grade

Based on the graph, answer the following questions.

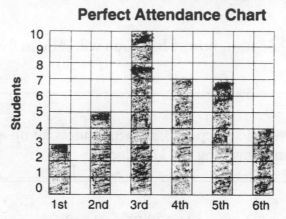

Perfect Attendance Chart

1. Which grades had more than 6 students with perfect attendance? _____

2. How many grades are tracked in this chart?
   ❑ 34   ❑ 6   ❑ 3

3. Which grade had the highest number of students with perfect attendance?
   ❑ 2nd   ❑ 6th   ❑ 3rd

4. Which grade had the lowest number of students with perfect attendance?
   ❑ 1st   ❑ 6th   ❑ 4th

5. How many students with perfect attendance are there all together?
   ❑ 36   ❑ 6   ❑ 10

---

0 to 1 ✖, put a check in the chart on page 427 and go to the next page. 2 or more ✖s, stop here and review skills; retest at a later date.

Division & Remainders　　　*Third Grade*

Solve the following division problems.

1.　　$5\overline{)6}$　　　　　　6.　　$3\overline{)23}$

2.　　$4\overline{)41}$　　　　　7.　　$8\overline{)31}$

3.　　$7\overline{)55}$　　　　　8.　　$6\overline{)71}$

4.　$9\overline{)200}$　　　　　9.　　$2\overline{)55}$

5.　　$5\overline{)98}$　　　　10.　　$9\overline{)17}$

---

0 to 2 ✗ s, put a check in the chart on page 427 and go to the next page. 3 or more ✗ s, stop here and review skills; retest at a later date.

Mixed Word Problems

Third Grade

Read the following questions and write the correct answer.

1. If there are 7 days in a week and 4 weeks in a month, how many days are in that month?

   _____

2. If there are 8 shelves and each shelf holds 20 books, how many books are there?

   _____

3. The computer was on for 2 hours per day. At the end of 16 days, how long had it been on?

   _____

4. The marathon bike race was 60 miles long. The children rode an even amount each day for 5 days. How many miles did they ride each day?

   _____

5. Write the following words in number form: Seven hundred twenty nine thousand four hundred sixty eight

   _____

0 to 1 ✖, put a check in the chart on page 427 and go to the next page. 2 or more ✖ s, stop here and review skills; retest at a later date.

Rounding Off & Estimating

Fourth Grade

Round off each number to the nearest 10:

1. 7 _____   2. 32 _____

Round off each number to the nearest 100:

3. 225 _____   4. 369 _____

Estimate

5. 13 feet is approximately how many yards?

_____

6. 35 inches is approximately how many feet?

_____

7. 70 days is approximately how many months?

_____

Average

8. Ben is 6 feet tall. Tim is 4 feet tall. Fred is 5 feet tall. What is the average height?

_____

9. The holiday schedule is as follows: 7 days in March, 9 days in May, 3 days in June, 1 in July. What is the average?

_____

10. Edgar earns $7 per day, working 4 days a week. What does that average per day for a 7-day week?

_____

0 to 2 ✗ s, put a check in the chart on page 427 and go to the next page. 3 or more ✗ s, stop here and review skills; retest at a later date.

Multiple Digit Computing　　　*Fourth Grade*

Solve the following problems.

1.　　　25
　　　x 53

6.　　8 $\overline{)354}$

2.　　　29
　　　x 48

7.　　55 $\overline{)855}$

3.　　　57
　　　x 49

8.　　22 $\overline{)\$3.30}$

4.　　　83
　　　x 91

9.　　87 $\overline{)\$2.61}$

5.　　　11
　　　x 11

10.　　40 $\overline{)500}$

> 0 to 2 ✗ s, put a check in the chart on page 427 and go to the next page. 3 or more ✗ s, stop here and review skills; retest at a later date.

Computing with Fractions   *Fourth Grade*

Reduce each fraction to its lowest terms.

1. $\dfrac{6}{8}$ 2. $\dfrac{16}{24}$ 3. $\dfrac{80}{100}$

Compare using >, <, = .

4. $\dfrac{1}{2}$ $\dfrac{1}{4}$ 5. $\dfrac{8}{9}$ $\dfrac{3}{4}$ 6. $\dfrac{1}{12}$ $\dfrac{2}{24}$

Reduce and write a mixed number or a whole number.

7. $\dfrac{5}{3}$ 8. $\dfrac{16}{4}$

9. $\dfrac{8}{3}$ 10. $\dfrac{9}{6}$

Add or subtract these fractions and reduce to lowest terms.

11.   2/5 + 2/5 =   12.   7 3/8 + 4 5/8 =

13.   5/9 − 3/9 =   14.   1 6/10 + 3 2/10 =

---

0 to 3 ✘s, put a check in the chart on page 427 and go to the next page. 4 or more ✘s, stop here and review skills; retest at a later date.

Measurements

Fourth Grade

Read the following questions and mark the correct answer.

1. If there are 4 kids playing and they need drinks, about how much juice would be needed for them altogether?

   ❑ a pint ❑ a quart ❑ a gallon

2. To measure how much carpeting would be needed to carpet your classroom floor, which measurement would be best to use?

   ❑ inches ❑ feet ❑ miles

3. To measure the weight of a serving of ice cream, which unit of measurement should be used?

   ❑ ounces ❑ pounds ❑ quarts

4. To measure how tall you are, which unit of measurement should be used?

   ❑ mm ❑ cm ❑ m ❑ km

5. Compare using > or <.

   33 feet _____ 3 yards

---

0 to 1 ✖, put a check in the chart on page 427 and go to the next page. 2 or more ✖s, stop here and review skills; retest at a later date.

Mixed Word Problems   *Fourth Grade*

Read the following questions and check the correct answer.

1. What is the chance of drawing a silver coin from a can that has one silver coin and four gold ones?

    ❑ even   ❑ 1 in 4   ❑ 1 in 5

2. There are 12 children at the playground. Each one is then joined by one friend. Most of the children are on the swings, but four are at the slide. What portion of the kids are at the slide?

    ❑ 1/4   ❑ 1/5   ❑ 1/6

3. 68 children are going on a class trip. Each bus they're taking holds 20 children. How many buses are needed?

    ❑ 3 buses   ❑ 5 buses   ❑ 4 buses

4. Jack spent a quarter of his allowance on baseball cards, an eighth on bubble gum, and the rest on a gift for his mom. How much of his allowance did he spend on his mom?

    ❑ 1/2   ❑ 5/8   ❑ 3/6

5. Half of the kids in class had on white shirts, a quarter had on yellow shirts, an eighth had on blue shirts, and the rest had on orange shirts. How many kids had on orange shirts?

    ❑ 1/4   ❑ 1/8   ❑ 1/2

---

0 to 1 ✗, put a check in the chart on page 427 and go to the next page. 2 or more ✗s, stop here and review skills; retest at a later date.

Multiplying & Dividing Fractions *Fifth Grade*

Multiply or divide these fractions. Reduce if necessary.

1. 1/3   x   2/3   =

2. 3/4   x   1/5   =

3. 5/6   x   2/3   =

4. 1/8   x   1/8   =

5. 1/2   x   3/1   =

6. 1/2   ÷   2/3   =

7. 1/8   ÷   7/10 =

8. 3/4   ÷   1/2   =

9. 1/3   ÷   3/1   =

10. 1/5   ÷   1/5   =

---

0 to 2 ✗ s, put a check in the chart on page 427 and go to the next page. 3 or more ✗ s, stop here and review skills; retest at a later date.

Graphs

Fifth Grade

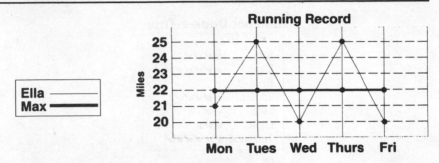

1. How many miles did Ella run on Tuesday? _____

2. How many more miles did Ella run on Thursday than on Monday? _____

3. Who ran further, Ella or Max? _____

4. What fraction of the time is spent at the beach?
   ❑ 1/8   ❑ 1/4   ❑ 1/2   ❑ 1   ❑ 2   ❑ 4

5. How much more time is spent at school than at the park?
   ❑ 1/8   ❑ 1/4   ❑ 1/2   ❑ 1   ❑ 2   ❑ 4

0 to 1 ✖, put a check in the chart on page 427 and go to the next page. 2 or more ✖s, stop here and review skills; retest at a later date.

Tables

Fifth Grade

Summer Book-a-Thon

Nick	✔✔✔✔
Cindi	✔✔✔✔✔✔
Paul	✔
James	✔✔✔✔✔
Lola	✔✔
Olga	✔✔✔
Terrence	✔✔✔✔✔

1. How many books did the children read in all?

   _____

2. If Cindi received 25 cents for every book she read, how much money did she bring in?

   _____

3. What is the average number of books read?

   _____

	# of Days		# of Days
January	31	July	31
February	28	August	31
March	31	September	30
April	30	October	31
May	31	November	30
June	30	December	31

4. If today is January 2, how many more days until Valentines Day (February 14?) _____

5. What is the average number of days per month in the second half of the year? _____

---

0 to 1 ✘, put a check in the chart on page 427 and go to the next page. 2 or more ✘s, stop here and review skills; retest at a later date.

Measurements   *Fifth Grade*

1. Yesterday the temperature was 40° C. Was it hot or cold? _____

2. To measure the thickness of a quarter, which unit of measurement would be used?

   ❏ mm   ❏ cm   ❏ km   ❏ m

3. How many ounces are in 2 gallons? _____

4. On the grid below, shade in an area of 16 square units.

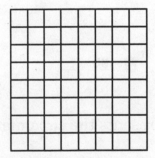

5. How many ounces are in 2 pounds?

   ❏ 16   ❏ 8   ❏ 32

> 0 to 1 ✖, put a check in the chart on page 427 and go to the next page. 2 or more ✖ s, stop here and review skills; retest at a later date.

Geometry   *Fifth Grade*

1. If a circle has a radius of 4 1/2 inches, what would the diameter be?

   _____

2. What is the perimeter of an octagon where each size measures four inches?

   _____

3. How many faces does a pyramid have?

   _____

4. Which of the following is an obtuse angle? Circle your answer.

   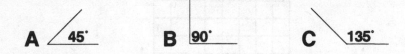

5. Which letter represents the circumference of the circle?

   ❏ A   ❏ B   ❏ C   ❏ D

   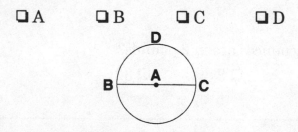

---

0 to 1 **✗**, put a check in the chart on page 427 and go to the next page. 2 or more **✗**s, stop here and review skills; retest at a later date.

Fractions & Decimals

Fifth Grade

Write the decimal or fraction for each problem.

1. $\dfrac{1}{20}$ _____

2. .20 _____

3. $\dfrac{3}{4}$ _____

Solve the following decimal problems.

4. .75 + .5 = _____

5. .5 − .25 = _____

Write the following as percentages.

6. 6/8 _____

7. .66 _____

8. 15/25 _____

9. 4/10 _____

10. .17 _____

---

0 to 2 ✖s, put a check in the chart on page 427 and go to the next page. 3 or more ✖s, stop here and review skills; retest at a later date.

Word Problems
Fifth Grade

Read the following questions and write the correct answer.

1. Nick spent 1 hour and 15 minutes washing 75 dishes. what was the average time spent on each dish?_____

2. Each gray pebble in a box of 20 pebbles weighs 22 grams. Each black pebble in another box of 20 pebbles weighs 0.5 as much. How much do the black pebbles weigh altogether?_____

3. Sarah sold 3 large shiitake mushrooms for $10 a pound. They weigh 21 oz., 23 oz., 20 oz. How much did she make?_____

4. Kathleen had 27 concerts during January and February. She had twice as many concerts in February as in January. How many concerts did she have in February?_____

5. The baseball game started at 1:17 p.m. The two teams played for 2 hours and 54 minutes. At what time did the game end?_____

> 0 to 1 ✘, put a check in the chart on page 427 and go to the next page. 2 or more ✘s, stop here and review skills; retest at a later date.

Answer Key

Fourth grade assessment

page

415	1. 40	2. 30	3.100	4. 500	5. 3
	6. 2	7. 4	8. 3 feet	9. 5 days	10. $8
416	1. 416	2. 2623	3. 1053	4. 3640	5. 2275
	6. 5 R50	7. .13	8. .07	9. 5 R1	10. 4 R40
417	1. 1/2	2. 1/3	3. 3/4	4. >	5. >
	6. =	7. 1	8. 4	9. 4 1/2	10. 1 5/6
	11. 1 1/2	12. 7	13. 1/2	14. 4 5/6	
418	1. a gallon	2. 1,000	3. cm	4. km	5. <
419	1. 1 in 3	2. 150 ft	3. 5 vans	4. 1/2	5. three

Fifth grade assessment

page

420	1. 1 or 1/3	2. 6/25	3. 9/81 or 1/9	4. 8/24 or 1/3	
	5. 3/4	6. 4/3 or 1 1/3	7. 10/12 or 5/6		
	8. 20/24 or 5/6	9. 70/10 or 7	10. 6/5 or 1 1/5		
421	1. 24	2. 5	3. 23	4. 1/4	5. 1/8
422	1. 27	2. $3.50	3. 6 3/4	4. 147	5. 30.4
423	1. 2.9 cm	2. 3.3 cm	3. ---	4. 8	5. 20
424	1. 240cm	2. 16 in.	3. 6	4. 90°	5. AC

425	**1.** .6	**2.** 2/5	**3.** .25	**4.** .75	**5.** .5
	6. 70%	**7.** 80%	**8.** 25%	**9.** 55%	**10.** 78%
426	**1.** 3 min.	**2.** 3	**3.** $12	**4.** 12:05	**5.** 1/4

Fourth grade reassessment

page

521	**1.** 10	**2.** 30	**3.** 200	**4.** 400	**5.** 4
	6. 3	**7.** 2	**8.** 5 feet	**9.** 5 days	**10.** $4

522	**1.** 1325	**2.** 1392	**3.** 2793	**4.** 7553	**5.** 121
	6. 44 R2	**7.** 15 R30	**8.** .15	**9.** .03	**10.** 12R20

523	**1.** 3/4	**2.** 2/3	**3.** 4/5	**4.** >	**5.** >
	6. =	**7.** 1 2/3	**8.** 4	**9.** 2 2/3	**10.** 1 1/2
	11. 4/5	**12.** 12	**13.** 2/9	**14.** 4 4/5	

524	**1.** a quart	**2.** feet	**3.** ounces	**4.** cm	**5.** >
525	**1.** 1 in 5	**2.** 1/6	**3.** 4 buses	**4.** 5/8	**5.** 1/8

Fifth grade reassessment

page

526	**1.** 2/9	**2.** 3/20	**3.** 10/18 or 5/9	**4.** 1/64
	5. 3/2 or 1 1/2		**6.** 3/4	**7.** 10/56
	8. 1/2	**9.** 1/9	**10.** 1	

527	**1.** 25	**2.** 4	**3.** Ella	**4.** 1/4	**5.** 1/8
528	**1.** 28	**2.** $1.75	**3.** 4	**4.** 43	**5.** 30.6
529	**1.** hot	**2.** mm	**3.** 256	**4.** ----	**5.** 32
530	**1.** 9 in.	**2.** 32 in.	**3.** 4	**4.** 135°	**5.** D
531	**1.** .05	**2.** 1/5	**3.** .75	**4.** 1.25	**5.** .25
	6. 75%	**7.** 66%	**8.** 60%	**9.** 40%	**10.** 17%
532	**1.** 1 min.	**2.** 220 gr.	**3.** $40	**4.** 18	**5.** 4:11

NAEP Math
Achievement
Standards

The National Assessment of Educational Progress (NAEP) is an arm of the U.S. Department of Education that monitors academic achievement through periodic testing of 4th, 8th, and 12th graders. It serves the vital function of reporting to educators, parents, policy makers, and the general public how well our students are achieving in the area of math proficiency.

The 1996 NAEP Math Assessment was administered to national samples of 4th-, 8th-, and 12th-grade students attending public and nonpublic schools, and to samples of 4th graders in the jurisdictions that participated in the 1992 Trial State Assessment. Nearly 250,000 students were assessed in the national and jurisdiction samples. Students' math performance is described on a proficiency scale ranging from 0 to 500, and in relation to three achievement levels: *Basic, Proficient,* and *Advanced*. The assessment results are reported based on the performance of students at each of the three grades and within specific subgroups of the population. For each grade, the definitions are cumulative from *Basic* through *Advanced*. One level builds on the previous level. That is, knowledge at the *Proficient* level presumes mastery of the *Basic* level, and knowledge at the *Advanced* level presumes mastery of both the *Basic* and *Proficient* levels. The 5 NAEP content areas are:

1. Numbers and Operations
2. Measurement
3. Geometry
4. Data Analysis, Statistics, and Probability
5. Algebra and Functions

At the 4th grade level, algebra, and functions are treated in informal and exploratory ways, often through the study of patterns.

NAEP Scoring System: Fourth Grade Math Achievement Levels

Fourth-grade students performing at the *Basic* level should be able to estimate and use basic facts to perform simple computations with whole numbers, show some understanding of fractions and decimals, and solve some simple real-world problems in all NAEP content areas. Students at this level should be able to use—though not always accurately—four-function calculators, rulers, and geometric shapes. Their written responses are often minimal and presented without supporting information. Fourth graders performing at the *Proficient* level should be able to use whole numbers to estimate, compute, and determine whether results are reasonable. They should have a conceptual understanding of fractions and decimals be able to solve real-world problems in all NAEP content areas and use four-function calculators, rulers, and geometric shapes appropriately. They should employ problem-solving strategies such as identifying and using appropriate information. Their written solutions should be organized and presented both with supporting information and explanations of how they were achieved.

Fourth-grade students performing at the *Advanced* level should be able to solve complex and nonroutine real-world problems in all NAEP content areas. They should display mastery in the use of four-function calculators, rulers, and geometric shapes. These students are expected to draw logical conclusions and justify answers and solution processes by explaining why, as well as how, they were achieved. They should go beyond the obvious in their interpretations and be able to communicate their thoughts clearly and concisely.

Math achievement levels: United States
Grade 4: NAEP Trial State Assessments in Math

1996 Assessment, Public Schools Only

State	At or Above Basic	Below Basic
Alabama	48%	52%
Alaska	65%	35%
Arizona	57%	43%
Arkansas	54%!	46%!
California	46%	54%
Colorado	67%	33%
Connecticut	75%	25%
Delaware	54%	46%
District of Columbia	20%	80%
Florida	55%	45%
Georgia	53%	47%
Hawaii	53%	47%
Idaho	64%*	36%*

How Well Does Your Child Do Math?

Indiana	72%	28%
Iowa	74%	26%
Kentucky	60%	40%
Louisiana	44%	56%
Maine	75%	25%
Maryland	59%	41%
Massachusetts	71%	29%
Michigan	68%	32%
Minnesota	76%	24%
Mississippi	42%	58%
Missouri	66%	34%
Montana	71%	29%
Nebraska	70%	30%
Nevada	57%	43%
New Hampshire	74%*	26%*
New Jersey	68%	32%
New Mexico	51%	49%
New York	64%	36%
North Carolina	64%	36%
North Dakota	75%	25%
Ohio	59%*	41%*
Oklahoma	62%*	38%*
Oregon	65%	35%
Pennsylvania	68%	32%
Rhode Island	61%	39%
South Carolina	48%	52%
Tennessee	58%	42%
Texas	69%	31%
Utah	69%	31%
Vermont	67%	33%
Virginia	62%	38%
Washington	67%	33%
West Virginia	63%	37%
Wisconsin	74%	26%
Wyoming	64%	36%
Guam	28%	72%

! Statistical tests involving this value should be interpreted with caution. Standard error estimates may not be accurately determined and/or the sampling distribution of the statistics does not match statistical test assumptions. (See NAEP Report Appendix A)

* 1992 data

Source: NAEP 1996 Math Report Card for the Nation and the States. U.S. Department of Education, Office of Educational Research and Improvement

Math achievement levels: International
TIMSS Third International Math & Science Study

1996 Assessment, 41 Countries, Grades 7 and 8

8th Grade Average Country	Achievement	7th Grade Average Country	Achievement
Singapore	643	Singapore	601
Korea	607	Korea	577
Japan	605	Japan	571
Hong Kong	588	Hong Kong	564
Belgium (Fl)	565	Belgium (Fl)	558
Czech Republic	564	Czech Republic	523
Slovak Republic	547	Netherlands	516
Switzerland	545	Bulgaria	514
Netherlands	541	Austria	509
Slovenia	541	Slovak Republic	508
Bulgaria	540	Belgium (Fr)	507
Austria	539	Switzerland	506
France	538	Hungary	502
Hungary	537	Russian Federation	501
Russian Federation	535	Ireland	500
Australia	530	Slovenia	498
Ireland	527	Australia	498
Canada	527	Thailand	495
Belgium (Fr)	526	Canada	494
Thailand	522	France	492
Israel	522	Germany	484
Sweden	519	Sweden	477
Germany	509	England	476
New Zealand	508	United States	476
England	506	New Zealand	472
Norway	503	Denmark	465
Denmark	502	Scotland	463
United States	500	Latvia(LSS)	462
Scotland	498	Norway	461
Latvia (LSS)	493	Iceland	459
Spain	487	Romania	454
Iceland	487	Spain	448
Greece	484	Cyprus	446
Romania	482	Greece	440
Lithuania	477	Lithuania	428
Cyprus	474	Portugal	423
Portugal	454	Iran, Islamic Rep.	401
Iran, Islamic Rep.	428	Colombia	369
Kuwait	92	South Africa	348

Index

Appendix 1

Online Educational Resources

Activities for Reading and Writing

http://www.ed.gov/Family/RWN/Activ97/title.html

This is the basic literacy kit to get children preschool through 6th grade and reading partners started. The kit includes an activities book, a vocabulary log, a bookmark, & two certificates. Every public library in the country will have kits.

Early Childhood Educator's and Family Web Corner

http://www.nauticom.net/www/cokids

This sunny site has loads of information—family pages, teacher pages, educational debate, and links to other sites.

EdLinks

http://webpages.marshall.edu/~jmullens/edlinks.html
http://webpages.marshall.edu/~jmullens/lang.html

This is a wonderful compilation of links to an astonishing variety of sites, all related somehow to language—from Walt Whitman to Chinese lessons.

Educational Online Sources (EOS)

http://netspace.students.brown.edu/eos/main_image.html

How Well Does Your Child Read, Write, and Do Math?

Welcome to the world wide web of educational online sources. This is a space where everyone can contribute and build a clearinghouse for educational information.

Family Education Network
http://www.familyeducation.com
This is an interesting site with a lot of information for parents. It is very browsable, like the family magazine that it is.

The Just Add Kids! Resource Directory
http://www.ed.gov/Family/JustAddKids/
A compilation of national organizations that can be useful in starting and supporting community reading projects. From Just Add Kids.

National Education Association
http://www.nea.org
Interested in great schools? You've come to the right place. We're the more than 2.4 million members of the National Education Association, and we hope this page can help public education work for every child and every family.

Parenting of K-6 Children
http://childparenting.miningco.com
http://daycare.miningco.com
A very friendly, accessible site with many great ideas and commendations.

The Read Write Now Partner Tutoring Program
http://www.udel.edu/ETL/RWN/Tutorman.html
A guide to tutoring for learning partners to help children develop their reading and writing skills.

Research and Reference Resources

The AskERIC Virtual Library
http://www.askeric.org/Virtual/
ERIC/AskERIC's information server contains select resources for both education and general use. Includes lesson plans, ERIC digests,

infoguides and publications, reference tools, government information, and educational archives.

Internet Resources Relating to Education
http://www.ilt.columbia.edu/net/guides/ILTeduc.html
Columbia University's education resource list. ILT is the Institute for Learning Technologies.

Library of Congress
http://lc.loc.gov
Every book that has ever been published is referenced here.

Researcher's Guide to the U.S. Department of Education
http://www.ed.gov/pubs/ResearchersGuide/Services.html
A list of services and resources administered by the U.S. Department of Education to advance research, information, and communication about educational issues.

United States Department of Education
http://www.ed.gov
http://www.ed.gov/index.html
The site of the U.S. Department of Education. It lists news, grant and contract information, programs and services, publications and products, and other sites among more.

The U.S. Education Department/OERI
gopher://gopher.ed.gov
An information server that acts as a reference desk for all things educational. Includes educational software, Goals 2000 information, and primary, secondary, and vocational information.

Voluntary National Tests—Department of Education
http://www.ed.gov/nationaltests
The President proposed in his State of the Union Address on February 4, 1997 a voluntary, annual reading test in English at grade 4 and a math test at grade 8. These tests will, for the first time in history, provide parents and teachers with information about how their students are progressing compared to other states, the nation, and other countries.

State-by-State Information

American Federation of Teachers (AFT)
http://www.aft.org
http://www.aft.org//research/reports/standards/iv.htm

The American Federation of Teachers (AFT) issued *Making Standards Matter 1996 an Annual 50-State Report on Efforts to Raise Academic Standards*. Nearly every state is working to set common academic standards for their students, but the AFT report makes it clear that most states have more work to do to strengthen their standards. For a report on an individual state, go online for the AFT state-by-state analysis.

Developing Educational Standards: Overview
http://putwest.boces.org/Standards.html#TOC

An annotated list of Internet sites with K-12 educational standards and curriculum frameworks documents, run by Putnam Valley Schools, Putnam Valley, NY. The three main sections are: governmental and general resources, listing by subject, listing by state.

Developing Educational Standards: Math
http://putwest.boces.org/StSu/Math.html

Developing Educational Standards is an annotated list of Internet sites with K-12 educational standards and curriculum frameworks documents.

State Curriculum Frameworks and Content Standards
http://www.ed.gov/offices/OERI/statecur

Brief description of various proposed frameworks and standards projects prepared with funding from DOE and Eisenhower National Program for Math and Science Education.

National Network of Regional Educational Laboratories

Appalachian Region (AEL) Specialty: Rural Education
http://www.ael.org

Western Region (WestEd) Specialty: Assessment and Accountability
http://www.fwl.org

Central Region (McREL) Specialty: Curriculum, Learning and Instruction
http://www.mcrel.org

Midwestern Region (NCREL) Specialty: Technology
http://www.ncrel.org

Northwestern Region; Specialty: School Change Processes
http://nwrel.org

Pacific Region; Specialty: Language and Cultural Diversity
http://w3.prel.hawaii.edu/

Northeastern Region; Specialty: Language and Cultural Diversity
http://www.lab.brown.edu

Southeastern Region; Specialty: Early Childhood Education
http://www.serve.org

Southwestern Region; Specialty: Language and Cultural Diversity
http://www.sedl.org

Mathematics

American Mathematics Competitions (AMC)
http://www.unl.edu/amc

The American Mathematics Competitions (AMC) seek to increase interest in mathematics through friendly mathematics competitions for junior/middle and senior high school students.

Curriculum Consumers Education Service
http://www.rdc.udel.edu/CCIS/ccis_math.html

This site from the University of Delaware contains standards-based instructional resource profiles of various elements of a mathematical curriculum.

Eisenhower National Clearinghouse for Mathematics and Science Education (ENC)
http://www.enc.org

The Eisenhower National Clearinghouse has put together one of the richest and most valuable instructional resources for math and science education on the Internet. Short of having an extensive personal library, you cannot beat the breadth and quality of information ENC has made available here.

Math Archives K-12 Index
http://archives.math.utk.edu/k12.html

A comprehensive listing of Internet sites containing significant collections of materials that can be used in the teaching of mathematics at the K-12 level.

Mathematics for Parents
http://www.wcer.wisc.edu/Projects/Mathematics_and_Science/Modeling_i
_Math_and_Science/Newsletters/Table_of_Content.html

An extension of the Cognitively Guided Instruction (CGI) program. The goal of CGI is to inform teachers about how children think about simple arithmetic in the primary grades.

Math Mania—Exploring the Frontiers of Mathematics
http://csr.uvic.ca/~mmania

This site has sections on knots, graphs, sorting networks, and finite state machines.

NASA Education Sites
http://quest.arc.nasa.gov
http://k12mac.larc.nasa.gov

NASA and the High-Performance Computing and Communications Program offers a collection of servers specifically geared for teachers, students, and administrators. They offer math and science education resources, connectivity to numerous education servers, journals, and grant and project participation information.

National Council of Teachers of Mathematics (NCTM)
http://www.nctm.org

Founded in 1920 as a not-for-profit professional and educational association, NCTM is the largest organization dedicated to the improvement of mathematics education and to meeting the needs of teachers of mathematics. This site offers curriculum and evaluation standards for school mathematics.

National Science Foundation
http://stis.nsf.gov

NSF provides this site as a source for educators and administrators. Contains information on NSF education projects, grants and publications.

Third International Math and Science Study (TIMSS)
http://ustimss.msu.edu

This site is funded by the National Science Foundation in conjunction with the National Center for Education Statistics. It contains a great deal of information about the Math and Science Study, as well as a wide range of links to other related sites.

Appendix 2

Services
and
Resources

The services that follow are administered by the U.S. Department of Education to advance research, information, and communication about educational issues. Organizations should be contacted directly for more information about their research agenda and available services.

1. National Research and Development Centers

To help improve and strengthen student learning in the United States, the Office of Research supports 21 university-based national educational research and development Centers. The Centers are addressing specific topics such as early childhood education, student achievement in core academic subjects, teacher preparation and training, systemic education reform and restructuring, school governance and finance, postsecondary education and lifelong learning. In addition, most of the Centers are also focusing on the education of disadvantaged children and youth. Many Centers are collaborating with other universities, and many work with elementary and secondary schools. All are encouraged to make sure the information they produce makes a difference and reaches parents, teachers, and others who can use it to make meaningful changes in America's schools. Some of the centers include:-

National Center for Research on
  Educational Accountability and
  Teacher Evaluation
Western Michigan University
401 B. Ellsworth Hall
Kalamazoo, MI 49008
616-387-5895

National Center for Improving
  Student Learning and
  Achievement in Mathematics and
  Science
University of Wisconsin at Madison
Center for Education Research
1025 West Johnson St.
Madison, WI 53706
608-263-3605

National Research Center on
  Education in the Inner Cities
Temple University
933 Ritter Hall Annex
1301 Cecil B. Moore Ave.
Philadelphia, PA 19122
215-204-3001

Center for Research on Evaluation,
  Standards, and Student Testing
  (CRESST)
University of California LA
Center for the Study of Evaluation
301 GSE & IF
Los Angeles, CA 90095-1522
310-206-1532

National Research Center on the
  Gifted and Talented
University of Connecticut
362 Fairfield Rd. U-7
Storrs, CT 06269-2007
860-486-4826

Center for the Social Organization of
  Schools
Johns Hopkins University
3505 North Charles St.
Baltimore, MD 21218-3888
410-516-0370

National Center on Postsecondary
  Teaching, Learning, and
  Assessment
Pennsylvania State University
Center for the Study of Higher
  Education
403 S. Allen St., Ste. 104
University Park, PA 16801-5252
814-865-5917

National Research Center on Student
  Learning
University of Pittsburgh
Learning Research and Development
  Center
3939 O'Hara St.
Pittsburgh, PA 15260
412-624-7457

2. ERIC Clearinghouses

Educational Resources Information Center (ERIC) is a nationwide information network that acquires, catalogues, summarizes, and provides access to education information from all sources. ERIC produces a variety of publications and provides extensive user assistance, including AskERIC, an electronic question answering service for teachers on the Internet (askeric@ericir.syr.edu). The ERIC system includes 16 subject-specific Clearinghouses (some of which are listed below), the ERIC Processing and Reference facility.

Access ERIC maintains links to ERIC Clearinghouses and Adjunct Clearinghouses with WWW and/or Gopher sites. For more information call ACCESS ERIC at 800-538-3742.

ERIC Clearinghouse on Science,
    Math & Environmental Ed.
Ohio State University
1929 Kenny Rd.
Columbus, OH 43210-1080
614-292-6717

ERIC Clearinghouse on Urban
    Education
Teachers College at Columbia
    University
Main Hall, Rm. 300
525 W. 120th St.
New York, NY 10027-6696

ERIC Clearinghouse on Information
    and Technology,
Syracuse University
Center for Science and Technology
4th Floor, Room 194
Syracuse, NY 13244-4100
315-443-3640

ERIC Clearinghouse on Rural
    Education and Small Schools
1031 Quarrier St.
Charleston, WV 25325-1348
800-624-9120

ERIC Clearinghouse on Higher
    Education
George Washington University
One Dupont Circle NW, Ste. 630
Washington, DC 20036-1183
202-296-2597

ERIC Clearinghouse on Disabilities
    and Gifted Education
Council for Exceptional Children
1920 Association Dr.
Reston, VA 22091-1589
800-328-0272

3. National Center for Education Statistics Data Sets

The National Center for Education Statistics collects data on many educational areas. What follows are brief descriptions of some NCES data sets. For a complete description of all of their data sets, contact OERI at 800-424-1616 for a copy of NCES Programs and Plans.

National Assessment of Educational Progress (NAEP) provides data on the educational attainment of U.S. students. It serves as a "report card" on the national condition of education. Students are assessed at grades 4, 8, and 12 in reading and writing and subject areas that include math, science, U.S. history, and world geography. Contact: Education Assessment Division, 202-219-1761.

Common Core of Data (CCD) is a comprehensive, annual, national statistical database of all public elementary and secondary schools and school districts, which contains data that are comparable across all states. Contact: Elementary and Secondary Education Statistics Division, 202-219-1335.

National Education Longitudinal Study of 1988 (NELS:88) follows children starting at 8th grade and will update information throughout the 1990s. NELS:88 is designed to provide trend data about critical transitions experienced by young people as they develop, attend school, and embark on their careers. Contact: Elementary and Secondary Education Statistics Division, 202-219-1777.

4. National Information Center for Children and Youth with Disabilities (NICHCY)

NICHCY provides information and technical assistance free of charge to families, professionals, caregivers, advocates, agencies, and others in helping children and youth with disabilities to become participating members of the community. NICHCY offers databases, publications and newsletters, updated fact sheets, briefing papers, and parents' guides. Contact: NICHCY/Suzanne Ripley, P.O. Box 1492, Washington, DC 20013, 800-695-0285.

5. Eisenhower National Clearinghouse for Mathematics and Science Education (ENC)

The Eisenhower National Clearinghouse for Mathematics and Science Education is the National Repository for K-12 mathematics and science instructional materials and an online searchable resource of descriptions of those materials and virtual resources, hot links to outstanding virtual resources for math and science teaching, and Federal programs supporting math and science education improvement. Contact: ENC/Len Simutis, Eisenhower National Clearinghouse, The Ohio State University, 1929 Kenny Rd., Columbus, OH 43210-1079, 614-292-7784.